I0063147

INNOVATING THE FUTURE:

TECHNOLOGY AND TRANSFORMATION IN MANUFACTURING

BY DR. ALI CHALHOUB

DEDICATION

This book is dedicated to the countless engineers, technicians, and factory workers who have tirelessly driven innovation and progress in the manufacturing industry. Their dedication, ingenuity, and unwavering commitment to excellence have shaped the modern manufacturing landscape and continue to pave the way for an innovative, more sustainable future. To their tireless efforts, often unseen yet profoundly impactful, this work is humbly offered as a testament to their contributions and a springboard for continued exploration and advancement. This dedication extends to the future generations of innovators, who will inherit and further refine the legacy of innovative manufacturing, pushing the boundaries of what is possible and shaping a more efficient and responsible industrial world. Their creativity and passion will be the key to unlocking the full potential of the technologies described herein, ushering in an era of unprecedented productivity and global collaboration. With profound respect and gratitude, we acknowledge the past and future contributions that make the journey toward innovative manufacturing a reality.

TABLE OF CONTENTS

PREFACE

The transformation of manufacturing is not just an incremental shift—it is a profound **revolution** reshaping the foundations of how industries operate. Over the years, I have had the privilege of **witnessing and contributing to this evolution firsthand**. From my early days in **manufacturing engineering and IT management** to leading **digital transformation initiatives**, my journey has been one of continuous learning, adaptation, and innovation.

This book, **Innovative Manufacturing: The Future Now**, is deeply personal. It reflects my **two decades of experience** navigating the ever-changing landscape of **industrial automation, innovative factories, and digital transformation**. I have worked on the frontlines, implementing **AI-driven automation, IoT integration, and robotics** in real-world manufacturing environments. I have seen the immense **opportunities these technologies bring** and the **challenges companies face**—from resistance to change and workforce adaptation to cybersecurity threats and sustainability concerns.

Throughout my career, I have had the opportunity to **collaborate with brilliant minds in engineering, IT, and operations**, tackling complex problems and driving **innovation in manufacturing environments**. These experiences have given me a unique vantage point—not just from a technical perspective but also from a **strategic and human-centered approach**. The most successful transformations are not just about technology; they require **leadership, vision, and a commitment to empowering people**.

This book goes beyond **technical overviews**. It delves into the **practical applications** of innovative manufacturing, examining **real-world case studies** and **lessons learned from the field**. It highlights the **critical role of workforce training**, the **importance of cybersecurity**, and the **imperative of sustainable manufacturing practices**. These aspects are often overlooked but just as crucial as the technologies themselves.

I wrote this book with a diverse audience in mind: **students eager to learn, engineers striving to innovate, executives making strategic decisions, and researchers shaping the future of manufacturing**. I hope this work will serve as a **guide, a resource, and a source of inspiration** for those looking to navigate this dynamic landscape, contribute to its advancement, and ultimately play a role in shaping an **innovative, more resilient, and more sustainable** manufacturing ecosystem.

This book is not just about **technology** but the **people, strategies, and vision** that drive transformation. It reflects **my journey**, and I hope it serves as your valuable roadmap.

INTRODUCTION

The manufacturing industry stands at a crossroads, poised on the precipice of a technological revolution unlike before. The convergence of Artificial Intelligence (AI), the Internet of Things (IoT), advanced robotics, and sophisticated data analytics fundamentally alters how goods are designed, produced, and delivered.

This book, Innovative Manufacturing: The Future Now, explores the transformative power of these converging technologies and their impact on the global manufacturing landscape. We journey through the history of automation, tracing its evolution from basic programmable logic controllers (PLCs) to the sophisticated AI-driven systems of today. We examine the critical role of data analytics in optimizing production processes, predicting maintenance needs, and improving overall efficiency. Moreover, we delve into the ethical considerations and challenges inherent in implementing these technologies, including workforce displacement, cybersecurity risks, and the need for responsible innovation.

The book explores real-world case studies of companies successfully leveraging these technologies to enhance productivity, improve product quality, and build more sustainable manufacturing operations. These case studies illustrate the practical application of the principles and technologies discussed, showcasing both the successes and the challenges encountered in the journey towards innovative manufacturing.

Ultimately, this book aims to provide a comprehensive and insightful understanding of the current state and future potential of innovative manufacturing, equipping readers with the knowledge and perspective to navigate this rapidly evolving industry. It is not simply a chronicle of technological advancements but a strategic guide for navigating the complexities of this transformative era and building a future where humans and machines collaborate to build a more efficient, sustainable, and prosperous global manufacturing ecosystem.

CHAPTER 1
THE EVOLUTION OF
MANUFACTURING

FROM CRAFT PRODUCTION TO MASS PRODUCTION

The journey of manufacturing is a fascinating narrative of human ingenuity, evolving from meticulous individual craftsmanship to the highly automated, data-driven systems of today's innovative factories.

Understanding this evolution is crucial to grasping the transformative potential of innovative manufacturing and its impact on the global economy. Our story begins in a world where production was a deeply personal affair, a testament to the skill and dedication of individual artisans.

Craft production, prevalent for millennia, is characterized by creating goods primarily by hand, often employing simple tools and relying heavily on the artisan's skill and experience. Please think of the medieval blacksmith, meticulously shaping iron into tools and weapons, or the skilled weaver producing intricate tapestries, each piece uniquely expressing their artistry. These processes were slow, labor-intensive, and inherently limited in terms of output. The focus was on quality, uniqueness, and customization, with products often tailored to individual needs and preferences. While this approach allowed for exquisite craftsmanship, it also severely constrained the volume of goods that could be produced, making them expensive and accessible only to a limited segment of society.

The very nature of the process limited scalability. The training was a lengthy apprenticeship, passing down skills and knowledge across generations within a tightly knit community of craftspeople. This intimate, localized production was the bedrock of the economy for centuries.

The Industrial Revolution, beginning in the late 18th century, dramatically altered this landscape. Fueled by groundbreaking machinery innovations, particularly the steam engine and power loom, manufacturing transitioned from manual labor to machine-based production. This shift marked the birth of mass production, characterized by the standardization of processes, the use of specialized machinery, and the division of labor. The factory system emerged as the dominant model, bringing together workers and machines in a centralized location to produce large quantities of standardized goods. The assembly line, famously pioneered by Henry Ford, further revolutionized mass production, enabling unparalleled efficiency and speed in the manufacturing process. Instead of one individual creating a complete product, tasks were broken down into smaller, more straightforward steps, with each worker specializing in a particular operation. This approach dramatically increased output, reduced production costs, and made goods more accessible. The profound impact led to significant economic growth, urbanization, and societal transformation.

However, the mass-production model also had its limitations. The emphasis on standardization often resulted in a lack of product variety and customization. It created rigid, inflexible systems vulnerable to disruptions in the supply chain. Quality control could be challenging due to the high volume and speed of production. Furthermore, the repetitive work on assembly lines often led to worker dissatisfaction and alienation. The inherent inflexibility of mass production processes meant that adapting to changing market demands or incorporating customer feedback could be slow and costly. In essence, while mass production succeeded in providing affordable goods to a large population, its inherent limitations paved the way for ongoing innovations and refinements in manufacturing processes.

The next significant phase in the evolution of manufacturing was the rise of automation. Initially, this involved the introduction of automated machines to perform specific tasks previously carried out by human workers. These automated systems ranged from simple programmable logic controllers (PLCs) controlling individual machines to more complex systems integrating multiple machines and processes. The benefits were immediately apparent: increased efficiency, improved consistency, and reduced labor costs. Early examples included automated welding systems in automotive plants and numerically controlled (NC) machine tools for precise metalworking. While these initial forays into automation focused on replacing human labor in repetitive tasks, they laid the foundation for today's more sophisticated and integrated automation systems. This transition, however, wasn't without its challenges. The initial investment costs for automation equipment were significant, requiring considerable capital expenditure. There were also training and integration challenges as existing workforces needed to adapt to working alongside new automated systems. The potential for disruptions and the need for robust maintenance protocols added to the complexity.

Lean manufacturing principles, born from the Toyota Production System, introduced a paradigm shift in the 20th century. This philosophy emphasized the elimination of waste, continuous improvement (Kaizen), and Just-in-Time (JIT) inventory management. Lean manufacturing focuses on streamlining processes, reducing unnecessary steps, and maximizing efficiency throughout the entire production system. The principles of Lean, unlike the often rigid structures of mass production, encouraged flexibility, adaptability, and continuous improvement – key factors that prepared the manufacturing industry for the digital revolution that was soon to follow. Lean Manufacturing also highlighted the importance of employee involvement in problem-solving and process improvement, creating a collaborative environment focused on continuous efficiency gains. Adopting Lean practices in numerous industries demonstrated significant cost savings and increased productivity, making it a cornerstone of modern manufacturing.

The digital revolution dramatically altered the manufacturing landscape yet again, introducing computer-aided design (CAD), computer-aided manufacturing (CAM), and enterprise resource planning (ERP) systems. CAD revolutionized product design, allowing faster iterations, more complex designs, and enhanced collaboration between designers and engineers. CAM integrated computer control into manufacturing processes, improving precision, speed, and efficiency. ERP systems provided a centralized platform for managing all aspects of the manufacturing process, from planning and procurement to production and distribution. These digital technologies greatly enhanced data management and analysis, laying the foundation for the data-driven decision-making that characterizes innovative manufacturing. Integrating these systems within organizations significantly improved

10

the coordination and communication among different departments, leading to more streamlined and efficient operations. They also facilitated better inventory management, reduced lead times, and improved responsiveness to market demands. The limitations of these earlier systems were primarily in their integration – they were often standalone applications, hindering seamless data flow across the entire manufacturing process.

The convergence of these historical trends – craft production's focus on quality, mass production's drive for scale, automation's quest for efficiency, Lean's emphasis on waste reduction, and the digital revolution's data-driven decision-making – sets the stage for innovative manufacturing. Innovative manufacturing leverages advanced technologies like the Internet of Things (IoT), artificial intelligence (AI), cloud computing, and robotics to create highly interconnected and responsive production systems. This is the subject of the next chapter, where we delve into the individual pillars supporting this modern manufacturing marvel.

THE RISE OF AUTOMATION AND ITS IMPACT

The rise of automation represents a pivotal moment in the ongoing evolution of manufacturing. While the Industrial Revolution ushered in mass production, automation indeed reshaped the fundamental nature of factory work. The initial steps involved the integration of automated machines to handle specific tasks previously performed by human workers. These were often discrete operations, replacing repetitive, physically demanding, or hazardous jobs. Early examples included automated welding systems in the burgeoning automotive industry. These systems, often employing simple programmable logic controllers (PLCs), demonstrated the potential for increased efficiency and improved consistency in production. The precision achievable through automation surpassed what was humanly possible in many cases, particularly in intricate metalworking processes using numerically controlled (NC) machine tools. The benefits were immediate and significant: reduced labor costs, increased production rates, and improved product quality, consistency, and precision.

However, this initial wave of automation was not without its challenges. The capital expenditure required to acquire and install automated systems was substantial, presenting a significant barrier to entry for many smaller manufacturers. Furthermore, integrating these new systems into existing production lines often proved complex, requiring specialized expertise and potentially disrupting existing workflows. Training existing workforces to operate and maintain this new technology added another layer of complexity and cost. The risk of downtime due to malfunctioning equipment was also a significant concern, underscoring the need for robust maintenance programs and skilled technicians capable of troubleshooting and repair. This highlighted the crucial role of skilled human capital alongside the new automated systems, creating a need for upskilling and workforce retraining programs.

The evolution of automation progressed rapidly, driven by continuous advancements in computing power, control systems, and robotics. Developing more sophisticated programmable logic controllers (PLCs) enabled the control of increasingly complex manufacturing processes. These PLCs provided a centralized platform for controlling multiple machines and processes simultaneously, enhancing coordination and efficiency. The emergence of industrial robots marked another significant milestone. Early robots were primarily used for simple, repetitive tasks like material handling, welding, and painting. However, they could perform increasingly complex and dexterous operations as robotic technology advanced. Their ability to work tirelessly, without fatigue or error, greatly enhanced productivity and improved product quality. The development of vision systems allowed robots to "see" their environment, enhancing their flexibility and adaptability. This meant that robots could handle a broader range of tasks and adapt to variations in the materials or components they were handling. This capability opened the doors to greater automation in more varied and complex manufacturing operations.

The integration of advanced sensors and data analytics transformed the automation landscape further. Sensors embedded within machines and production lines provided real-time data on performance, enabling predictive maintenance and optimizing production processes. This data-driven approach to manufacturing allowed for proactively identifying potential problems before they resulted in downtime or quality defects. Applying machine learning and artificial intelligence (AI) further enhanced this capability, automating more complex decision-making processes. AI algorithms could analyze vast quantities of data to identify patterns and anomalies, improving overall efficiency and optimizing resource allocation. This shift towards a more data-driven, intelligent approach to automation enhanced manufacturing systems' overall flexibility and responsiveness.

They were no longer merely rigid, pre-programmed machines performing repetitive tasks but instead became adaptive and self-learning systems capable of responding to changing conditions and optimizing their performance accordingly.

The impact of automation on productivity has been profound. Automated systems have increased production rates, improved product quality, and reduced labor costs. This has resulted in significant gains in efficiency and competitiveness for many manufacturers. However, implementing automation has also raised concerns about the displacement of human workers. As automated systems take over more tasks previously performed by humans, concerns about job security and the need for workforce retraining have become increasingly important. This necessitates a proactive approach to managing this transition, focusing on upskilling and reskilling programs to equip workers with the skills needed for the jobs of the future. This requires collaboration between industry, government, and educational institutions to ensure a smooth transition and minimize automation's negative social and economic impacts. Investing in education and training becomes crucial in this environment, preparing the workforce to adapt to new roles that require collaboration with automated systems rather than direct competition.

Furthermore, the security of automated systems has become a critical concern. The increasing interconnectedness of manufacturing systems through networks and the internet exposes them to cyber threats. Protecting these systems from cyberattacks is crucial, not only to prevent production disruptions but also to safeguard sensitive data. Robust cybersecurity measures, including firewalls, intrusion detection systems, and regular security audits, are essential to maintaining the security and integrity of automated manufacturing systems. The vulnerability of automated systems extends beyond cyberattacks; physical security must also be considered. Protecting automated equipment and processes from unauthorized access and physical damage requires robust physical security measures. This multifaceted approach ensures the safety and integrity of the entire system.

The ongoing evolution of automation continues to redefine the manufacturing landscape. Integrating advanced robotics, AI, and machine learning leads to more flexible, adaptable, and intelligent manufacturing systems. These systems can handle increasingly complex tasks, adapt to changing conditions, and optimize their performance in real-time. The focus is shifting towards human-machine collaboration, where humans and robots work together to achieve optimal efficiency and productivity. This collaborative approach recognizes the unique strengths of humans and machines, combining human creativity, problem-solving skills, and adaptability with automated systems' precision, speed, and tireless nature. This synergistic approach to automation leverages the advantages of both while mitigating the potential risks associated with solely relying on either one. The future of manufacturing lies in this intelligent, collaborative approach to automation. The careful integration of advanced technologies and human expertise will define the success of manufacturers in the increasingly competitive global marketplace. This requires strategic planning, investment in technology and training, and a long-term vision focused on sustainable growth and adaptation to the ever-evolving landscape of the manufacturing industry.

THE EMERGENCE OF LEAN MANUFACTURING PRINCIPLES

The journey toward innovative manufacturing didn't emerge in a vacuum. It was built upon decades of incremental improvements and paradigm shifts in manufacturing philosophy. One of the most influential was the development and widespread adoption of Lean manufacturing principles. Lean, often associated with Toyota's production system, represents a fundamental departure from traditional mass production methodologies. Instead of focusing solely on maximizing output, Lean prioritizes the elimination of waste and continuously improving processes to achieve optimal efficiency and customer value.

The genesis of Lean can be traced back to post-World War II Japan, where companies like Toyota faced significant challenges in a resource-constrained environment. Unlike the vast industrial complexes of the United States and Europe, Japanese manufacturers had to be more resourceful, squeezing maximum value from limited resources. This necessity fostered a relentless focus on efficiency and eliminating all forms of waste – a concept that became the cornerstone of Lean manufacturing.

Central to Lean is the concept of *Muda*, which encompasses seven types of waste: Transportation, Inventory, Motion, Waiting, Overproduction, Over-processing, and Defects. Each form of waste represents an inefficiency that adds cost and reduces value without contributing to the final product. Eliminating Muda is not merely about cost reduction but creating a more streamlined, efficient, and responsive production system.

Transportation waste is the unnecessary movement of materials or products within the factory. This can involve inefficient layouts, excessive handling, or unnecessary movement of materials between different workstations. Optimizing factory layout, utilizing efficient material handling systems, and minimizing unnecessary movements are crucial to eliminating this type of waste. For instance, implementing a cellular manufacturing layout, where related machines are grouped, significantly reduces the distance materials need to travel.

Inventory waste, often called excess inventory, represents a significant drain on resources. Excessive stock ties up capital, increases storage costs and risks obsolescence. Lean emphasizes Just-in-Time (JIT) inventory management, where materials are delivered only when needed for production. This minimizes storage space, reduces holding costs, and reduces the risk of waste from obsolete inventory. The implementation of Kanban systems and visual signaling methods to manage inventory flow is a key component of JIT implementation. These systems provide real-time feedback on inventory levels, allowing for timely replenishment and preventing overstocking.

Motion waste refers to the unnecessary movement of workers.

Inefficient workspaces, poorly designed workstations, or inadequate tools can waste time and effort. Lean principles advocate for ergonomic workstation design, optimized workflows, and the provision of appropriate tools to minimize unnecessary worker movement. This translates to improved worker efficiency, reduced fatigue, and fewer workplace injuries.

Waiting waste occurs when workers or machines are idle due to bottlenecks, lack of materials, or other delays. Lean aims to identify and eliminate these bottlenecks through process analysis and improvement. This can involve streamlining workflows, optimizing machine setups, or improving communication to minimize waiting time. Value stream mapping, a technique used to visualize the entire production process, is crucial in identifying these bottlenecks and developing solutions.

Overproduction waste refers to producing more than is needed or ahead of demand. This leads to excess inventory, increased storage costs, and the risk of obsolete products. Lean advocates for producing only what is needed, when it's needed, and in the quantity required. This requires accurate demand forecasting and close coordination with customers. Pull systems, where production is initiated by customer demand rather than a pre-set schedule, effectively eliminate overproduction.

Over-processing waste means performing more work than is necessary to satisfy customer requirements. This can involve unnecessary steps, complex processes, or sophisticated equipment requiring more straightforward methods. Lean focuses on simplifying processes, reducing steps, and using the most appropriate tools for the task. This minimizes cost, improves efficiency, and reduces the risk of defects. Value stream mapping is crucial in identifying and eliminating unnecessary processing steps.

Defect waste encompasses all product defects, including errors, scrap, rework, and repairs. Lean emphasizes quality control and prevention to reduce defects. This involves implementing robust quality control systems, proactive defect detection, and a focus on continuous improvement to minimize errors. Statistical process control (SPC) and other quality control techniques are instrumental in minimizing defects and improving product quality.

The application of Lean principles extends beyond the factory floor.

It encompasses all aspects of the organization, including procurement, design, and customer relations. By focusing on continuous improvement (Kaizen), a philosophy of incremental, ongoing improvement, Lean organizations strive to refine and optimize their processes constantly. Kaizen involves regular review of processes, identifying areas for improvement, and implementing small, incremental changes to achieve ongoing efficiency gains. This approach to continuous improvement fosters a culture of problem-solving and innovation throughout the organization.

The relationship between Lean and Innovative Manufacturing is synergistic. Lean principles provide a foundation for optimizing processes, eliminating waste, and improving efficiency. Innovative Manufacturing technologies, such as sensors, data analytics, and automation, provide the tools to implement and enhance Lean practices. Data collected from sensors can provide real-time visibility into production processes, enabling faster identification and elimination of waste. Predictive maintenance, enabled by data analytics, can prevent machine downtime and reduce waste due to equipment failures.

Automation can enhance efficiency by automating repetitive tasks and reducing human error, directly contributing to the reduction of several Muda categories.

However, a purely technology-driven approach to Lean implementation can fall short. Technology alone cannot address cultural aspects crucial to successful Lean adoption. A deep understanding of Lean philosophy, employee engagement, and a commitment to continuous improvement are equally vital for effective implementation. Innovative Manufacturing technologies should be seen as tools to enhance and accelerate Lean principles, not as a replacement for them. Successful implementation requires a holistic approach that combines Lean principles with advanced technology to create a highly efficient, responsive, and sustainable manufacturing system. In essence, Innovative Manufacturing builds upon the foundations laid by Lean, augmenting its capabilities with advanced technologies to create a genuinely transformative manufacturing paradigm. This combined approach has significant benefits, such as reduced lead times, improved quality, enhanced flexibility, and increased profitability. The integration is not about a simple overlay; it's a profound shift towards a more agile, data-driven, and human-centered approach to manufacturing. This convergence of Lean principles and technologies marks a crucial step in the evolution of the manufacturing industry, paving the way for a future characterized by optimized efficiency, sustainable practices, and enhanced competitiveness. The challenge lies in successfully integrating these two powerful forces to achieve a synergistic outcome. This involves addressing organizational culture, empowering employees, and providing the proper training and technological infrastructure to support the transition. It's a journey that demands continuous learning, adaptation, and a commitment to operational excellence.

THE DIGITAL REVOLUTION AND ITS INFLUENCE

The groundwork for today's innovative factories was laid not in a single revolutionary moment but through a gradual yet profound digital transformation spanning several decades. This transformation began with computer-aided design (CAD) systems, which significantly departed from traditional drafting methods. Before CAD, designs were meticulously drawn by hand, a time-consuming process, prone to errors, and limited in its capacity for revision and modification. The advent of CAD brought about a paradigm shift, enabling engineers to create, modify, and analyze designs digitally, dramatically accelerating the design process and enhancing its precision. The ability to easily manipulate three-dimensional models, simulate product performance, and conduct virtual testing significantly reduced design iterations and lead times, contributing to faster product development cycles and reduced costs. Furthermore, CAD systems facilitated better collaboration among designers and engineers, allowing for simultaneous access to designs and seamless integration of feedback. Companies could now efficiently manage complex designs with greater accuracy, fostering innovation and pushing the boundaries of product design capabilities.

The impact of CAD extended beyond the design phase, seamlessly integrating with the subsequent manufacturing stages. This integration was facilitated mainly by developing and adopting computer-aided manufacturing (CAM) systems. CAM systems automated computer numerical control (CNC) machine programming, enabling precise and efficient machining of complex parts. Unlike traditional manual programming, CAM systems use CAD data directly, eliminating the need for manual transcription and reducing the risk of errors. This resulted in improved machining accuracy, reduced production times, and greater consistency in the quality of manufactured parts. Moreover, CAM systems can optimize machining parameters, minimizing material waste and maximizing efficiency. This enhanced productivity led to cost savings and enabled manufacturers to respond more effectively to market demands. The combined effect of CAD and CAM drastically reshaped the manufacturing landscape, paving the way for greater automation, precision, and efficiency.

However, the integration of CAD and CAM was only the beginning of the digital transformation. The next major leap involved implementing enterprise resource planning (ERP) systems. ERP systems represented a significant advancement in information management, bringing together disparate functional areas of a business – from finance and human resources to manufacturing and supply chain management – onto a single, integrated platform. Before ERP, these functions operated in relative isolation, leading to information silos and a lack of coordination across the organization. ERP systems effectively broke down these silos, enabling real-time information sharing and better collaboration between departments.

This enhanced visibility into all aspects of the business provided greater control and efficiency. Manufacturers gained a clear overview of their inventory levels, production schedules, and sales orders, empowering them to make more informed decisions and optimize their operations.

ERP systems provided a centralized database containing crucial information about materials, production processes, and customer orders. This centralized repository eliminated the need for manual data entry and reconciliation, reducing the risk of errors and increasing the accuracy of information. Further, ERP systems incorporated sophisticated planning and scheduling tools, enabling manufacturers to optimize their production schedules, minimize bottlenecks, and improve on-time delivery. This improved operational efficiency directly translated into cost savings and increased customer satisfaction. Moreover, the ability to integrate real-time data from the manufacturing floor with other aspects of the business provided managers with greater insight into operational performance, allowing them to identify improvement areas and promptly implement corrective actions.

The introduction of CAD, CAM, and ERP systems established the foundational elements of the digital revolution in manufacturing. These technologies improved individual processes and fostered greater integration between various stages of manufacturing, ultimately creating a more streamlined and efficient value chain. This level of integration and the subsequent accumulation of operational data formed the fertile ground upon which the current era of innovative manufacturing blossomed. The ability to collect and analyze large volumes of data from across the manufacturing ecosystem became a central driver of innovation, allowing manufacturers to identify patterns, predict potential problems, and optimize operations in ways that were unimaginable just a few decades ago.

However, the initial stages of this digital transformation were often characterized by a lack of complete integration between systems. Data often resided in separate databases, limiting its usefulness for comprehensive analysis and decision-making. The transition to more integrated systems, utilizing standardized data formats and communication protocols, played a crucial role in enhancing the value of the accumulated data. This shift toward seamless data exchange between different systems has allowed for a more holistic view of the manufacturing process, providing a deeper understanding of efficiency bottlenecks and potential improvements. The ability to connect CAD, CAM, and ERP data with real-time sensor data from the shop floor further enhanced this information's richness and contextual relevance.

The subsequent development of advanced analytics and machine learning algorithms further amplified the impact of this integrated data. These technologies enabled extracting meaningful insights from vast datasets, helping manufacturers identify patterns, predict equipment failures, and optimize resource allocation.

Predictive maintenance, enabled by analyzing sensor data, became a crucial application, reducing downtime and enhancing production efficiency. The ability to anticipate potential problems before they occur minimized disruptions and improved operational resilience. This proactive approach to maintenance significantly reduced the costs associated with unplanned downtime and repairs, contributing to increased profitability.

The move towards a data-driven approach to manufacturing profoundly impacted the role of human operators. While concerns about automation replacing human jobs were legitimate, the reality proved more nuanced. The shift was not about replacing human workers entirely but about augmenting their capabilities with intelligent technologies. Operators were no longer tasked with repetitive and mundane tasks but instead were empowered to focus on higher-value activities such as problem-solving, process improvement, and strategic decision-making. This involved training and upskilling the workforce, equipping them with the necessary skills to effectively leverage new technologies and maximize their value. The successful integration of these technologies required a focus on human-centered design, considering not only the technological aspects but also the human factors that played a crucial role in the overall success of the digital transformation.

The evolution of manufacturing, fueled by the digital revolution, has resulted in significant transformations that continue to reshape the industry landscape. From the initial introduction of CAD and CAM to the widespread adoption of ERP systems and the emergence of innovative manufacturing technologies, the journey has been one of continuous progress and adaptation. The successful integration of these digital technologies has not only enhanced efficiency and productivity but has also fostered a greater level of collaboration and transparency across the organization. The capacity to collect, analyze, and leverage vast data has led to a new paradigm of data-driven decision-making, enabling manufacturers to optimize operations and enhance competitiveness in a global market. This journey, however, is ongoing, with further technological advancements and strategic shifts promising continued evolution in the years to come. The future of manufacturing undoubtedly lies in the ongoing integration of technologies, coupled with a dedicated workforce equipped to embrace the challenges and opportunities of this ever-evolving landscape.

SETTING THE STAGE FOR INNOVATIVE MANUFACTURING

The groundwork laid by CAD, CAM, and ERP systems created a fertile ground for the next evolutionary leap: innovative manufacturing.

This wasn't a single technological breakthrough but rather the convergence of several powerful technologies, each contributing to a fundamentally different approach to manufacturing. Central to this shift is the Internet of Things (IoT), a network of interconnected physical devices, vehicles, buildings, and other items embedded with electronics, software, sensors, actuators, and network connectivity that enables these objects to collect and exchange data.

In manufacturing, IoT manifests as sensors placed on machines, robots, and even individual products, continuously collecting data on performance, status, and environmental conditions. This data provides unprecedented real-time visibility into every aspect of the manufacturing process.

Imagine a scenario before the widespread adoption of IoT.

Troubleshooting a malfunctioning machine involved manual inspection, often relying on the operator's experience and intuition. The process could be time-consuming, leading to production delays and potential quality issues. With IoT, sensors on the machine monitor various parameters—temperature, vibration, pressure, power consumption—and transmit this data to a central system. Anomalies detected in these parameters can trigger alerts, allowing for proactive maintenance before a complete failure occurs. This predictive maintenance capability significantly reduces downtime, improves operational efficiency, and minimizes the risk of costly repairs. Moreover, the data collected can be analyzed to identify recurring patterns, suggesting potential design improvements or process adjustments for enhanced efficiency.

The sheer volume of data generated by the IoT necessitates sophisticated data management and analytical capabilities. This is where cloud computing plays a pivotal role. Cloud computing provides scalable, on-demand computing resources, including storage, processing power, and data analytics tools, allowing manufacturers to manage and analyze the massive datasets generated by IoT devices. Cloud platforms offer the flexibility to scale resources up or down depending on demand, eliminating the need for expensive on-site infrastructure investments. Moreover, they provide access to advanced analytics tools and machine learning algorithms that can identify patterns and anomalies in the data, revealing valuable insights for process improvement and decision-making.

CHAPTER 2
THE PILLARS OF INNOVATIVE
MANUFACTURING

Integrating IoT and cloud computing is further enhanced by incorporating artificial intelligence (AI). AI algorithms can analyze the vast amounts of data collected to identify trends, predict potential problems, and optimize production processes. For example, AI-powered systems can analyze sensor data from multiple machines to identify optimal production schedules, minimizing bottlenecks and maximizing throughput. They can also predict potential equipment failures, allowing for proactive maintenance and preventing costly downtime. Furthermore, AI can automate quality control processes, identifying defects in real-time and reducing the need for manual inspection.

Combining IoT, cloud computing, and AI represents a powerful synergy transforming traditional manufacturing processes. Consider the example of a large-scale automotive manufacturing plant. Historically, monitoring the performance of individual machines and tracking materials throughout the assembly line involved considerable manual effort. With manufacturing technologies, sensors on each machine transmit real-time performance data to a central system hosted in the cloud. AI algorithms analyze this data to identify potential bottlenecks, predict maintenance needs, and optimize production schedules. The system can also track the location and status of each component throughout the assembly line, ensuring that materials are available when and where needed. This level of visibility and control dramatically reduces waste, improves efficiency, and enhances overall productivity.

The integration of these technologies extends beyond the factory floor. Innovative manufacturing also impacts supply chain management, logistics, and customer service. Real-time visibility into inventory levels allows for better demand forecasting and optimized supply chain planning. Automated tracking systems monitor shipments, providing real-time updates on location and status. Data-driven insights can improve customer service by anticipating customer needs and proactively addressing potential issues.

However, the transition to innovative manufacturing isn't merely about technology implementation. It requires a holistic approach that addresses organizational culture, workforce skills, and business processes. Companies must invest in training and development programs to equip their workforce with the necessary skills to manage and utilize manufacturing technologies. Data security and privacy are critical, demanding robust cybersecurity measures to protect sensitive information. Integration with legacy systems can present significant challenges, requiring careful planning and execution. Finally, a successful innovative manufacturing strategy must align with the company's overall business goals, ensuring that the implemented technologies contribute directly to enhanced productivity, profitability, and competitiveness.

The potential benefits of innovative manufacturing are substantial.

Improved productivity and efficiency lead to significant cost savings. Predictive maintenance reduces downtime and improves operational resilience. Real-time data insights enhance decision-making, enabling companies to respond quickly to market changes. Enhanced product quality and reduced defects increase customer satisfaction and brand loyalty. The ability to innovate faster and bring new products to market more quickly strengthens competitive advantage.

Despite the numerous advantages, challenges remain. The initial investment in hardware, software, and training can be substantial. Data security and integration with legacy systems pose significant hurdles. The need for skilled personnel necessitates investing in workforce development programs. Addressing these challenges requires careful planning, strategic partnerships, and a long-term commitment to digital transformation.

In conclusion, innovative manufacturing represents a paradigm shift in the manufacturing industry. The convergence of IoT, cloud computing, and AI creates unprecedented opportunities for enhanced efficiency, productivity, and competitiveness. While challenges remain, the potential benefits are too significant to ignore. Companies that embrace this digital transformation and invest in the necessary infrastructure, skills, and processes will be well-positioned to succeed in the increasingly competitive global market. The journey toward innovative manufacturing is ongoing, but the direction is clear: a future where data-driven insights empower manufacturers to optimize operations, innovate continuously, and deliver superior value to their customers. This evolution is not just a technological advancement; it's a fundamental restructuring of the manufacturing value chain, demanding re-evaluating processes, workflows, and even the skillsets required for a successful operation in the 21st century. The ultimate success of innovative manufacturing hinges on a commitment to continuous improvement, embracing both the technological capabilities and the human potential necessary to leverage them effectively.

UNDERSTANDING THE INTERNET OF THINGS IOT IN MANUFACTURING

The transformative potential of the Internet of Things (IoT) in manufacturing lies in its theoretical capabilities and tangible, real-world applications. This section will explore the practical implementations of IoT, focusing on how sensor networks, data acquisition, and real-time monitoring capabilities are revolutionizing manufacturing processes. We will examine the benefits, challenges, and real-world examples illuminating IoT-driven data's power in improving decision-making and overall operational efficiency.

One of the most significant contributions of IoT in manufacturing is the creation of highly sophisticated sensor networks. These networks are not simply a collection of sensors; they are strategically deployed systems designed to gather comprehensive data on various aspects of the manufacturing process. Sensors are integrated into machinery, equipment, and even products, continuously monitoring parameters such as temperature, pressure, vibration, humidity, and power consumption. This granular data provides unprecedented detail, offering a real-time, holistic view of the manufacturing environment that was previously impossible to achieve.

The data acquisition process itself is crucial. Sophisticated software systems are employed to collect, process, and store vast data streamed from these sensor networks. This data is typically transmitted wirelessly, using Wi-Fi, Bluetooth, or cellular networks, ensuring seamless data flow to central servers or cloud-based platforms. This data's efficient and reliable acquisition is critical, as its value hinges on its timeliness and accuracy. Any delays or inaccuracies can compromise the effectiveness of subsequent analysis and decision-making. Therefore, robust data management systems are essential to ensure data integrity and availability.

Real-time monitoring capabilities are arguably the most impactful outcome of this data acquisition. Manufacturers gain immediate insight into the performance of their equipment and processes through dedicated dashboards and visualization tools. Anomalies are instantly identified, allowing for swift intervention and proactive problem-solving. Imagine a scenario where a machine's temperature begins to rise unexpectedly. In a traditional setting, this might go unnoticed until a catastrophic failure occurs. With IoT-enabled monitoring, an alert is automatically generated, alerting maintenance personnel to the issue before it escalates, thus preventing costly downtime and potential damage. This proactive approach significantly improves operational efficiency and reduces maintenance costs.

Beyond simple alerts, real-time monitoring allows for sophisticated predictive maintenance. By analyzing historical data and identifying patterns, AI algorithms can predict potential equipment failures before they occur. This allows for scheduled maintenance during periods of low production, minimizing disruptions and maximizing uptime. The ability to anticipate and address potential problems before they manifest is a game-changer for manufacturers, reducing downtime, enhancing operational efficiency, and improving overall profitability.

However, implementing IoT solutions in manufacturing is not without its challenges. The initial investment in sensors, software, and infrastructure can be significant, requiring careful planning and justification. Data security and privacy are paramount, necessitating robust cybersecurity measures to protect sensitive operational data from unauthorized access or cyberattacks. Integrating IoT systems with legacy systems can also be complex and time-consuming, potentially requiring significant modifications to existing infrastructure. Finally, skilled personnel are needed to manage and interpret the massive datasets generated by IoT devices, emphasizing the need for ongoing training and development within the workforce.

Despite these challenges, the advantages far outweigh the obstacles. The improved decision-making capabilities enabled by IoT data are transformative. Manufacturers can make data-driven choices concerning production scheduling, inventory management, and quality control, leading to significant improvements in efficiency and productivity. Tracking and tracing materials throughout the supply chain enhances visibility and allows for faster response to disruptions. Furthermore, the detailed performance data collected by IoT sensors provides valuable insights into process optimization, allowing manufacturers to identify and eliminate bottlenecks, reduce waste, and improve overall yields.

Let's consider a few real-world examples. In the automotive industry, IoT sensors embedded in assembly line robots monitor their performance, identifying potential malfunctions before they impact production. In pharmaceuticals, IoT sensors in storage facilities ensure optimal temperature and humidity conditions, preventing spoilage and ensuring product quality. In food processing, sensors monitor hygiene parameters, enhancing food safety and compliance with regulatory requirements. These are just a few examples of IoT transforming manufacturing across diverse industries.

The impact of IoT extends beyond the factory floor. By connecting manufacturing processes with supply chain partners and customers, IoT enables greater transparency and collaboration. Real-time tracking of shipments allows manufacturers to monitor goods in transit, anticipating potential delays and ensuring timely delivery. Product usage and performance data can be collected, providing valuable feedback for product development and improvement. This interconnectedness transforms the entire value chain, enhancing efficiency, responsiveness, and customer satisfaction.

In conclusion, the Internet of Things represents a significant paradigm shift in manufacturing. IoT enables proactive decision-making, predictive maintenance, and enhanced operational efficiency by providing real-time visibility into every aspect of the production process. While challenges exist, the potential benefits are immense, promising significant cost savings, improved product quality, and enhanced competitiveness. Companies embracing IoT technologies and investing in the necessary infrastructure, skills, and processes are positioning themselves for success in the increasingly data-driven landscape of modern manufacturing. The ongoing evolution of IoT, coupled with advancements in artificial intelligence and machine learning, will undoubtedly continue to shape the future of manufacturing, pushing the boundaries of efficiency, productivity, and innovation. The key to success lies in a strategic and comprehensive approach to implementation, considering the technological aspects and the organizational, cultural, and human capital dimensions of this profound transformation.

ARTIFICIAL INTELLIGENCE AI AND MACHINE LEARNING APPLICATIONS

The seamless integration of the Internet of Things (IoT) lays the groundwork for the next level of manufacturing evolution: the intelligent factory empowered by Artificial Intelligence (AI) and Machine Learning (ML). While IoT provides the raw data – the nervous system of the innovative factory – AI and ML act as the brain, processing this information to make informed decisions, optimize processes, and predict future outcomes. This synergy unlocks unprecedented levels of efficiency, productivity, and overall profitability.

Predictive maintenance is perhaps the most widely recognized application of AI and ML in innovative manufacturing. The massive datasets generated by IoT sensors – encompassing vibration levels, temperature fluctuations, pressure readings, and operational parameters – are fed into sophisticated algorithms that can identify patterns indicative of impending equipment failures. These algorithms, often employing techniques such as time series analysis, deep learning, and anomaly detection, go beyond simple threshold-based alerts. They can forecast the likelihood of failures with remarkable accuracy, allowing for proactive maintenance scheduling. Instead of reactive repairs that cause costly downtime, manufacturers can strategically plan maintenance during periods of low production, minimizing disruption to operations and maximizing equipment uptime. This translates directly to significant cost savings and improved overall equipment effectiveness (OEE).

The benefits extend beyond simply preventing equipment failures.

Predictive maintenance using AI and ML can also optimize maintenance schedules themselves. By analyzing historical maintenance data and equipment performance, the AI can determine the optimal maintenance intervals for different types of equipment, moving away from fixed-interval maintenance towards condition-based maintenance. This dynamic approach ensures that maintenance is performed only when necessary, further reducing downtime and extending the lifespan of equipment.

Moving beyond predictive maintenance, AI and ML are revolutionizing quality control in manufacturing. Traditional quality control methods often rely on manual inspection, a process that is time-consuming, labor-intensive, and prone to human error.

AI-powered vision systems and machine learning algorithms provide a far more efficient and accurate alternative.

These systems can analyze images and videos from cameras positioned throughout the production line, identifying defects with a speed and precision unmatched by human inspectors. Moreover, AI algorithms can identify subtle flaws that might be overlooked by the human eye, ensuring higher quality standards and reduced defect rates. This enhanced quality control improves product quality, reduces waste, and increases customer satisfaction.

The application of AI and ML is not limited to individual machines or processes; it extends to optimizing entire production lines and supply chains. By analyzing data from various sources, including IoT sensors, ERP systems, and CRM platforms, AI algorithms can identify bottlenecks, inefficiencies, and areas for improvement within the manufacturing process. This data-driven approach enables manufacturers to optimize production schedules, resource allocation, and inventory management, resulting in smoother operations and reduced production costs. Moreover, AI can predict and mitigate supply chain disruptions, ensuring timely delivery of materials and components. This predictive capability minimizes delays and reduces the risk of production stoppages due to supply chain issues.

Implementing AI and ML in innovative manufacturing requires careful consideration of various factors. Data quality is paramount – garbage in, garbage out, as the saying goes. The accuracy and reliability of the AI's predictions directly depend on the data quality fed into the algorithms. Therefore, robust data acquisition and pre-processing techniques are essential to ensure the data is clean, consistent, and representative of the manufacturing process.

Furthermore, the selection of appropriate algorithms is critical.

Different AI and ML algorithms are suited for different tasks. For instance, deep learning algorithms are particularly effective for image recognition and anomaly detection, while time series analysis is better suited for predicting equipment failures. Choosing the correct algorithm for the specific application is crucial to ensure the effectiveness of the AI system.

Integrating AI and ML into existing manufacturing infrastructure can also present challenges. Legacy systems might not be compatible with the latest AI technologies, requiring significant investment in infrastructure upgrades and system integration. Furthermore, implementing AI requires skilled personnel to manage and interpret the results of the algorithms. This emphasizes the importance of investing in training and development programs for the manufacturing workforce to acquire the necessary skills to work effectively with these advanced technologies.

However, the potential benefits far outweigh the challenges. The cost savings alone, resulting from reduced downtime, improved quality control, and optimized production processes, can justify the investment in AI and ML technologies. Moreover, enhanced efficiency and productivity create a competitive advantage, enabling manufacturers to meet ever-increasing customer demands and maintain a leading position in the market.

Consider, for example, the automotive industry. Manufacturers use AI to optimize robotic assembly lines, reducing production time and increasing throughput. In the semiconductor industry, AI algorithms detect minute defects in chips, improving product yield and reducing waste. Pharmaceutical companies leverage AI for real-time monitoring of production processes, ensuring product quality and compliance with stringent regulatory requirements. These are just a few examples of how AI and ML are transforming manufacturing across various sectors, showcasing the vast potential of these technologies to revolutionize the industry.

The future of innovative manufacturing hinges on the continued development and integration of AI and ML. As algorithms become more sophisticated and computing power increases, the capabilities of AI in manufacturing will only expand, leading to even greater levels of efficiency, productivity, and innovation. The manufacturers who embrace these technologies and invest in the necessary infrastructure, skills, and processes will be best positioned for success in the increasingly competitive global marketplace. This proactive approach, embracing data-driven decision-making and leveraging the power of AI and ML, is no longer a luxury but a necessity for survival and thriving in the intelligent factory of tomorrow. These technologies' continuous learning and adaptation will ensure that manufacturing remains at the forefront of technological advancement, driving further innovation and efficiency gains. The data-driven revolution is not just transforming manufacturing but defining its future.

ROBOTICS AND AUTOMATION IN INNOVATIVE FACTORIES

The integration of Artificial Intelligence and Machine Learning (AI/ML) lays a robust foundation for innovative manufacturing, but the actual realization of this intelligent factory relies heavily on advanced robotics and automation. These technologies aren't simply replacing human workers but fundamentally reshaping the manufacturing landscape, enabling unprecedented efficiency, flexibility, and productivity. This transformation hinges on the strategic deployment of several key robotic systems.

One of the most significant advancements is the rise of collaborative robots or cobots. Unlike traditional industrial robots operating in isolated, caged environments for safety reasons, cobots are designed to work alongside human employees. This collaborative approach requires sophisticated safety mechanisms, including force-limiting sensors and advanced programming that allows the robot to stop or adjust its movements in response to human presence or unexpected obstacles. This interaction is crucial, as it allows for the optimal blending of human dexterity and creativity with robotic systems' precision and tireless work ethic. A human's judgment remains invaluable for tasks requiring intricate manipulation or complex decision-making. Cobots, therefore, become extensions of the human workforce, boosting output without entirely replacing human involvement. This collaborative nature also promotes a more adaptable and responsive manufacturing environment. Cobots can be easily reprogrammed and redeployed to handle different tasks, allowing manufacturers to swiftly adjust to changing production demands or new product designs. This agility is a critical advantage in today's dynamic market conditions.

The benefits of this human-robot collaboration extend beyond increased efficiency. By working side-by-side, humans and robots learn from each other. Workers can identify areas for improvement in the robot's performance, leading to refinements in programming and operational strategies. Conversely, observing the robot's precise and consistent execution can inspire workers to optimize their processes and techniques. This synergistic relationship fosters continuous improvement across the entire production line, constantly pushing the boundaries of what is possible.

Beyond cobots, Autonomous Guided Vehicles (AGVs) are revolutionizing material handling within innovative factories. These self-navigating vehicles automate the transporting of materials, components, and finished goods throughout the facility. Unlike traditional conveyor belts or forklifts, AGVs offer greater flexibility, dynamically adapting their routes to optimize traffic flow and avoid congestion. This adaptability is especially crucial in large or complex manufacturing environments where the layout changes. Integrating AGVs into an innovative factory's logistics network streamlines the material flow, minimizing delays and ensuring a consistent supply of materials to the production line.

Real-time tracking systems provide complete visibility into the location and status of each AGV, enhancing efficiency and allowing for proactive adjustments to logistics operations. This precision and automation drastically reduce the risk of errors associated with manual material handling, such as misplaced items or delays caused by human error. Furthermore, AGVs can operate continuously, 24/7, maximizing productivity and minimizing downtime.

Automated Storage and Retrieval Systems (AS/RS) represent another vital component of the automated innovative factory. These systems automate the storage and retrieval of materials, using robotic cranes or other automated mechanisms to access and move inventory within high-density storage racks. AS/RS significantly reduces the need for vast warehouse spaces, optimizes storage capacity, and minimizes manual handling of materials. The automation also improves inventory accuracy, reducing the risk of stockouts or overstocking. Manufacturers can gain real-time insights into their inventory levels through sophisticated inventory management software integrated with the AS/RS system, allowing for optimized ordering and reducing the risk of material shortages that could disrupt production. This level of control and transparency minimizes waste, reduces storage costs, and improves the overall supply chain efficiency.

The implementation of these advanced robotic systems requires careful planning and integration. Consideration must be given to the factory layout, existing infrastructure, and the specific requirements of the manufacturing process. Interoperability between robotic systems and other elements of the innovative factory, such as the ERP and MES systems, is essential for seamless data flow and optimal performance. This integration often requires significant investment in new software and hardware and extensive training for personnel to operate and maintain these advanced systems.

However, the long-term benefits often far outweigh the initial investment. The improved efficiency, reduced errors, and enhanced productivity resulting from implementing robotics and automation significantly impact the bottom line. Moreover, these technologies often enhance worker safety by handling dangerous or repetitive tasks, reducing the risk of workplace injuries. This creates a safer, more productive, and more efficient working environment.

The integration of robotics and automation is not a one-size-fits-all solution. The optimal approach depends on the specific requirements of each manufacturing environment, including the type of products being manufactured, the production volume, and the existing infrastructure. For example, a small-batch manufacturing facility might benefit more from the flexibility of cobots, while a high-volume production line might be better suited to a highly automated system with AS/RS and AGVs. A thorough assessment of the company's needs and resources is vital to ensure that the chosen robotic systems are effectively integrated into the existing operations.

Furthermore, the successful implementation of robotics and automation depends on the availability of skilled workers who can program, operate, and maintain these advanced systems. This highlights the importance of investing in education and training programs to develop the necessary skills within the workforce. A workforce equipped with the necessary skills to effectively utilize and troubleshoot these robotic systems is essential for the long-term success of factory initiatives.

The continuous evolution of robotics and automation technologies presents both opportunities and challenges. Emerging technologies like AI-powered vision systems further enhance the capabilities of robots, enabling them to perform more complex tasks with greater precision and adaptability. These advancements drive further innovation in manufacturing, pushing the boundaries of efficiency and productivity. However, careful consideration must be given to the ethical implications and potential impact on the workforce. The responsible implementation of robotics and automation requires a strategic approach that balances technological advancement with the needs and well-being of the human workforce. A human-centered approach that prioritizes worker training and upskilling is vital to ensure a successful integration of these advanced technologies and a positive impact on the workforce. The innovative factory of the future relies not only on deploying advanced robotic systems but also on a skilled and adaptable workforce capable of working effectively alongside these advanced technologies. This partnership between humans and robots will define the future of manufacturing, driving innovation and ensuring a competitive advantage in the global marketplace.

CYBERSECURITY IN INNOVATIVE MANUFACTURING ENVIRONMENTS

As discussed previously, the seamless integration of advanced robotics and automation forms the backbone of the modern innovative factory. However, this interconnectedness, while driving efficiency and productivity, also introduces significant cybersecurity vulnerabilities. The very features that make innovative manufacturing so powerful – the extensive network of interconnected devices, systems, and software – create an expansive attack surface ripe for exploitation. A successful cyberattack on an innovative factory can have devastating consequences, ranging from minor production disruptions to catastrophic failures with significant financial and reputational damage.

There are numerous potential entry points for cyberattacks. Industrial Control Systems (ICS), which govern the physical processes within the factory, are often legacy systems with outdated security protocols. These systems, designed decades ago, were not built with modern cybersecurity threats in mind. Their vulnerability increases exponentially when connected to the broader enterprise network, creating a pathway for malicious actors to access and manipulate critical manufacturing processes. Moreover, the proliferation of Internet of Things (IoT) devices – sensors, actuators, and other intelligent devices that collect and transmit data – adds to the complexity and expands the attack surface. These devices, often with limited security capabilities, can become easy targets for hackers seeking access to the factory network.

50

One significant concern is the potential for ransomware attacks. A successful ransomware attack can cripple a factory's operations, halting production and causing substantial financial losses. The attackers can encrypt critical data, rendering it inaccessible, and demand a ransom for its release. The longer the factory remains offline, the greater the economic damage. Furthermore, the disruption can impact supply chains, leading to delays and potentially harming customer relationships. This highlights the critical need for robust backup and recovery systems, regularly tested and updated, to ensure business continuity during a ransomware attack.

Beyond ransomware, the potential for sabotage is a serious threat. Malicious actors could manipulate ICS to damage equipment, alter production processes, or even cause physical harm to personnel. Imagine a scenario where a hacker remotely manipulates a robotic arm to perform actions outside its normal parameters, leading to damage to the equipment or injury to nearby workers. Such attacks can have severe consequences, requiring extensive repairs, potentially leading to production delays, and creating significant safety hazards.

The sophistication of these attacks is constantly evolving. Advanced Persistent Threats (APTs) – stealthy, long-term attacks – are particularly concerning. APTs often involve network infiltration over an extended period, allowing attackers to gather intelligence and plan more impactful strikes. These attacks can go undetected for months or even years, giving the attacker ample time to execute their malicious plan.

Mitigating these risks requires a multi-layered approach to cybersecurity. One crucial strategy is network segmentation. By dividing the factory network into isolated segments, attackers who manage to compromise one segment are prevented from accessing other critical areas. This limits the potential impact of a successful attack. Similarly, strict access control measures, including strong passwords, multi-factor authentication, and regular security audits, are essential to limit who can access the network and its sensitive data. This includes not just employees but also external contractors and vendors who may need access to the system.

Regular security assessments and penetration testing are critical. These tests simulate real-world attacks, identifying network defenses' vulnerabilities and weaknesses. This proactive approach allows companies to address potential security flaws before malicious actors can exploit them. The results of these assessments should be carefully analyzed and prioritized for remediation. Furthermore, continuous network activity monitoring is essential to detect and respond quickly to suspicious behavior. Intrusion Detection Systems (IDS) and Security Information and Event Management (SIEM) tools can be crucial in identifying and alerting security personnel to potential threats.

A comprehensive incident response plan is paramount. This plan should outline procedures for responding to cyberattacks, from relatively minor incidents to significant breaches. This plan must be regularly tested and updated to ensure its effectiveness in responding to the evolving threat landscape. This plan should include clearly defined roles and responsibilities, communication protocols, and procedures for containing and mitigating the impact of an attack. Regular training for personnel on cybersecurity best practices is also critical, empowering employees to identify and report suspicious activity.

Furthermore, adopting secure coding practices throughout the development lifecycle of software and applications used within the innovative factory is crucial. Secure coding minimizes vulnerabilities introduced during the software development process. Regular software updates and patches are essential to address known vulnerabilities and protect against emerging threats. These updates need to be carefully managed and rolled out, minimizing disruption to production.

Finally, collaboration and information sharing are vital.

Manufacturers should actively participate in information-sharing initiatives, sharing knowledge and insights about cyber threats and best practices with other organizations in the industry. This collective effort can help build a more vigorous, resilient defense against the constantly evolving threat landscape. The cybersecurity of an innovative factory is not a one-time implementation; it is an ongoing process that requires constant vigilance, adaptation, and investment. Ignoring these critical aspects can lead to significant financial losses, reputational damage, and even endanger personnel. A proactive and comprehensive cybersecurity strategy is not simply a cost; it is an investment in the innovative factory's long-term security, stability, and success.

CLOUD COMPUTING AND DATA ANALYTICS FOR MANUFACTURING

The robust cybersecurity measures discussed previously are critical for protecting the valuable data generated within an innovative factory.

However, the sheer volume and velocity of data produced by interconnected devices, AI algorithms, and advanced automation systems present unique storage, processing, and analytical challenges. This is where cloud computing emerges as a transformative technology, offering scalable and cost-effective solutions to manage and leverage this data deluge.

Cloud computing provides a flexible and adaptable infrastructure for storing and processing massive datasets an innovative factory generates. Unlike on-premise solutions, which require significant upfront investments in hardware and IT infrastructure, cloud computing offers a pay-as-you-go model, enabling manufacturers to scale their computing resources up or down based on their needs. This scalability is crucial in a dynamic manufacturing environment where data volumes can fluctuate significantly depending on production levels and operational demands. The elasticity of cloud resources allows manufacturers to easily handle peak loads without incurring the costs associated with over-provisioning on-premise infrastructure.

The cloud's capacity to handle Big Data is another key advantage.

The vast amounts of data generated by IoT sensors, machine learning models, and other sources within an innovative factory often exceed the capabilities of traditional on-premise systems. With their distributed architecture and massive storage capacity, cloud platforms can easily accommodate this data influx, ensuring that no valuable information is lost or overlooked. This is particularly crucial for advanced analytics applications that require the analysis of large historical datasets to identify trends, predict failures, and optimize production processes.

Furthermore, cloud computing facilitates the deployment of advanced data analytics tools and techniques. Many cloud providers offer pre-built analytics platforms and services that can be readily integrated into the innovative factory ecosystem. These platforms offer a range of capabilities, from basic data visualization and reporting to sophisticated machine-learning algorithms for predictive maintenance and process optimization. Manufacturers can leverage these services to gain deeper insights into their operational data, identifying areas for improvement and driving continuous optimization.

Consider, for instance, the application of cloud-based predictive maintenance. By analyzing data from sensors embedded in machines, predictive maintenance models can identify anomalies and predict potential failures before they occur. This proactive approach enables manufacturers to schedule maintenance proactively, minimizing downtime and preventing costly production disruptions. Cloud computing provides the necessary infrastructure to process vast amounts of sensor data in real-time, generating timely alerts and enabling swift remedial action. Deploying and scaling these predictive models rapidly is a significant advantage of cloud-based solutions.

Real-time monitoring is another crucial application of cloud computing in innovative manufacturing. Cloud-based dashboards and visualization tools enable manufacturers to monitor key performance indicators (KPIs) across the factory floor. This real-time visibility provides valuable insights into production efficiency, machine utilization, and potential bottlenecks. Operators can quickly identify and address issues, ensuring smooth and uninterrupted operations. The scalability of cloud infrastructure ensures that even the largest and most complex factories can be effectively monitored in real-time.

The capabilities of cloud computing significantly enhance the integration of AI and machine learning algorithms. The computational power required for training and deploying complex AI models is often substantial. Cloud computing offers the necessary resources, allowing manufacturers to leverage the full potential of AI for tasks such as defect detection, quality control, and process optimization. Cloud-based AI platforms also offer pre-trained models and libraries that can accelerate the development and deployment of AI solutions, reducing time-to-market and development costs.

Data security is paramount in any cloud deployment, particularly in innovative manufacturing.

Manufacturers must carefully evaluate cloud providers' security features and certifications, ensuring that their data is protected against unauthorized access and cyber threats. This includes robust access control mechanisms, data encryption in transit and at rest, and compliance with relevant industry regulations. A multi-layered security approach, including network segmentation and intrusion detection systems, is critical in mitigating potential risks.

Beyond the technical aspects, adopting cloud computing in innovative manufacturing requires a strategic data management and governance approach. Manufacturers must establish clear policies and procedures for data collection, storage, processing, and access, ensuring compliance with data privacy regulations. A well-defined data governance framework is essential for ensuring the integrity, accuracy, and security of the data used for decision-making. This includes establishing clear roles and responsibilities for data management and implementing robust data quality control measures.

Furthermore, the successful implementation of cloud computing in innovative manufacturing requires a cultural shift within the organization. Employees need to be trained to utilize cloud-based tools and platforms effectively. A collaborative approach involving IT professionals, operations managers, and data scientists is essential for ensuring seamless integration and maximizing the benefits of cloud computing. This collaboration should extend to the supply chain, integrating cloud-based systems with suppliers and customers to enhance communication, visibility, and collaboration across the entire value chain.

Transitioning to a cloud-based infrastructure may involve significant IT systems and workflow changes.

Manufacturers must develop a phased implementation plan, starting with pilot projects to test and validate the chosen cloud solutions. This approach allows for iterative improvements and minimizes the risk of disruptions to existing operations. A thorough assessment of existing IT infrastructure is crucial to identify areas requiring upgrades or replacements to ensure seamless integration with cloud services.

Finally, choosing a cloud provider is a critical decision.

Manufacturers should carefully evaluate the offerings of different providers, considering factors such as scalability, security, cost, and geographic location. Choosing a provider with robust support and expertise in the manufacturing industry is essential for successful implementation. It's also crucial to consider the provider's compliance with relevant industry standards and regulations, particularly data privacy and security. Continuous monitoring and evaluation of the cloud solution are essential to ensure ongoing performance and security. The cloud is not a static entity, and its capabilities constantly evolve, requiring manufacturers to adapt and optimize their cloud strategies accordingly to remain competitive. The investment in cloud computing and data analytics represents a significant step toward realizing the full potential of innovative manufacturing.

The benefits of embracing cloud computing in innovative manufacturing extend beyond the mere storage and processing of data. It fosters a data-driven culture, empowering decision-making based on real-time insights and predictive analytics. This facilitates proactive problem-solving, improved operational efficiency, and the development of products and services. Ultimately, the strategic deployment of cloud computing and data analytics represents a cornerstone of an ingenious and competitive manufacturing enterprise.

CHAPTER 3
INNOVATIVE FACTORY DESIGN AND IMPLEMENTATION

DESIGNING AN INNOVATIVE FACTORY ARCHITECTURE

Building a successful, innovative factory requires a well-defined architecture that integrates various technologies and systems seamlessly. This architecture serves as the blueprint for the digital transformation journey, ensuring that all components work together harmoniously to achieve the desired efficiency, productivity, and agility levels. The design must consider several key elements, including the network infrastructure, the data management system, and the integration strategies that bind these elements together.

A robust and reliable network infrastructure is the foundation of any factory architecture. This network must handle the massive amounts of data generated by the interconnected devices and systems throughout the factory. A high-bandwidth, low-latency network is critical for real-time data acquisition, processing, and communication. Consideration must be given to the choice of networking technologies, such as Ethernet, Industrial Ethernet (e.g., Profinet, EtherCAT), and wireless technologies (e.g., Wi-Fi, 5G), depending on the specific needs of the factory and the capabilities of individual machines. A layered approach to network design, with separate networks for different functionalities (e.g., control networks, data acquisition networks, enterprise networks), is often recommended to enhance security and reliability.

Furthermore, network security is paramount. Implementing firewalls, intrusion detection systems, and robust access control mechanisms is crucial to protect the network from cyber threats and ensure data confidentiality, integrity, and availability. Regular security audits and penetration testing should be part of the ongoing maintenance strategy.

The data generated within an innovative factory is a valuable asset that needs to be effectively managed and leveraged. A comprehensive data management system is crucial for collecting, storing, processing, and analyzing this data. This system should integrate data from various sources, including machines, sensors, PLCs, ERP, and MES systems. The choice of data management technology will depend on the volume, velocity, and variety of data generated. In many cases, combining on-premise and cloud-based solutions is the most effective approach, leveraging each of their strengths. On-premise systems can be used for real-time data acquisition and processing, while cloud-based solutions provide scalability, elasticity, and advanced analytics capabilities. A crucial aspect of data management is data quality. Implementing robust data quality control measures is crucial to ensure the accuracy, completeness, and consistency of the data used for decision-making. This involves establishing clear data governance policies and procedures, including data validation, cleansing, and standardization processes.

Data integration is critical to factory architecture, ensuring that data from different systems and sources can be seamlessly accessed and analyzed. Enterprise service buses (ESBs) or integration platforms as a service (PaaS) solutions can streamline this process. These platforms facilitate the exchange of data between various systems, eliminating data silos and providing a unified view of the factory floor. The choice of integration technology will depend on factors such as the system's complexity, the number of systems to be integrated, and the need for real-time data integration. APIs (Application Programming Interfaces) facilitate data integration between systems and applications. Well-defined APIs ensure interoperability and enable developers to create custom applications leveraging data from various sources.

Furthermore, developing standardized data formats and protocols can facilitate seamless data exchange, reducing integration complexities and promoting interoperability.

The choice of factory architecture also depends heavily on the type of manufacturing processes involved. For example, a batch production environment may require a different architecture than a mass production environment. Batch production, characterized by producing small quantities of customized products, may benefit from a more flexible and adaptable architecture that can handle frequent changes in production schedules and product configurations. In contrast, mass production, where large quantities of identical products are manufactured, may require a more streamlined and standardized architecture optimized for speed and efficiency. Modular architectures, which break down the factory into smaller, independent modules, offer greater flexibility and scalability, making them particularly suitable for environments with evolving production requirements. This modularity allows for easier upgrades, expansion, and reconfiguration as needed, mitigating the risk of significant downtime during technological updates.

Another important consideration is the level of automation desired. Some innovative factories may be largely automated, with minimal human intervention, while others may retain significant human involvement in specific processes. This choice will impact the architecture's design, with highly automated factories requiring more sophisticated control systems and data analytics capabilities. The architecture should support the integration of robotic systems, automated guided vehicles (AGVs), and other automation technologies seamlessly. Integrating human-machine interfaces (HMIs) is crucial to ensure that human operators can effectively interact with the automated systems and monitor the production process. Effective HMIs are crucial for real-time monitoring of key performance indicators (KPIs), allowing operators to promptly identify and address potential problems, contributing to enhanced productivity and reduced downtime.

Cybersecurity is a paramount concern throughout the factory architecture. Given the increasing interconnectedness of systems and the reliance on data networks, securing the factory's digital infrastructure is essential to protect against cyber threats. A layered security approach, incorporating various security measures at different levels of the architecture, is crucial for protecting the factory from potential attacks. This approach includes firewalls, intrusion detection systems, robust access control mechanisms at the network level, data encryption at the data level, and secure software development practices at the application level.

Regular security audits and penetration testing are essential to identify vulnerabilities and mitigate potential risks. Moreover, the factory's cybersecurity strategy must consider compliance with relevant industry standards and regulations, ensuring that data is protected and privacy is respected. Employee training and awareness programs are critical to ensure all personnel understand their roles in protecting the factory's cybersecurity.

Implementing a factory architecture is an iterative process that requires careful planning and execution. Starting with a pilot project on a limited scale can help assess the feasibility of the chosen architecture and identify potential challenges before a full-scale deployment. This phased approach allows for iterative improvements and minimizes the risk of disruptions to existing operations. A thorough assessment of existing IT infrastructure and processes is crucial to identify potential bottlenecks and incompatibilities. The migration to a new architecture should be carefully planned to minimize downtime and ensure the smooth transition of existing systems and processes.

Furthermore, continuous monitoring and evaluation of the architecture's performance is necessary to identify areas for improvement and ensure its effectiveness. Analytics dashboards can help visualize key metrics and track progress toward the desired outcomes, facilitating data-driven decision-making in refining and enhancing the factory's architecture. Regular updates and upgrades are also necessary to maintain the efficiency and security of the architecture in the face of ever-evolving technological advancements and emerging security threats. The dynamic nature of technology necessitates a continuous improvement mindset, with regular reviews and updates to maintain optimal performance.

Finally, successfully implementing an innovation factory architecture requires a collaborative effort involving various stakeholders, including IT professionals, operations managers, engineers, and data scientists. Effective communication and collaboration are crucial to ensure the alignment of goals and the efficient execution of the implementation plan. A well-defined project management framework is also necessary to track progress, manage risks, and ensure the project stays on track. Training and support are essential to enable personnel to utilize the new systems and processes effectively. Adopting an innovation factory architecture necessitates a cultural shift within the organization, encouraging a data-driven mindset and a collaborative approach to problem-solving. Investing in employee training and development is crucial to building the necessary skills and knowledge for operating and maintaining an innovative factory effectively. Manufacturers can create a robust, efficient, and secure innovative factory that delivers significant value by engaging all stakeholders throughout the process.

IMPLEMENTING INNOVATIVE MANUFACTURING TECHNOLOGIES

Implementing manufacturing technologies is a multifaceted undertaking that demands a structured approach. It's not simply about acquiring the latest technologies; it's about integrating them strategically into existing operational workflows, fostering a culture of data-driven decision-making, and managing the inevitable change that accompanies such a significant transformation. This process can be broken down into several key phases, each with its challenges and best practices.

The initial phase involves meticulous project planning. This begins with a thorough assessment of the current manufacturing processes, identifying bottlenecks, inefficiencies, and areas ripe for improvement. This assessment isn't merely a technical exercise; it also requires understanding the organization's strategic goals and aligning technology investments with those objectives. For instance, a company aiming for increased production speed will prioritize technologies like automated guided vehicles (AGVs) and high-speed robotics, whereas a company focused on enhanced product quality might invest heavily in advanced quality inspection systems and predictive maintenance software. A detailed cost-benefit analysis should also be conducted, factoring in the initial investment in hardware and software and the ongoing costs of maintenance, training, and support. This detailed planning phase lays the foundation for a successful implementation, minimizing costly mistakes and ensuring alignment with broader business strategies. A robust project management plan, incorporating Gantt charts, resource allocation strategies, and risk mitigation protocols, is critical for effective execution. This plan must address potential risks, including integration challenges, unexpected downtime, and employee resistance to change.

Following the planning phase comes technology selection. This requires a deep understanding of the various manufacturing technologies available and their applicability to the specific manufacturing environment. For example, the choice of a manufacturing execution system (MES) will depend on factors such as the complexity of the manufacturing processes, the volume of data generated, and the level of integration required with other enterprise systems. Similarly, the selection of industrial IoT (IIoT) platforms will be guided by the need for scalability, security, and real-time data analytics. Consideration must also be given to interoperability between different technologies. Selecting technologies from different vendors can introduce integration complexities, potentially hindering data sharing and creating data silos. Considering their track record, technical expertise, and support capabilities, a strategic approach to vendor selection is crucial. Moreover, a thorough evaluation of the technology's scalability and ability to adapt to future needs is essential to avoid premature obsolescence and costly replacements. Proof-of-concept projects can be invaluable in assessing the viability and performance of specific technologies before a full-scale deployment.

The successful implementation of manufacturing technologies necessitates a robust change management strategy. This involves preparing the workforce for the transition to new technologies and processes. Resistance to change is a common hurdle in digital transformation initiatives, and effective change management mitigates this risk. This involves open communication, clearly explaining the benefits of the new technologies, and addressing employees' concerns and anxieties. Comprehensive training programs ensure that employees have the necessary skills and knowledge to operate and maintain the new systems effectively. The training should be tailored to different roles and skill levels, empowering employees to participate actively in the innovative factory's operation. Moreover, a well-structured communication plan keeps employees informed throughout the implementation process, minimizing uncertainty and fostering a sense of ownership in the transformation journey. Change management also encompasses the redefinition of roles and responsibilities, considering the implications of automation on workforce structure. This may involve reskilling or upskilling existing employees to handle new roles or redeploying employees to areas where human expertise remains valuable.

A phased implementation approach is often the most effective strategy. Instead of a disruptive, "big bang" approach that risks significant disruption to operations, a phased approach allows for incremental implementation, starting with a pilot project on a smaller scale. This allows testing and refinement of the chosen technologies and processes before full-scale deployment. The pilot project serves as a valuable learning experience, providing insights into potential challenges and identifying areas for improvement before investing heavily in a complete factory-wide transformation.

This iterative approach minimizes risk, allows for continuous improvement, and reduces the potential for costly mistakes. The insights gained from the pilot project can be used to refine the implementation plan for subsequent phases, ensuring a smoother and more efficient rollout. Continuous monitoring and evaluation are crucial throughout the implementation process, enabling data-driven adjustments to optimize the performance of the innovative factory. Regular review of key performance indicators (KPIs) allows for early identification of potential problems and facilitates proactive adjustments to the implementation strategy.

Real-world examples highlight the importance of careful planning and a phased approach. Consider a large automotive manufacturer that attempted a full-scale implementation of a new MES without a pilot project. The complexity of integrating the new system with existing legacy systems led to significant downtime and production delays, resulting in considerable financial losses. In contrast, a smaller electronics manufacturer took a phased approach, starting with a pilot project in a single production line. This allowed them to identify and address integration challenges before expanding the implementation to other lines, resulting in a much smoother and more successful transition. The successful implementation of manufacturing technologies often requires collaboration with external partners, including technology providers, integration specialists, and consulting firms. These partners bring specialized expertise, accelerating the implementation process and ensuring the effective integration of different systems. Effective communication and collaboration are crucial, ensuring that all stakeholders are aligned on the goals and objectives of the project.

The journey toward a fully operational innovative factory is rarely linear; it's an iterative process demanding constant adaptation and improvement. Data analytics play a crucial role in this ongoing optimization. Sophisticated data analytics tools allow manufacturers to monitor key performance indicators (KPIs) in real-time, identifying areas for improvement and enabling data-driven decision-making. Manufacturers can identify bottlenecks, predict equipment failures, and optimize production schedules by analyzing data from various sources, including machines, sensors, and ERP systems. This data-driven approach to process optimization is a hallmark of successful innovative factories, continuously enhancing efficiency and productivity. Moreover, continuous improvement initiatives, incorporating feedback from employees, operations managers, and other stakeholders, refine the innovative factory's capabilities over time.

Finally, the ongoing maintenance and security of the implemented technologies are paramount. Innovative factories rely on a complex network of interconnected devices and systems, making them vulnerable to cyber threats. Therefore, a robust cybersecurity framework is essential to protect the factory's digital infrastructure and sensitive data. This includes regular security audits, penetration testing, and the implementation of appropriate security measures to safeguard against potential attacks. The ongoing maintenance of the implemented technologies is also critical to ensure their continued reliability and efficiency. Regular updates, preventive maintenance schedules, and employee training programs all contribute to the long-term success of the innovative factory. The ever-evolving nature of technology demands continuous learning and adaptation, ensuring that the innovative factory remains at the cutting edge of manufacturing innovation. The successful implementation of manufacturing technologies is not a destination but a continuous journey of improvement and optimization.

INTEGRATING LEGACY SYSTEMS WITH NEW TECHNOLOGIES

The transition to an innovative factory is rarely a clean slate operation. Most manufacturers invest significantly in legacy systems – equipment, software, and control systems that have served the company faithfully for years, perhaps even decades.

While perhaps outdated in terms of modern technological capabilities, these systems represent a substantial sunk cost and often possess unique functionalities crucial to the current production processes. Simply discarding these assets is often impractical, economically unfeasible, and strategically unwise.

Instead, the challenge becomes seamless integration: connecting these legacy systems with the new, cutting-edge technologies that define the factory paradigm. This integration is arguably one of factory transformation's most complex and critical phases.

The first hurdle lies in assessing the legacy systems. This isn't just about identifying the hardware and software in use; it requires a deep understanding of their functionalities, limitations, and interdependencies within the existing production workflows. A comprehensive audit is crucial, detailing the age, condition, performance metrics, and potential risks associated with each legacy system. This assessment should also thoroughly evaluate the data these systems generate, their communication protocols, and the potential for data integration with the new innovative factory infrastructure. Detailed documentation of the legacy system's architecture, including data flow diagrams, network maps, and functional specifications, forms the foundation for the integration process. Failing to document these systems meticulously can lead to unforeseen complications and delays during the integration phase.

Once the assessment is complete, a strategic integration plan must be formulated. This plan should outline how each legacy system will be connected to the new innovative factory infrastructure. Several approaches are possible, each with its advantages and disadvantages. One common strategy involves deploying gateways or adapters to bridge the communication gap between the legacy systems and the new technologies. These gateways translate data from the legacy systems' proprietary protocols into industry-standard formats like OPC UA or MQTT, allowing them to communicate seamlessly with modern platforms such as cloud-based MES systems or IIoT platforms. This approach avoids the need for complete replacement of the legacy systems, preserving their existing functionalities while enabling integration with the new innovative factory ecosystem. However, this approach can be technically complex, requiring specialized expertise in legacy system protocols and modern integration technologies. The cost of developing and implementing custom gateways can also be significant.

Another approach involves modernizing or upgrading the legacy systems. This might entail replacing outdated hardware components, upgrading software to newer versions with improved functionalities, or implementing software patches to enhance security and interoperability. Such modernization can significantly extend the lifespan of legacy systems, reducing the overall cost of the factory transformation. However, upgrading legacy systems can be time-consuming and expensive, especially if extensive software customization is required. It also risks introducing unforeseen issues or incompatibilities if not managed carefully. Thorough testing and validation are essential to ensure the system's stability and reliability after any upgrade.

In some instances, complete replacement of legacy systems may be the most effective solution. This is particularly true when the legacy systems are obsolete, unreliable, or significantly hindering the integration of new technologies. While this represents a significant financial investment, it can bring significant long-term benefits in improved efficiency, productivity, and reduced maintenance costs. The decision to replace a legacy system should be based on a careful cost-benefit analysis, weighing the investment costs against the potential returns from improved performance and streamlined operations. The choice between these approaches isn't always binary; a hybrid approach is often optimal, combining partial modernization, gateway implementation, and selective replacement of components to achieve the desired level of integration.

Regardless of the chosen approach, careful consideration must be given to data security and integrity. Legacy systems might lack the robust security measures found in modern technologies, creating vulnerabilities that could compromise the security of the entire factory network. Integrating legacy systems demands a comprehensive cybersecurity strategy, including thorough risk assessments, vulnerability scans, and the implementation of appropriate security controls, such as firewalls, intrusion detection systems, and access control policies. This approach is crucial to mitigate risks associated with legacy system vulnerabilities. Data migration also requires careful planning and execution to ensure data accuracy and integrity during the transition. Inconsistent data formats between legacy systems and the new innovative factory infrastructure can lead to integration problems and compromised data quality. Data cleaning, transformation, and validation procedures are crucial to address these issues.

One of the critical considerations often overlooked is the human element. Experienced personnel are typically intimately familiar with legacy systems' nuances, quirks, and limitations. This knowledge is invaluable during integration, yet their expertise might not readily translate to the new factory technologies. A robust change management strategy is essential to mitigate this risk. Training programs should be designed to upskill existing personnel in operating and maintaining the new systems while retaining their experience with legacy systems to ensure a smooth transition. Furthermore, communication and collaboration between IT personnel, operations teams, and integration specialists are vital for successful integration.

Regular meetings, progress reports, and open communication channels are crucial to address any challenges or concerns that may arise throughout the process. These meetings should foster a sense of shared ownership and responsibility among all stakeholders involved in the integration process.

Finally, the ongoing maintenance and support of the integrated legacy systems are critical to the long-term success of the innovative factory. Regular maintenance schedules, software updates, and security patches are necessary to ensure these systems' ongoing reliability and security. The integration process isn't a one-off project; it's an ongoing optimization, adaptation, and refinement process. Continuous monitoring, data analysis, and feedback loops are essential to identify potential issues, optimize system performance, and enhance the overall efficiency of the innovative factory. This ongoing process demands continuous learning and improvement, adapting to the ever-evolving landscape of manufacturing technologies. The successful integration of legacy systems is a crucial step in the journey toward a brilliant and efficient factory, requiring a well-defined strategy, meticulous planning, and a commitment to ongoing adaptation and improvement. This integration is not just a technical challenge but a strategic imperative that requires careful consideration of all aspects of the manufacturing environment, including the human element and the company's long-term vision.

OPTIMIZING PRODUCTION PROCESSES WITH INNOVATIVE TECHNOLOGIES

The successful integration of legacy systems, as discussed in the previous section, lays the groundwork for implementing technologies to optimize production processes. This optimization goes beyond simply connecting disparate systems; it involves leveraging the data generated by these integrated systems to drive significant efficiency improvements, reduce waste, and enhance product quality. This section explores how technologies can be deployed to achieve these goals, offering practical examples and analyzing their impact on manufacturing performance.

One of the most impactful applications of technologies is in predictive maintenance. Traditional maintenance strategies rely on scheduled or reactive repairs, leading to downtime and increased costs. By integrating sensors on machinery and equipment, coupled with advanced analytics, innovative factories can predict potential equipment failures before they occur. This predictive capability allows for proactive maintenance, minimizing downtime and optimizing the lifespan of expensive machinery. For example, a manufacturer of automotive parts might deploy vibration sensors on their CNC milling machines. These sensors collect data on vibrations, temperature, and power consumption.

This data is then analyzed using machine learning algorithms to identify patterns indicative of impending failures. The system can then alert maintenance personnel in advance, allowing them to schedule repairs during planned downtime, preventing costly emergency shutdowns and production delays. The economic benefits are significant, reducing maintenance costs, minimizing production disruptions, and extending equipment lifespan. Implementing predictive maintenance requires careful consideration of sensor placement, data acquisition methods, and the development of appropriate predictive models. The accuracy and effectiveness of the predictive model directly impact the value proposition of the predictive maintenance strategy.

Real-time production monitoring is another area where technologies deliver significant improvements. A comprehensive view of the production process can be established by integrating data from various sources – including PLCs, SCADA systems, and even manual data entry. This real-time data provides actionable insights into bottlenecks, inefficiencies, and potential quality issues. For instance, a consumer electronics manufacturer could utilize real-time production monitoring to track the throughput of each assembly line. Any slowdown or deviation from the expected output can be immediately identified and addressed, minimizing production delays and ensuring timely delivery of products.

Furthermore, real-time data allows for identifying defects in real-time, reducing scrap rates and improving overall product quality. This is made possible by implementing automated quality control systems that integrate vision systems and other sensors to identify defects during the manufacturing process. Such systems can instantly halt production if a defect is identified, preventing the creation of numerous defective products. The overall effect is a considerable waste reduction, resulting in cost savings and higher profit margins.

The use of advanced analytics goes beyond simply monitoring production. Manufacturers can gain deeper insights into their operations by applying sophisticated statistical techniques and machine learning algorithms to the accumulated data. This allows for optimizing production parameters, process improvements, and enhanced decision-making. For example, a food processing company might analyze temperature, humidity, and ingredient quality data to identify the optimal conditions for maximizing product yield and shelf life. This data-driven approach allows the company to refine its processes, improving efficiency and product quality continually. These improvements can be subtle, such as minor adjustments to processing temperatures or ingredient ratios, accumulating over time to yield substantial improvements in overall performance.

The successful implementation of such analytical tools requires skilled data scientists and engineers who can extract meaningful insights from large datasets and translate these insights into actionable strategies.

Technologies also play a significant role in optimizing supply chain management. By integrating systems across the entire supply chain, manufacturers can better see inventory levels, transportation logistics, and supplier performance. This improved visibility allows for better inventory management, reduced lead times, and enhanced responsiveness to changing market demands.

Consider a pharmaceutical manufacturer integrating its production systems with its suppliers' systems. This integration enables the real-time monitoring of raw material availability, leading to more accurate demand forecasting and just-in-time inventory management. This reduces the risk of stockouts, minimizing production disruptions and enhancing overall supply chain efficiency. The improved communication and coordination across the supply chain translate into cost savings, reduced lead times, and enhanced customer satisfaction. These benefits are amplified by using blockchain technology, which improves transparency and traceability within the supply chain.

Furthermore, adopting augmented reality (AR) and virtual reality (VR) technologies is transforming manufacturing processes.

AR overlays digital information in the real world, providing workers with real-time guidance and instructions. This can be particularly helpful in complex assembly processes, minimizing errors and increasing efficiency. For example, technicians performing maintenance on complex equipment can use AR headsets to access interactive diagrams and instructions, minimizing downtime and ensuring the correct procedures are followed. VR, on the other hand, allows for the simulation of manufacturing processes, enabling the identification of potential bottlenecks and inefficiencies before they impact production. This proactive approach to process optimization is crucial in reducing errors and improving overall productivity. Investing in AR/VR technologies requires careful consideration of the specific needs of the manufacturing processes and the integration with existing systems.

Finally, the human element remains crucial in the success of factory initiatives. The implementation of innovative technologies should empower employees, not replace them. Training programs ensure that workers have the necessary skills to operate and maintain the new systems. Moreover, continuous feedback loops should be established to incorporate workers' insights and expertise in the ongoing optimization of processes. A culture of continuous improvement, where employees are encouraged to contribute to improving processes, is essential. Integrating technologies shouldn't be viewed as a replacement for human expertise but rather as an augmentation that enhances capabilities and productivity.

In conclusion, optimizing production processes with technologies is a multifaceted endeavor involving integrating various technologies, data analysis, and a commitment to continuous improvement. By adopting a holistic approach that considers legacy system integration, predictive maintenance, real-time production monitoring, advanced analytics, supply chain optimization, and AR/VR technologies, manufacturers can significantly improve efficiency, reduce waste, and enhance product quality. This journey, however, requires careful planning, a strong focus on data security, and a dedicated effort to train and empower the workforce. The transition to an innovative factory is not just a technological upgrade; it's a strategic transformation that requires a long-term vision and a commitment to continuous learning and adaptation.

MEASURING AND EVALUATING THE ROI OF INNOVATIVE MANUFACTURING

The transition to an innovative factory, while promising significant improvements in efficiency and profitability, demands a rigorous approach to measuring and evaluating its return on investment (ROI). Implementing technologies isn't enough; a robust framework for assessing their impact is crucial for justifying the initial investment and demonstrating ongoing value to stakeholders. This involves establishing key performance indicators (KPIs), meticulously tracking relevant metrics, and employing appropriate ROI calculation methodologies. A comprehensive ROI analysis goes beyond simple cost-benefit comparisons; it encompasses a holistic assessment of the tangible and intangible benefits accrued through manufacturing initiatives.

One of the primary challenges in measuring the ROI of innovative manufacturing lies in the multifaceted nature of its benefits. The improvements aren't always immediately apparent or easily quantifiable. For instance, enhanced product quality might lead to increased customer satisfaction and brand loyalty, which are difficult to translate directly into monetary figures. Similarly, reduced downtime due to predictive maintenance might prevent costly production delays, yet this benefit is only realized by preventing potential losses. Therefore, a multifaceted approach is necessary to capture both direct and indirect benefits.

To effectively measure the ROI, it's crucial to establish clear and measurable KPIs aligned with the strategic objectives of the manufacturing initiative. These KPIs should be specific, measurable, achievable, relevant, and time-bound (SMART). Examples of such KPIs include:

Overall Equipment Effectiveness (OEE): This metric quantifies the effectiveness of equipment utilization, encompassing availability, performance, and quality rate. An increase in OEE directly translates to increased production output and reduced downtime. Improvements in OEE following innovative factory implementation should be carefully tracked and attributed to specific technologies or processes. For example, implementing predictive maintenance can directly impact the availability component of OEE, leading to a measurable improvement.

Similarly, real-time production monitoring can identify and rectify performance bottlenecks, leading to higher performance rates. The data from predictive maintenance and real-time monitoring systems should be integrated to demonstrate the combined effect on OEE.

Manufacturing Cost Reduction: Innovative manufacturing initiatives often lead to significant cost reductions through improved efficiency and reduced waste. These cost reductions can be tracked by comparing the manufacturing costs before and after implementing technologies. Specific cost categories, such as labor costs, energy consumption, material waste, and maintenance expenses, should be analyzed separately to identify where the most significant cost savings have been achieved. For instance, reducing material waste due to real-time quality control systems can be calculated by comparing the scrap generated before and after implementation. Similarly, the reduction in maintenance costs due to predictive maintenance can be determined by comparing maintenance expenditures before and after implementing the predictive maintenance system. It's vital to delineate the cost savings directly attributable to specific manufacturing implementations.

Product Quality Improvement: Innovative manufacturing technologies, such as automated quality control systems, can lead to significant improvements in product quality, resulting in reduced defect rates and fewer returns. This improvement can be measured by tracking the defect rate, customer returns, and warranty claims. A decrease in these metrics represents a significant improvement in product quality, translating into reduced costs and increased customer satisfaction. For example, implementing advanced vision systems in a packaging line can significantly reduce the number of products with packaging defects. The reduction in defective products can be quantified and translated into cost savings.

Lead Time Reduction: Innovative manufacturing can streamline production processes, leading to a reduction in lead times. This improved efficiency can enhance customer satisfaction and faster response to market demands. The reduction in lead times should be carefully monitored and attributed to specific manufacturing technologies or process improvements. For example, improved inventory management through real-time data integration can lead to a shorter procurement lead time. This should be documented and quantified.

Improved Inventory Management: manufacturing enables more accurate inventory management by integrating systems and enhancing visibility across the supply chain. This reduces inventory holding costs, minimizes stockouts, and improves responsiveness to demand fluctuations. Quantifying the reduction in inventory holding costs, the decrease in stockout incidents, and the improvement in fill rates can demonstrate the positive impact of innovative manufacturing on inventory management.

Employee Productivity: While often overlooked, the impact of innovative manufacturing on employee productivity should be evaluated. Technologies can automate repetitive tasks, freeing employees to focus on higher-value activities. Measuring employee productivity improvements requires careful consideration of the specific tasks and roles impacted by manufacturing initiatives. This could involve comparing output per employee before and after implementation or the time spent on specific tasks.

Once the relevant KPIs have been identified and tracked, various methodologies can be used to assess the ROI of manufacturing initiatives. The most straightforward approach is a cost-benefit analysis, comparing the total implementation costs against the total benefits realized. However, this approach often overlooks intangible benefits, such as improved brand reputation or employee morale. More sophisticated methodologies, such as discounted cash flow (DCF) analysis, consider the time value of money, providing a more accurate picture of the long-term ROI. Sensitivity analysis can help assess the impact of uncertainties on the ROI, providing a more robust and realistic assessment.

Furthermore, implementing a robust data analytics platform is crucial for collecting, storing, and analyzing the data required to measure the ROI of manufacturing initiatives. This platform should be capable of integrating data from various sources, including PLCs, SCADA systems, sensors, and ERP systems. Advanced analytics techniques, such as machine learning, can identify trends and patterns in the data, providing further insights into the performance of manufacturing technologies.

A well-designed data analytics platform ensures that the data needed for ROI calculations is readily available and accurate.

In conclusion, measuring and evaluating the ROI of manufacturing initiatives requires a holistic and data-driven approach. Manufacturers can effectively demonstrate the value of their investments in manufacturing technologies by establishing clear KPIs, meticulously tracking relevant metrics, and employing appropriate ROI calculation methodologies. This necessitates a dedicated effort to build data infrastructure and cultivate the expertise required to extract meaningful insights from the generated data. Ignoring the ROI assessment can lead to underinvestment or misallocation of resources. A clear understanding of the financial implications allows for strategic decision-making, fostering continuous improvement and maximizing the return on investment in innovative manufacturing. The ongoing monitoring and adjustment of the implementation based on the data-driven ROI analysis ensures that innovative manufacturing delivers its promised transformative results.

CHAPTER 4
CASE STUDIES IN INNOVATIVE MANUFACTURING

TESLAS GIGAFACTORY: A PARADIGM OF INNOVATIVE MANUFACTURING

Tesla's Gigafactory, a sprawling complex initially conceived for battery production but rapidly expanding to encompass the entire vehicle manufacturing process, is a compelling case study in innovative manufacturing. Its success isn't merely about scale; it's a testament to a meticulously planned and executed integration of advanced technologies, a commitment to vertical integration, and a data-driven optimization approach. This paradigm shift in manufacturing challenges conventional wisdom and offers valuable lessons for other industries seeking to leverage manufacturing principles.

The foundation of Tesla's innovative manufacturing strategy rests upon its extensive automation and robotics deployment. Gigafactories utilize a vast network of robots for tasks ranging from welding and painting to assembly and material handling. These aren't simply standalone robotic arms; they're intricately coordinated through sophisticated control systems, forming a highly interconnected and responsive production ecosystem. The integration of robotics isn't just about replacing human labor; it's about achieving precision, consistency, and speed unattainable through traditional methods. The robots operate accurately and minimize errors and waste, a critical factor in maintaining high production efficiency and ensuring product quality.

Beyond the robotic workforce, Tesla leverages sophisticated AI-powered systems for various aspects of the production process.

Predictive maintenance algorithms, trained on massive datasets gathered from sensors embedded throughout the factory, anticipate potential equipment failures and schedule maintenance proactively.

This dramatically reduces downtime, optimizes equipment utilization, and prevents costly disruptions to the production line. The ability to predict failures before they occur prevents significant production delays and minimizes the need for reactive, emergency maintenance – a considerable cost-saving measure. Further illustrating the capabilities of AI, Tesla also employs machine vision systems for quality control, automatically identifying defects and ensuring that only high-quality components and finished vehicles leave the factory.

Tesla's approach to vertical integration is another defining characteristic of its innovative manufacturing strategy. It manufactures many crucial parts in-house rather than relying on external suppliers for key components like batteries. This strategy offers several advantages. It enhances control over the supply chain, mitigating risks associated with supplier dependencies and ensuring timely component availability. Moreover, vertical integration allows for more significant production process optimization, streamlining workflows and reducing logistical complexities. The ability to fine-tune components manufacturing to match the final product's requirements ideally improves overall efficiency. This level of control also facilitates innovation, enabling Tesla to iterate on designs and incorporate new technologies rapidly.

Data analytics plays a pivotal role in Tesla's innovative manufacturing success. An extensive network of sensors across the Gigafactories continuously collects data on various aspects of production, from machine performance and energy consumption to material flow and quality metrics. This raw data is processed and analyzed using advanced analytics techniques, including machine learning and statistical modeling. These analyses provide real-time insights into the production process, enabling Tesla to identify bottlenecks, optimize workflows, and proactively address potential problems.

The insights derived from data analytics are not simply used for reactive problem-solving; they're integral to continuous improvement efforts, allowing Tesla to continuously refine its manufacturing processes and push the boundaries of efficiency.

The sheer scale of data generated by Tesla's Gigafactories necessitates robust data storage and processing infrastructure. This necessitates a sophisticated data management system capable of handling vast volumes of data in real-time, ensuring that crucial information is readily available to decision-makers. This system is not simply a repository of raw data; it's a dynamic platform that facilitates the seamless integration of data from various sources and provides tools for analyzing and visualizing the data. Visualizing trends and patterns in the data empowers operators to make informed decisions, driving further optimization.

Tesla's focus on data-driven decision-making extends beyond the confines of its production facilities. Data collected from the performance of its vehicles in the field is fed back into the manufacturing process. This information contributes to continuous improvement in design and manufacturing, ensuring that future vehicles are even more reliable and efficient. This closed-loop system, where real-world usage data informs the manufacturing process, underscores Tesla's commitment to continuous improvement and highlights the interconnectedness of data across its entire value chain.

However, Tesla's innovative manufacturing approach isn't without challenges. The complexity of its integrated systems necessitates a highly skilled workforce capable of managing and maintaining these advanced technologies. This calls for significant investment in employee training and development to ensure personnel possess the necessary expertise to operate and troubleshoot these sophisticated systems. The reliance on advanced technologies also introduces a certain level of vulnerability to system failures. Robust cybersecurity measures and redundancy systems are crucial to mitigate the risk of disruptions caused by technical issues or cyberattacks. Ensuring the resilience of its systems is paramount to maintaining the smooth operation of the Gigafactories.

Furthermore, the constant drive for innovation and improvement requires a culture of experimentation and adaptation. Tesla's approach involves continuous iteration and refinement of its processes based on ongoing data analysis and feedback. This requires a flexible and adaptable organizational structure capable of quickly responding to changes and incorporating new technologies.

The high level of automation also raises concerns about job displacement. Tesla addresses this by focusing on upskilling its workforce and providing training opportunities for employees to transition into new roles requiring higher expertise.

In summary, Tesla's Gigafactory represents a significant advancement in innovative manufacturing, demonstrating the potential of integrating advanced automation, robotics, AI, and data analytics to achieve unprecedented efficiency and productivity. Its vertically integrated model and its data-driven approach to continuous improvement provide a compelling blueprint for other manufacturers seeking to transform their operations.

However, it also highlights the challenges associated with implementing such complex systems, emphasizing the importance of workforce development, robust cybersecurity, and organizational adaptability. The lessons learned from Tesla's journey offer invaluable insights into the possibilities and complexities of building a brilliant factory, setting a high benchmark for others to follow. The evolution of Tesla's manufacturing approach will undoubtedly continue to shape the future of industrial automation and provide further examples of how innovative manufacturing can revolutionize industries. The constant refinement of their process, driven by data and continuous improvement, is a powerful example of the ongoing potential within innovative manufacturing, offering valuable lessons for future advancements. Tesla's proactive investment in data analytics infrastructure and its commitment to a culture of continuous improvement is key to understanding its sustained success in this evolving technological landscape.

SIEMENS DIGITAL TWIN TECHNOLOGY AND ITS APPLICATIONS

Siemens, a global leader in industrial automation and digitalization, offers a compelling example of how digital twin technology reshapes manufacturing processes. Their implementation goes beyond simple visualization; it's a deeply integrated approach encompassing virtual commissioning, predictive maintenance, and comprehensive process optimization across diverse industrial sectors. Siemens leverages its extensive portfolio of hardware and software solutions to create holistic digital twins, mirroring the physical performance and behavior of their machinery and entire production lines. This allows for a level of operational understanding and control previously unattainable.

The application of digital twins in virtual commissioning represents a significant advancement in the manufacturing lifecycle.

Traditionally, commissioning involved physically assembling and testing equipment, a time-consuming and often error-prone process.

Siemens utilizes digital twins to virtually commission complex machinery and control systems, allowing engineers to identify and resolve design flaws or integration issues before the physical equipment is built. This virtual environment provides a safe space for experimentation, allowing for testing different operating parameters and scenarios without the risk of damaging expensive physical assets. The ability to simulate realistic operating conditions significantly reduces commissioning time, minimizes disruptions during startup, and ensures a smoother transition to full-scale production. This virtual testing capability is particularly valuable for complex systems with numerous interconnected components, where traditional commissioning methods can be unwieldy and expensive. For instance, in the automotive industry, Siemens has assisted manufacturers in virtually commissioning intricate robotic assembly lines, predicting potential bottlenecks, and optimizing the movement of robots to improve efficiency before physical installation. This has led to significant cost savings and accelerated production timelines.

Predictive maintenance is another key area where Siemens' digital twin technology shines. By integrating sensor data from physical assets into the digital twin, Siemens can monitor the real-time performance of equipment and predict potential failures before they occur. Advanced algorithms analyze sensor data, identifying subtle changes indicative of impending malfunctions. This predictive capability enables proactive maintenance scheduling, minimizing downtime and extending the lifespan of expensive machinery. The digital twin provides detailed insights into the root cause of potential failures, guiding maintenance personnel toward efficient repair strategies and reducing the need for extensive troubleshooting. Imagine a scenario where a critical piece of manufacturing equipment is predicted to fail within the next 72 hours. Using Siemens' digital twin, maintenance teams can proactively schedule repairs, order necessary parts, and prepare for downtime, minimizing production disruption. This proactive approach to maintenance is far more cost-effective than reactive maintenance, where failures cause unscheduled downtime and costly emergency repairs. Moreover, using digital twins to track equipment health allows manufacturers to optimize their maintenance schedules, moving from fixed interval maintenance to a condition-based approach.

Process optimization is another vital application of Siemens' digital twins. By simulating various production scenarios within the digital environment, engineers can identify bottlenecks, inefficiencies, and potential areas for improvement. This virtual experimentation allows for the rapid testing of different process parameters and configurations without disrupting ongoing production. The ability to analyze data from the digital twin provides insights into the overall performance of the manufacturing process, allowing for data-driven decisions that optimize throughput, reduce waste, and improve product quality. For example, in a chemical manufacturing plant, Siemens may utilize a digital twin to simulate chemical reaction process parameter changes. This virtual experimentation allows them to optimize reaction yield, reduce energy consumption, and minimize waste by-products, significantly impacting production costs and environmental impact. The ability to rapidly iterate on process improvements using the digital twin significantly reduces the time and resources required for optimizing production processes.

However, the implementation of digital twin technology isn't without its challenges. One major hurdle is the integration of data from disparate sources. Manufacturing facilities often utilize various equipment and software systems, creating a complex data landscape. Integrating data from these diverse sources is essential for creating a comprehensive and accurate digital twin.

Siemens addresses this by leveraging its industry expertise and software and hardware solutions portfolio to establish seamless data integration. However, careful planning and execution are crucial to ensure compatibility and data integrity.

Another challenge involves acquiring and managing the vast quantities of data needed to create and maintain an accurate digital twin. Sensors, control systems, and other data sources continuously generate large volumes of data. Effective data management is essential to prevent data overload and ensure the efficient processing of this information. Siemens utilizes advanced data management systems capable of handling this data volume, but investment in robust infrastructure is vital for ensuring the effectiveness of digital twin technology. Furthermore, adequate data security measures are crucial to protect sensitive manufacturing data from unauthorized access or cyberattacks.

Implementing digital twin technology also requires a skilled workforce capable of operating and maintaining the digital environment. Engineers, technicians, and other personnel need the expertise to interpret data, identify potential problems, and effectively leverage the insights the digital twin provides.

Siemens addresses this by providing comprehensive training programs and supporting its customers throughout the digital transformation journey. However, a company's internal commitment to upskilling employees is critical for successful digital twin implementation.

In conclusion, Siemens' successful deployment of digital twin technology highlights the transformative potential of this approach in manufacturing. Its application in virtual commissioning, predictive maintenance, and process optimization provides significant benefits, enhancing efficiency, reducing costs, and driving continuous improvement. However, successful implementation requires careful planning, robust data management systems, and a skilled workforce capable of interpreting and leveraging the insights the digital twin provides. The ongoing evolution of digital twin technology, coupled with Siemens' continued investment in its development and implementation, is poised to revolutionize manufacturing processes across various industries. The complexity of creating and implementing a reliable digital twin necessitates an ongoing commitment to data management, continuous improvement, and investment in a skilled workforce capable of adapting to the ever-evolving technological landscape. The success of Siemens' approach underscores the importance of a holistic strategy that integrates technological advancements with organizational readiness and a dedication to continuous learning and improvement within the manufacturing environment. The long-term benefits of this technology far outweigh the initial investment and challenges, paving the way for a more efficient, adaptable, and sustainable manufacturing future.

GE APPLICATION OF ADDITIVE MANUFACTURING TECHNOLOGIES

GE's pioneering efforts in additive manufacturing (AM), commonly known as 3D printing, represent a significant shift in how the company designs, manufactures, and delivers its products. Unlike traditional subtractive manufacturing methods, which involve removing material from a larger block, AM builds parts layer by layer from a digital design, offering unparalleled design freedom and efficiency. GE's embrace of this technology showcases its commitment to innovation and its strategic understanding of the transformative potential of innovative manufacturing.

GE's journey into additive manufacturing began with a focus on addressing specific challenges within its existing production processes. The company recognized the limitations of traditional methods when dealing with complex geometries and intricate designs. While established techniques, casting and forging often resulted in excess material, extended lead times, and increased costs, mainly when producing high-value, complex components. Additive manufacturing offered a potential solution, enabling the creation of intricate parts with internal channels and complex geometries that would be impossible or prohibitively expensive to manufacture using conventional methods.

One notable application of AM within GE is the production of aircraft engine components. The company's aviation division has been at the forefront of adopting this technology to manufacture fuel nozzles, turbine blades, and other critical engine components. Traditionally produced through time-consuming and expensive casting processes, these parts are now created through AM with significantly reduced lead times and improved performance. For instance, the ability to create complex internal cooling channels within turbine blades significantly improves engine efficiency and performance. These intricate cooling channels are nearly impossible to create using traditional manufacturing techniques. The precision and control offered by AM allowed GE to optimize the cooling system design, leading to higher engine thrust and fuel efficiency. This, in turn, translates directly into significant cost savings for airlines and improved environmental performance.

Beyond the manufacturing of engine components, GE has leveraged AM to create lightweight and high-strength parts for its power generation and healthcare divisions. AM has enabled the production of complex components for power generation for gas turbines, optimizing performance and reducing weight. This reduces the overall strain on the turbine, enhancing its operational lifespan and reducing maintenance requirements. The weight reduction also translates into fuel efficiency, lowering operational costs and a smaller environmental footprint. In the healthcare sector, GE's adoption of AM has created customized implants and medical devices tailored to individual patient needs. The ability to create highly personalized medical devices opens up opportunities for improved patient outcomes and reduced recovery times.

GE's strategy extends beyond merely adopting the technology; it involves developing its AM capabilities and expertise. The company has invested heavily in research and development, collaborating with leading universities and research institutions to push the boundaries of AM technology. This investment in R&D has been crucial in enabling GE to tailor the technology to its specific needs and overcome the inherent limitations of AM. For example, the company has invested in developing new materials and printing processes specifically designed for high-performance applications, such as those found in aircraft engines. These proprietary materials and processes offer improved performance characteristics compared to off-the-shelf solutions.

Implementing AM within GE also required a significant shift in its manufacturing processes and organizational structures. The company recognized that adopting new technology was not enough; it also needed to adapt its design processes, manufacturing workflows, and quality control procedures to fully realize the full potential of AM. This involved training personnel on using new software and equipment, establishing new quality control protocols for AM parts, and integrating AM seamlessly into existing manufacturing workflows. The transition involved more than just technological upgrades; it necessitated a change in mindset and a collaborative approach across various departments within GE. This holistic approach, encompassing technological innovation and organizational adaptation, has been vital to GE's success in implementing AM.

One of the key challenges GE faced in implementing AM was overcoming the perceptions of quality and reliability associated with 3D-printed parts. While AM offers numerous advantages, concerns about the strength and consistency of AM-produced parts have been a barrier to broader adoption. GE addressed this by rigorously testing its AM-produced components, conducting extensive stress tests, and employing advanced quality control methods. This commitment to rigorous testing and quality assurance has built trust in the reliability of GE's AM-produced parts and has served to overcome industry skepticism. The company's transparent approach to quality control and the successful performance of AM-produced components in demanding environments have played a critical role in overcoming the hesitancy surrounding AM adoption.

Another major hurdle was the need for advanced design tools and software. Traditional CAD software wasn't always well-suited to the unique design considerations of AM. GE invested heavily in developing advanced software capable of generating optimized designs for AM, taking full advantage of the design freedom offered by this technology. These proprietary software tools assist engineers in creating functional and manufacturable designs using AM, maximizing the benefits of the technology while minimizing potential limitations. Using these advanced design tools was instrumental in pushing the boundaries of AM capabilities and realizing its full potential.

The integration of AM into GE's manufacturing operations has profoundly impacted its production lead times. In many cases, AM has drastically reduced the time required to manufacture complex components. This shortened lead time translates directly into improved operational efficiency and the ability to respond more quickly to changes in market demand. Furthermore, the ability to produce parts on demand eliminates the need for extensive inventories of spare parts, resulting in significant cost savings. The on-demand manufacturing capabilities of

AM significantly improve supply chain resilience and reduce the risk of production delays due to parts shortages.

Despite the numerous successes, GE's experience with AM highlights the need for ongoing research and development. The technology constantly evolves, with new materials and printing processes developed regularly. GE's commitment to ongoing innovation ensures that the company remains at the forefront of AM technology, continuously improving its manufacturing processes and expanding the range of applications for this transformative technology. This commitment to continuous improvement is essential for maximizing the benefits of AM and adapting to the ever-changing technological landscape. The successful integration of AM into its production processes is a compelling case study for other companies considering adopting this transformative technology. The key takeaways for other organizations are the need for a holistic approach involving technological investment, significant organizational changes, rigorous quality control procedures, and a long-term commitment to research and development. The challenges GE encountered and the solutions they implemented offer valuable insights for other organizations that are considering embarking on their journey into the world of additive manufacturing. The long-term benefits – reduced lead times, cost savings, improved performance, and increased design flexibility – outweigh the initial investment and challenges. GE's successful adoption of AM is a testament to the transformative power of manufacturing technologies and their potential to revolutionize industries.

THE ROLE OF AI IN PREDICTIVE MAINTENANCE AT BOEING

Boeing, a global leader in aerospace manufacturing, has long recognized the critical importance of aircraft maintenance.

Minimizing downtime, ensuring passenger safety, and optimizing maintenance costs are paramount to its operational success.

Traditional, largely reactive maintenance practices often involved scheduled inspections and repairs based on pre-determined timelines. While providing a degree of predictability, this approach proved inefficient and costly, leading to unnecessary inspections and potential safety risks arising from undetected issues. The advent of sophisticated sensor technologies and the rapid advancements in artificial intelligence (AI) have offered a transformative solution: predictive maintenance. Boeing's adoption of AI-powered predictive maintenance systems represents a significant shift towards proactive, data-driven maintenance strategies.

The core of Boeing's AI-driven predictive maintenance initiative lies in the vast amounts of aircraft-generated data during operation.

Modern aircraft are equipped with extensive sensors that constantly monitor various parameters, including engine performance, flight dynamics, and structural integrity. This previously vastly underutilized data now serves as the lifeblood of Boeing's predictive maintenance algorithms. Sensors embedded within engines meticulously record temperature, pressure, vibration levels, and fuel consumption. Structural sensors monitor stress levels on critical components, detecting even minute changes that could signal developing problems. Flight data recorders capture comprehensive information about each flight, providing invaluable insights into aircraft performance under diverse operating conditions.

This deluge of data, however, requires sophisticated analytical tools to extract meaningful insights. This is where AI comes into play.

Boeing employs various AI techniques, including machine learning (ML) and deep learning (DL), to analyze this data in real-time. ML algorithms, trained on historical maintenance data and sensor readings from a vast fleet of aircraft, can identify patterns and correlations that indicate potential failures. These algorithms often learn to recognize subtle deviations from normal operating parameters before these deviations manifest as readily observable malfunctions. Deep learning models, with their ability to handle complex, high-dimensional data, further enhance the accuracy and predictive capabilities of the system. These models can identify subtle anomalies in sensor data that might be missed by simpler ML algorithms, providing even earlier warnings of potential problems.

Integrating AI into Boeing's predictive maintenance system extends beyond mere data analysis. The system incorporates advanced visualization tools that allow maintenance engineers to interpret the AI's predictions easily. Instead of sifting through vast amounts of raw data, engineers are presented with clear, concise visualizations highlighting potential issues and their severity. This allows for timely and targeted interventions, minimizing the risk of catastrophic failures and ensuring the safety of passengers and crew. The system predicts potential failures and prioritizes maintenance tasks based on their urgency and potential impact. This ensures that critical maintenance needs are addressed first, while less urgent tasks can be scheduled more conveniently.

One of the key advantages of Boeing's AI-powered predictive maintenance is the ability to anticipate problems before they become critical. This proactive approach drastically reduces downtime, a significant cost factor in the airline industry. Boeing minimizes costly aircraft grounding and delays by identifying and addressing potential failures before they lead to major malfunctions. The system enables airlines to optimize their maintenance schedules, ensuring that aircraft are available when needed while minimizing unnecessary maintenance expenses. This translates into significant cost savings for airlines and improved operational efficiency.

Furthermore, the early detection of potential problems afforded by AI-powered predictive maintenance enhances passenger safety. By identifying and addressing issues before they escalate into safety hazards, Boeing significantly mitigates the risk of in-flight emergencies. This proactive approach contributes to a safer and more reliable aviation ecosystem. The system also supports the development of more robust aircraft designs, as data collected from the predictive maintenance system can be used to identify areas for improvement in aircraft design and manufacturing.

Boeing's approach extends beyond advanced algorithms and involves significant investment in infrastructure and personnel. The company has invested heavily in building robust data infrastructure capable of handling its aircraft's massive volume of data. This includes high-performance computing clusters and advanced data storage solutions that ensure sensor data's reliable storage and processing. Moreover, Boeing has invested in training its engineers to effectively utilize AI-powered predictive maintenance tools. This training encompasses the technical aspects of using the AI system, the interpretation of its predictions, and the implementation of appropriate maintenance strategies. Boeing recognizes that successfully implementing AI-driven predictive maintenance requires a skilled workforce capable of understanding and utilizing the system's capabilities.

The deployment of AI-powered predictive maintenance at Boeing is not without its challenges. The sheer volume of aircraft-generated data requires sophisticated data management and processing techniques. Ensuring the accuracy and reliability of the AI models is crucial, as incorrect predictions could lead to unnecessary maintenance or potentially missed critical issues. Data security and privacy are also significant concerns, as the system handles sensitive aircraft performance and maintenance information.

Addressing these challenges requires a multi-faceted approach involving advanced data infrastructure, robust quality control procedures, and stringent security protocols.

One significant challenge lies in data heterogeneity. Data from various sensors and systems might be in different formats and contain inconsistencies or errors. Preprocessing this data to ensure consistency and accuracy is crucial for the effective functioning of the AI models. Moreover, the development and deployment of AI models require specialized expertise, a scarcity of which can be a significant hurdle in the industry. Boeing has proactively addressed this by investing in training and development programs for its workforce and collaborating with academic institutions and technology companies to ensure a continuous supply of skilled personnel.

Moreover, Boeing is continuously refining its AI-powered predictive maintenance system through ongoing research and development. The company is exploring new AI algorithms, sensor technologies, and data analytics techniques to enhance the accuracy and efficiency of the system. This continuous improvement is essential to keep pace with the aviation industry's evolving needs and ensure that the system remains effective in the long term. The data collected from the system provides invaluable insights into aircraft performance and maintenance needs, which can be used to improve future aircraft designs and optimize maintenance strategies.

The success of Boeing's AI-powered predictive maintenance initiative is a testament to the transformative potential of AI in the aerospace industry. It demonstrates how data-driven insights can significantly improve aircraft maintenance, enhance safety, and reduce costs. The company's commitment to innovation, investment in advanced technologies, and skilled personnel have been instrumental in its success. Implementing AI-powered predictive maintenance is not just a technological achievement; it's a paradigm shift in how Boeing approaches aircraft maintenance, representing a move from a reactive to a proactive and data-driven approach. The experience provides a compelling case study for other industries looking to leverage the power of AI to improve their operational efficiency and enhance safety. The lessons learned from Boeing's journey underscore the importance of data integration, robust AI algorithms, and skilled personnel in successfully implementing AI-powered predictive maintenance systems. The future of aircraft maintenance and many other industries lies in the effective harnessing of AI's predictive capabilities.

DATA-DRIVEN OPTIMIZATION IN PHARMACEUTICAL MANUFACTURING

With its stringent regulatory requirements and emphasis on patient safety, the pharmaceutical industry presents a unique challenge and opportunity for innovative manufacturing. Traditional manufacturing practices rely on batch processing and manual quality checks, leading to inconsistencies and inefficiencies.

However, the increasing availability of data from various sources within the manufacturing process—sensors on equipment, production logs, quality control reports, and even real-time environmental monitoring—provides a wealth of information that can be leveraged for significant optimization. This data-driven approach, enabled by advanced analytics and machine learning, transforms pharmaceutical manufacturing, improving quality, reducing waste, and increasing efficiency.

One central area of impact is quality control. In traditional pharmaceutical manufacturing, quality checks are often performed at the end of the production process, meaning defects might only be detected after significant resources have already been invested. A data-driven approach allows for real-time monitoring of critical parameters throughout the entire manufacturing process. Sensors on mixing tanks, for instance, can monitor temperature, pressure, and viscosity with high accuracy, instantly flagging any deviations from pre-defined specifications. Machine learning algorithms can be trained to identify patterns in the sensor data that correlate with product defects, allowing for proactive intervention before a batch is deemed unsuitable. This predictive capability enables preventative maintenance, reducing downtime and improving overall yield.

Furthermore, these algorithms can identify subtle trends and anomalies that human operators might miss. By analyzing historical data from previous batches, the system can identify specific combinations of process parameters that consistently lead to higher-quality products. This allows manufacturers to fine-tune their processes, simultaneously optimizing for yield and quality. For instance, a subtle change in mixing speed or temperature might significantly impact the final product's potency or stability, which would be difficult to identify through traditional methods. These subtle relationships can be uncovered and leveraged through advanced analytics to produce higher-quality pharmaceuticals consistently.

Beyond quality control, data-driven optimization extends to reducing waste throughout the manufacturing process.

Pharmaceutical manufacturing often involves the use of expensive raw materials and complex processes. Data analysis can help identify areas where materials are being unnecessarily consumed or process inefficiencies lead to waste. For example, analysis of raw material usage patterns can identify anomalies or deviations that suggest potential equipment malfunction or process inefficiencies, prompting timely intervention and preventing further wastage. Predictive modeling can anticipate potential issues, such as equipment failure or supply chain disruptions, allowing for proactive adjustments to minimize waste and production delays.

The real-time monitoring capabilities prevent the production of faulty batches, thereby eliminating the need to dispose of large quantities of unusable products, representing significant cost savings and reducing environmental impact.

The optimization also extends to improving overall production efficiency. Data analytics can identify bottlenecks in the manufacturing process, highlighting areas where improvements can be made to increase throughput. For instance, analysis of production logs can reveal which process stages are causing delays, allowing for targeted improvements in equipment or process design. This data-driven approach allows for a continuous improvement cycle, constantly refining processes to maximize efficiency and minimize production time. Optimization also extends to resource allocation, enabling companies to adjust their resource utilization dynamically to meet fluctuating demands, reducing costs and maximizing output. This dynamic management can be particularly valuable in the pharmaceutical industry, where demand can fluctuate significantly due to seasonal changes in disease prevalence or market conditions.

Another crucial aspect is the integration of data from various sources. The pharmaceutical manufacturing process generates data from diverse systems, including manufacturing execution systems (MES), enterprise resource planning (ERP) systems, and laboratory information management systems (LIMS). Integrating these disparate data sources into a unified platform is crucial for comprehensively understanding the manufacturing process. This integration can reveal hidden relationships between different process aspects, leading to more effective optimization strategies. For example, correlating data from MES on production parameters with data from LIMS on product quality can reveal critical relationships that improve understanding of process variables and product outcomes.

However, implementing data-driven optimization in pharmaceutical manufacturing is not without its challenges. Data quality is a significant concern. Inconsistent data entry, missing data, and data errors can significantly impact the accuracy of the analytical models. Robust data governance processes, including data validation and cleaning, are essential to ensure the reliability of the results. Furthermore, the regulatory environment in the pharmaceutical industry is highly stringent. Data security and compliance with GDPR and 21 CFR Part 11 regulations are paramount, necessitating secure data storage and access control mechanisms.

The human element is also crucial. The successful implementation of data-driven optimization requires skilled personnel capable of interpreting the data analysis results and implementing appropriate manufacturing process changes. Training programs and ongoing support are necessary to ensure the workforce has the skills and knowledge to use data-driven tools and insights effectively. Effective communication and collaboration between data scientists, engineers, and production personnel are essential for successfully implementing and adopting data-driven approaches within the organization.

Moreover, the technology itself requires ongoing investment. The data collection, storage, and analysis systems require regular updates and maintenance to keep pace with technological advancements. Cloud-based solutions can offer scalability and flexibility, but ensuring data security and compliance in a cloud environment remains critical. Furthermore, continuous monitoring and improvement of the algorithms are crucial to ensure they remain effective and accurate over time as the manufacturing process evolves.

Despite these challenges, the potential benefits of data-driven optimization in pharmaceutical manufacturing are substantial. By leveraging the power of big data analytics, pharmaceutical companies can improve quality control, reduce waste, increase efficiency, and ultimately deliver safer and more effective medications to patients. Implementing these strategies signifies a move toward a proactive, data-driven approach to manufacturing, representing a paradigm shift in how pharmaceuticals are produced, enhancing the quality of life for millions worldwide. This ongoing digital transformation in the industry requires continual investment in technology, data management, and skilled personnel. Long-term success relies on overcoming technological and human challenges, fostering a culture of continuous improvement, and embracing the opportunities presented by advanced analytics and AI. The ultimate goal is not simply efficiency improvement but a profound enhancement of patient safety and confidence in the reliability of pharmaceuticals, which are cornerstones of modern healthcare.

CHAPTER 5
HUMAN-MACHINE COLLABORATION
IN INNOVATIVE MANUFACTURING

THE ROLE OF HUMAN WORKERS IN INNOVATIVE FACTORIES

As highlighted in the previous discussion of data-driven optimization in pharmaceutical manufacturing, the transformative potential of innovative factories hinges not solely on technological advancements but critically on the human element. While sophisticated algorithms and interconnected systems drive efficiency and precision, the success of these "innovative" environments rests on the adaptability and skills of the workforce. The human worker is not rendered obsolete; their role is fundamentally redefined, shifting from repetitive manual tasks to more complex, strategic functions that demand a new skill set.

This transition necessitates a proactive approach to workforce development. Upskilling and reskilling initiatives are no longer optional but essential components of successful innovative factory implementation. Workers need data analysis, programming, robotics maintenance, and advanced control systems training. This is not simply about teaching workers to operate new machines but empowering them to understand the underlying data, identify potential problems, and optimize processes. For instance, a machine operator in a traditional factory might be solely responsible for monitoring a single machine. In an innovative factory, the same operator might oversee a network of interconnected machines, using data analytics tools to identify inefficiencies or potential malfunctions across the entire system. This requires a deeper understanding of the technology, the ability to interpret complex data visualizations, and the problem-solving skills to respond effectively to anomalies.

The complexity of modern automation systems also necessitates a shift in roles and responsibilities. The rise of collaborative robots (cobots) represents a prime example. Cobots work alongside human workers, performing tasks that are too dangerous, repetitive, or precise for human operators alone. This collaboration requires a different approach to safety training, emphasizing safe interaction and collaboration with robotic systems. Workers must understand cobot functionality, limitations, and safety protocols to ensure safe and efficient operation. Furthermore, integrating AI into manufacturing processes creates new opportunities for human-machine collaboration and necessitates new skills. Workers need to understand how to interact with AI systems, interpret their outputs, and identify potential biases or limitations in the AI's decision-making.

Integrating advanced analytics into decision-making processes requires higher analytical and critical thinking skills from the workforce. Instead of relying solely on experience and intuition, workers must be comfortable interpreting large datasets, identifying patterns and trends, and using this information to inform their decisions. This demands training in using data analysis tools and statistical reasoning, data interpretation, and problem-solving skills. For example, workers might need to analyze sensor data from a production line to identify the root cause of a recurring quality defect. This requires isolating relevant variables, identifying correlations, and developing solutions based on the data analysis.

Beyond technical skills, the human element in innovative factories also emphasizes the importance of soft skills. Effective communication, teamwork, and problem-solving are crucial for navigating the complexities of human-machine collaboration. Workers must effectively communicate with colleagues, engineers, and even the AI systems they interact with. Problem-solving skills are also crucial, as workers will need to identify and resolve problems that arise in the complex interconnected systems of an innovative factory. Teamwork and collaboration are paramount, as integrated systems and complex workflows require cross-functional collaboration to ensure seamless operations.

The shift towards a more data-driven environment also impacts the management style within innovative factories. The organization needs to foster a culture of continuous improvement and data-driven decision-making. This necessitates changes in management training and leadership development programs. Managers must be equipped to lead and mentor teams in this evolving technological landscape. Their roles shift from direct supervision of manual tasks to guiding and supporting teams in leveraging technology for continuous improvement. Training programs should focus on developing leadership skills emphasizing collaboration, communication, and workforce empowerment to embrace change. The change management process should involve significant employee participation to build trust and address automation-related anxieties.

Implementing these changes also requires a significant investment in education and training. Companies need to partner with educational institutions and training providers to develop customized programs that meet the specific needs of their workforce. This may include apprenticeships, on-the-job training, and online learning platforms. Government initiatives and industry collaborations can also support these upskilling and reskilling initiatives. Investing in workforce development is not merely a cost; it is a strategic investment that ensures the long-term success of innovative factories and fosters a highly skilled and adaptable workforce. Furthermore, this commitment demonstrates to employees that their value and expertise remain central to the organization's success, mitigating anxieties related to job displacement due to automation.

Addressing potential workforce displacement anxieties is vital for successfully transitioning to a factory environment. Open and transparent communication about the changes and the company's commitment to reskilling and upskilling is essential to build trust and reduce employee concerns. Transparency about the evolution of job roles, new opportunities, and support offered for retraining will alleviate anxieties and foster a positive mindset towards the transition. This includes clearly articulating how current skills will be leveraged in new roles and emphasizing the opportunities for career advancement within the evolving factory context.

Moreover, the human element extends beyond the immediate workforce. Successful innovative factory implementation requires skilled engineers, data scientists, and IT professionals capable of designing, implementing, and maintaining these complex systems. This highlights the growing demand for a skilled technical workforce in robotics, AI, and data analytics fields. Educational institutions must adapt curricula to meet this demand, producing graduates with the technical expertise needed to support the ongoing digital transformation in manufacturing. This underscores the need for collaboration between industry and academia to align educational programs with the evolving needs of the manufacturing sector.

In conclusion, while technology plays a central role in developing and implementing innovative factories, the human element remains paramount. The success of these factories hinges on the ability of workers to adapt to new roles, acquire new skills, and effectively collaborate with advanced technologies. Upskilling and reskilling initiatives, a supportive organizational culture, and proactive management of workforce anxieties are crucial for successfully transitioning to a factory environment. This requires a technological investment and a significant investment in human capital, which will ultimately drive the long-term success and sustainability of innovative manufacturing. The future of innovative factories is not about machines replacing humans but about humans and machines working together to achieve greater efficiency, productivity, and innovation.

DESIGNING ERGONOMICALLY SOUND WORKSPACES

As previously discussed, the seamless integration of humans and machines in innovative factories necessitates a profound shift in how we design and manage the work environment. While technological advancements drive productivity and efficiency, the well-being and safety of the human workforce remain paramount. This requires a meticulous focus on designing ergonomically sound workspaces, minimizing worker fatigue, preventing injuries, and maximizing overall productivity. Neglecting this aspect can negate the benefits of automation, leading to decreased efficiency, higher absenteeism, and increased healthcare costs.

Ergonomic design in innovative factories transcends the traditional considerations of office ergonomics. It must account for the unique challenges of integrating advanced robotics, collaborative robots (cobots), sophisticated control systems, and extensive data visualization interfaces. The workspace must be adaptable and intuitive, fostering a harmonious collaboration between human workers and automated systems.

A fundamental ergonomic design principle is optimizing the workspace layout to minimize unnecessary movement and strain. This involves carefully considering the placement of machinery, workstations, and supporting equipment. For instance, frequently accessed tools and materials should be within easy reach, avoiding awkward postures and excessive stretching. The arrangement should facilitate a smooth workflow, minimizing the need for workers to move excessively between tasks. Lean principles, focusing on eliminating waste and optimizing flow, are particularly relevant in this context. Applying lean manufacturing principles, such as 5S (sort, set in order, shine, standardize, sustain), can significantly enhance the efficiency and safety of the workspace. Regular audits of the workspace layout should be conducted to identify and address any potential ergonomic issues.

The physical design of the workstations themselves is crucial. Chairs should be adjustable to accommodate individual worker needs, offering proper lumbar support and encouraging a neutral posture. Work surfaces should be at an appropriate height to prevent strain on the neck, shoulders, and back. The use of adjustable height desks, or sit-stand workstations, allows for greater flexibility and helps to prevent fatigue associated with prolonged sitting.

Furthermore, the use of ergonomic keyboards and mice, as well as adjustable monitors, contributes significantly to minimizing musculoskeletal strain.

Beyond the physical arrangement of the workspace, lighting also plays a crucial role in ergonomics. Adequate lighting, both in intensity and quality, reduces eye strain and enhances worker alertness. Natural light, where feasible, should be maximized, as it contributes to improved mood and overall well-being. However, the integration of artificial lighting needs to consider potential glare and ensure a consistent, comfortable level of illumination across the workspace. Using task lighting to supplement general lighting in specific areas can be particularly beneficial.

Noise is another significant factor impacting worker comfort and safety in innovative factories. The operation of machinery and equipment can generate considerable noise, which, over prolonged exposure, can lead to hearing loss and reduced productivity. Noise reduction strategies are crucial, such as using sound-absorbing materials, noise barriers, and personal protective equipment (PPE).

Regular noise level monitoring is essential to ensure compliance with safety regulations and identify potential improvement areas.

The integration of advanced technology in innovative factories presents unique ergonomic challenges. The design of human-machine interfaces (HMIs) should prioritize ease of use and intuitive navigation. Complex systems should be designed with clear and concise displays, avoiding information overload and minimizing mental fatigue. Virtual reality (VR) and augmented reality (AR) technologies can significantly enhance the training and operation of complex machinery. However, implementing these technologies requires careful consideration of the potential for motion sickness and other ergonomic issues.

Integrating collaborative robots (cobots) demands a different approach to workspace design. Safety protocols and training programs are crucial to ensure humans and robots' harmonious and safe co-existence. The physical workspace should be designed to facilitate safe interactions, with clear zones of operation defined for both humans and robots. Sensor technologies and safety systems should be integrated to prevent accidents and collisions.

Moreover, the design should incorporate safety features that mitigate the risks associated with unexpected robot movements or malfunctions.

Data visualization in innovative factories is integral to efficient operations, but excessive screen time can lead to eye strain, neck pain, and other ergonomic issues. The design of dashboards and displays should follow principles of visual clarity and ease of interpretation. Using color coding, clear labels, and well-structured information hierarchies minimizes the need for extensive searching and reduces mental fatigue. Workers should be encouraged to take regular breaks to reduce prolonged screen time and prevent eye strain.

The ergonomic design of innovative factories is not a one-time project but an ongoing process. Regular ergonomic assessments and audits are necessary to identify and address potential hazards. These assessments should involve input from workers themselves, as they are the ones experiencing the workspace firsthand. Feedback mechanisms should be in place to encourage proactive reporting of ergonomic concerns and suggestions for improvements. Continuous improvement methodologies, similar to those employed in other aspects of factory operations, should be applied to the ergonomic design of the workspace.

Finally, the implementation of ergonomic design principles necessitates a holistic approach. It involves not only the physical design of the workspace but also considers the organizational culture and employee well-being. Companies should prioritize the training of employees on safe work practices and ergonomic principles. Management should actively promote a culture of safety and well-being, encouraging employees to report concerns and participate in the design and improvement of their workspaces. By investing in ergonomic design and actively promoting a culture of safety and well-being, companies can maximize the benefits of factory technologies while safeguarding the health and well-being of their workforce. This proactive approach leads to increased worker satisfaction, reduced absenteeism, improved productivity, and, ultimately, the sustained success of the innovative factory. The successful implementation of these strategies enhances productivity and fosters a healthier, more engaged, and more satisfied workforce.

IMPLEMENTING COLLABORATIVE ROBOTS COBOTS

Implementing collaborative robots (cobots) significantly advances human-machine collaboration within innovative manufacturing. Their inherent design, prioritizing safety and ease of interaction, allows for a more integrated and efficient workflow than traditional industrial robots. Unlike their industrial counterparts, Cobots are programmed to operate alongside human workers, sharing tasks and responsibilities rather than replacing them entirely. This paradigm shift necessitates rethinking workspace design, safety protocols, and employee training programs.

One of the key advantages of cobots is their enhanced safety features. Equipped with advanced sensors and sophisticated software, cobots can detect the presence of humans and adjust their movements accordingly. Force-limiting technology ensures that if a collision occurs, the impact is minimal, reducing the risk of injury to human workers. This inherent safety mechanism significantly reduces the need for extensive safety cages and barriers, often restricting traditional robotic systems' flexibility and efficiency. The open architecture of cobot workspaces promotes a more collaborative and less isolating work environment, fostering a sense of shared responsibility between humans and machines.

The increased safety offered by cobots translates directly into improved worker productivity. By automating repetitive or physically demanding tasks, cobots free up human workers to focus on more complex and value-added activities. This reallocation of labor can significantly increase overall output and efficiency. For instance, in assembly lines, cobots can assist with parts handling, fastening, and welding tasks, while human workers oversee the process, perform quality control, and handle exceptions. This division of labor optimizes the strengths of both humans and machines, creating a synergistic relationship that enhances productivity. Successful implementations of cobots across various manufacturing sectors illustrate their impact. Consider the automotive industry, where cobots are used extensively in assembly processes. They handle delicate components, apply precise amounts of adhesive, and perform intricate welding tasks while working alongside human technicians. This collaboration allows for faster assembly times, improved quality control, and reduced workplace injuries. Cobots are invaluable in handling small and fragile components in the electronics industry, performing delicate soldering and assembly operations with precision and speed exceeding human capabilities. The result is increased throughput and improved product quality. Similar benefits are observed in the food processing and pharmaceutical industries, where cobots aid in tasks requiring careful handling and precise movements.

The integration of cobots requires careful planning and implementation. A crucial element is the selection of appropriate cobot models based on the specific tasks and environment. Factors to consider include the payload capacity, reach, and speed of the cobot and the level of dexterity and precision required for the task. The cobot's software and programming interface also play a significant role, ensuring compatibility with existing manufacturing systems and ease of use for human operators. A poorly chosen cobot can lead to inefficiencies, safety concerns, and, ultimately, failure to achieve the desired productivity gains.

Training employees to work alongside cobots is another critical aspect of successful implementation. Comprehensive training programs should cover the safe operation of the cobots, emergency procedures, and essential maintenance. Workers need to understand the cobot's capabilities and limitations and the protocols for human-robot interaction. Practical training fosters confidence and trust in the cobot, encouraging collaboration and reducing apprehension. Moreover, regular refresher training ensures workers stay up-to-date with evolving technology and safety procedures. A well-trained workforce is essential to maximizing the benefits of cobot integration and minimizing the risks.

The design of the workspace is crucial for safe and efficient human-robot collaboration. The layout should facilitate smooth workflows, minimizing the need for humans and cobots to occupy the same space simultaneously. Clear zones of operation should be defined for humans and robots, with physical barriers or sensor systems used to prevent accidental collisions. The workspace should also be ergonomically designed, considering factors such as lighting, noise levels, and the placement of tools and materials. A well-designed workspace minimizes worker fatigue and improves overall comfort, enhancing productivity and safety. Regular audits of the workspace should be conducted to identify and address any potential safety or ergonomic issues.

Beyond the physical implementation, the successful integration of cobots requires a change in organizational culture. Managers and supervisors must foster a collaborative environment where humans and machines work together seamlessly. This necessitates shifting from a purely task-oriented approach to one that values human-robot teamwork. Open communication channels, allowing workers to express concerns and provide feedback, are essential for a smooth transition. The benefits of cobot integration should be communicated to the workforce, emphasizing enhanced safety and improved working conditions. A supportive and collaborative culture will ensure the smooth integration of cobots and the maximization of their potential.

Data analytics play a crucial role in optimizing cobot performance and identifying areas for improvement. Sensors and monitoring systems embedded within cobots collect data on various aspects of their operation, such as cycle times, task completion, and error rates. This data can be used to identify bottlenecks, optimize workflows, and predict potential maintenance needs. The insights gained from data analytics can inform decisions on cobot deployment, programming, and training, ensuring continuous improvement and maximizing return on investment. Furthermore, data analytics can track worker performance and identify potential ergonomic issues, ensuring a safe and productive work environment.

The long-term success of cobot implementation depends on continuous monitoring and improvement. Regular assessments of cobot performance, worker safety, and overall productivity are necessary to identify areas for optimization. This requires the implementation of robust monitoring systems and regular feedback mechanisms. Continuous improvement methodologies, such as Kaizen, can be applied to refine processes, improve efficiency, and ensure the long-term effectiveness of cobot integration. By embracing a culture of continuous improvement, manufacturers can fully realize the potential of cobots and maintain a competitive edge in the ever-evolving landscape of innovative manufacturing.

In conclusion, implementing collaborative robots marks a significant step forward in human-machine collaboration in innovative manufacturing. Their inherent safety features and ability to automate repetitive tasks lead to increased worker productivity and improved workplace safety. However, successful implementation requires careful planning, appropriate training programs, ergonomic workspace design, and a supportive organizational culture. Through technological advancements and strategic management practices, manufacturers can harness the full potential of cobots and create a truly synergistic and efficient production environment. The ongoing monitoring and refinement of cobot deployment strategies, supported by data analytics and a commitment to continuous improvement, ensure long-term success and a positive impact on the bottom line and the workforce's well-being. The evolution of human-robot collaboration continues, and cobots are at the forefront of this exciting transformation.

AUGMENTED REALITY AR AND VIRTUAL REALITY VR IN TRAINING

Integrating collaborative robots (cobots) and other advanced automation technologies in innovative manufacturing necessitates a highly skilled and adaptable workforce. Traditional training methods often struggle to keep pace with the rapid advancements in this field. This is where augmented reality (AR) and virtual reality (VR) technologies offer significant advantages, providing immersive and engaging training experiences that significantly enhance worker competency and safety.

AR overlays digital information onto the real world, allowing trainees to interact with virtual elements superimposed on physical equipment. For instance, AR applications can guide technicians through complex maintenance procedures by projecting step-by-step instructions directly onto the machine they are servicing. This hands-on approach, supported by interactive 3D models and real-time data overlays, allows trainees to learn at their own pace and in a risk-free environment. The visual and interactive nature of AR training enhances comprehension and retention compared to traditional textbook-based or lecture-style learning. Furthermore, AR can provide context-sensitive information, making the learning experience more relevant and immediately applicable.

Consider training a technician to replace a faulty sensor on a complex robotic arm. Traditional methods might involve consulting thick manuals, potentially deciphering cryptic diagrams, and navigating a potentially hazardous workspace. With AR, the technician could point their tablet or AR glasses at the robotic arm, and the system would project an interactive 3D model of the sensor, highlighting the steps involved in its removal and replacement. The AR system could even provide haptic feedback, guiding the technician's hand to ensure proper alignment and prevent accidental damage. This immersive approach drastically reduces the learning curve and enhances safety by mitigating potential errors.

The benefits extend beyond the initial training phase. AR can also be used for on-the-job support, providing real-time assistance to technicians as they perform complex tasks. Imagine a scenario where a technician encounters an unexpected malfunction. The technician can receive immediate expert guidance through an AR interface, with remote experts virtually guiding the process through real-time overlays and video conferencing. This streamlines problem-solving significantly reduces downtime, and enhances operational efficiency.

Virtual Reality (VR), on the other hand, immerses trainees in completely simulated environments, allowing them to practice complex procedures in a safe and controlled setting. VR training simulations can replicate the nuances of real-world scenarios, including potential malfunctions and emergencies, without the risk of equipment damage or personnel injury. This allows trainees to develop critical decision-making skills and build confidence in handling unforeseen circumstances. The ability to repeatedly practice scenarios and make mistakes without consequence accelerates the learning process and improves proficiency.

For example, a VR training module could simulate a complete shutdown of a manufacturing line due to a power failure. Trainees would be immersed in a realistic virtual environment, mimicking the sights and sounds of the factory floor under emergency conditions. They would then have to navigate the virtual environment, respond to alerts, troubleshoot problems, and execute emergency procedures. This immersive experience is considerably more effective than simply reading a procedural manual, fostering a deeper understanding of the processes and building crucial decision-making skills under pressure. The data collected from each trainee's performance within the simulation can be used to identify areas where additional training or reinforcement is needed, leading to more targeted and effective learning interventions.

Implementing AR/VR training programs requires careful planning and integration with existing training infrastructure. The selection of appropriate hardware and software is crucial, ensuring compatibility with existing systems and meeting the specific needs of the training program. This includes assessing the technical proficiency of the target audience and tailoring the user interface accordingly. A poorly designed interface can hinder the effectiveness of the training and may even lead to frustration and user rejection.

Furthermore, the successful implementation of AR/VR training programs hinges on effective curriculum design. The training content should be carefully curated to align with specific job roles and industry standards. This necessitates the close collaboration between training specialists, subject matter experts, and technology providers. The content should be engaging and relevant, incorporating interactive elements and gamified challenges to improve learner motivation and knowledge retention. Regular evaluation and feedback mechanisms are also vital to track the effectiveness of the training and make necessary adjustments.

A critical factor in successfully integrating AR/VR in training is the commitment and buy-in from management and employees. A phased rollout, starting with pilot programs in specific areas, can help to address any concerns and demonstrate the benefits of this technology. Providing comprehensive training on AR/VR equipment and software is essential, ensuring that employees are comfortable and confident using the technology. Furthermore, open communication channels and feedback mechanisms can help to address any challenges or issues that arise during implementation.

Several case studies demonstrate the positive impact of AR/VR training in innovative manufacturing. Companies like Siemens have implemented AR applications to support the maintenance and repair of their industrial equipment. This has reduced downtime, improved efficiency, and increased worker satisfaction. Similarly, Boeing has utilized VR to train its technicians on complex aircraft maintenance procedures, significantly reducing training time and improving the safety and accuracy of their work. In these examples, the quantifiable improvements in training efficiency, reduced error rates, and shortened onboarding times have demonstrated a significant return on investment.

The future of AR/VR in manufacturing training promises even more significant advancements. Developing more sophisticated hardware, such as lightweight and comfortable AR glasses and immersive VR headsets, will further enhance the training experience. Advances in artificial intelligence (AI) will allow for more personalized and adaptive training programs catering to individual workers' specific needs and learning styles. Integrating haptic feedback and other sensory technologies will make the training experience more realistic and engaging.

Beyond the immediate benefits of improved skills and safety, AR/ VR training fosters a more engaged and motivated workforce. These technologies' interactive and immersive nature makes learning more enjoyable and less daunting, leading to increased confidence and improved job satisfaction. This is particularly important in a rapidly evolving field such as innovative manufacturing, where continuous learning is essential for staying ahead of the curve. By embracing AR/VR, manufacturers can cultivate a more skilled, confident, and adaptable workforce, ensuring competitiveness in the global marketplace.

The cost of implementing AR/VR training programs can be a significant factor, but the long-term benefits often outweigh the initial investment. A thorough cost-benefit analysis, considering factors such as reduced training time, decreased error rates, and improved worker safety, can help to justify the investment. The potential for scalability is also a significant advantage. Once an AR/ VR training module has been developed, it can be easily deployed across multiple locations and to many trainees. This reduces the need for multiple instructors and physical training materials, resulting in significant cost savings over time.

In conclusion, integrating AR and VR technologies in manufacturing training represents a paradigm shift in workforce development. By providing immersive, engaging, and risk-free learning experiences, these technologies enhance worker competency, improve safety, and accelerate the adoption of advanced manufacturing technologies. While the implementation requires careful planning and investment, the long-term benefits, including increased efficiency, reduced costs, and a more skilled and satisfied workforce, solidify the role of AR/VR as a crucial component of the future of innovative manufacturing. The continuous evolution of these technologies promises to enhance their effectiveness further, making them an increasingly vital asset in fostering the highly skilled workforce needed to drive innovation and productivity in the manufacturing sector.

HUMAN FACTORS AND USER INTERFACE DESIGN

The seamless integration of humans and machines in innovative manufacturing hinges not only on the technological prowess of the automation systems but also on the design of the human-machine interface (HMI). A poorly designed interface, regardless of the sophistication of the underlying technology, can lead to errors, inefficiencies, and even safety hazards. Therefore, understanding and applying sound principles of human factors and user interface (UI) design is paramount in realizing the full potential of innovative manufacturing.

Human factors engineering, a discipline dedicated to optimizing the interaction between humans and systems, provides a crucial framework for HMI design. It considers various aspects of human capabilities and limitations, including cognitive abilities, physical dexterity, perceptual limitations, and ergonomic factors. These considerations directly influence the HMI's usability, learnability, and overall effectiveness. For instance, the placement of controls, the size and clarity of displays, and the overall layout of the interface should be designed to minimize cognitive load and physical strain on the operators.

One of the key principles of human factors engineering is to design for the user, not the technology. This means understanding the specific tasks performed by the operators, their skill levels, and their individual needs. Designing interfaces that cater to diverse user groups' specific needs and cognitive capabilities is crucial for inclusive and effective human-machine interaction. Consider the differences between experienced technicians and newly trained apprentices. An interface designed for an expert might be overwhelming and confusing for a novice, leading to errors and delays. Conversely, an overly simplistic interface might restrict the capabilities of more skilled workers. Therefore, adaptable interfaces that can be tailored to different skill levels are highly desirable.

The design of visual displays is another critical aspect of HMI design. Innovative manufacturing involves extensive data, ranging from real-time sensor readings to complex process parameters. The display of this information needs to be clear, concise, and readily interpretable by the operators. Avoid information overload by carefully selecting the most critical parameters to display and using visual cues, such as color-coding and graphical representations, to highlight important information.

Using intuitive icons and symbols can further improve comprehension and reduce the reliance on complex textual descriptions. The design should also consider factors such as ambient lighting conditions and the viewing distance, ensuring that the display remains legible under diverse circumstances.

Auditory feedback is equally important, particularly in noisy environments where visual displays may be difficult to see.

Auditory alerts should be distinct and easily recognizable, providing timely notifications of critical events or deviations from normal operating parameters. The design of these alerts should avoid unnecessary distractions, only providing information that is genuinely important and relevant to the operator's task. The volume and tone of auditory alerts should be carefully chosen to ensure they are heard clearly but do not contribute to auditory fatigue or stress.

The physical design of the HMI controls is also crucial, ensuring that they are easily accessible, comfortable to use, and ergonomically sound. The size, shape, and placement of buttons, switches, and other control elements should be optimized to minimize hand strain and facilitate efficient operation. Consider using tactile feedback to confirm button presses or other control actions. This helps to prevent errors caused by accidental presses or missed actions. Furthermore, the design should account for the potential for glove use, ensuring that controls remain easily operable even when wearing protective gear.

The integration of advanced technologies, such as augmented reality (AR) and virtual reality (VR), further complicates the design of the HMI. While these technologies offer immense potential for improving human-machine interaction, they also present unique design challenges. AR overlays digital information onto the real world, providing operators with context-sensitive information directly related to their task. This requires careful consideration of how this information is presented, ensuring it does not obscure the physical environment or overwhelm the operator with excessive data.

Conversely, VR immerses users in a simulated environment, allowing them to practice complex procedures or troubleshoot problems in a safe and controlled setting. The design of the VR environment must be realistic and intuitive, mimicking the physical and operational characteristics of the real-world system as closely as possible. The user interaction within the VR environment should also be natural and intuitive, using familiar control schemes that minimize the learning curve. Furthermore, the design should incorporate clear and concise visual cues and feedback mechanisms to guide the user through the simulation.

Developing effective HMIs in innovative manufacturing requires a collaborative approach involving engineers, designers, and, most importantly, the end users. Usability testing is crucial in ensuring that the design meets the needs of the operators and that the interface is both intuitive and efficient. Iterative design cycles involving user feedback and continuous improvement are critical for developing a user-friendly and effective HMI. This collaborative approach ensures that the final product results from a deep understanding of the human factors involved in the manufacturing process.

The increasing complexity of manufacturing systems necessitates the development of adaptable and intelligent HMIs. These interfaces should be able to adjust to changing conditions and operator skill levels dynamically, providing personalized information and support. Artificial intelligence (AI) can play a significant role in achieving this adaptability, enabling the HMI to learn from operator behavior and optimize its presentation of information. For example, an intelligent HMI could proactively alert the operator to potential problems or provide context-sensitive instructions, anticipating their needs and simplifying their tasks.

Furthermore, the HMI should facilitate seamless communication and collaboration between operators, supervisors, and remote experts. This may involve directly integrating communication tools, such as video conferencing or instant messaging, into the HMI. This capability is especially valuable in addressing unexpected malfunctions or emergencies, allowing immediate remote support and troubleshooting. The integration of these communication tools needs to be carefully considered to avoid cluttering the interface or hindering the operator's ability to focus on their primary task.

Security is another crucial factor in the design of HMI for innovative manufacturing. The interface should be designed to protect sensitive data and prevent unauthorized access. This might involve implementing robust authentication mechanisms, secure communication protocols, and regular security audits. The security features should be seamlessly integrated into the HMI without compromising usability or efficiency.

Ultimately, the success of innovative manufacturing depends not only on the technological advancements in automation and robotics but also on the ability to integrate human operators into the system effectively. The design of the HMI is the critical interface where this integration takes place. By carefully considering human factors and applying sound UI design principles, we can create HMIs that are safe, efficient, and empowering, maximizing the potential of human-machine collaboration at the heart of innovative manufacturing. The future of innovative manufacturing is not just about machines but about the intelligent, harmonious collaboration between humans and machines facilitated by well-designed and user-centered HMIs.

Continuous research and development in this area is essential for ensuring that innovative factories remain safe, productive, and adaptable to the ever-evolving demands of the global market.

CHAPTER 6
SUSTAINABILITY AND THE
CIRCULAR ECONOMY

INTEGRATING SUSTAINABILITY INTO INNOVATIVE MANUFACTURING

Integrating sustainability into innovative manufacturing is no longer a niche concern; it's a strategic imperative. The pressure from consumers, investors, and regulators to adopt environmentally responsible practices is intensifying, and for manufacturers, this translates into both opportunities and challenges. Innovative manufacturing, emphasizing data-driven optimization and automation, offers a powerful platform for implementing sustainable practices, but realizing this potential requires a deliberate and integrated approach.

One of the most significant areas where innovative manufacturing can contribute to sustainability is energy efficiency. Traditional manufacturing processes often suffer from energy waste due to inefficient equipment, suboptimal process control, and a lack of real-time monitoring. Innovative factories with sensors, data analytics, and advanced control systems can significantly improve energy efficiency. For example, real-time monitoring of energy consumption across various production lines allows for identifying energy-intensive processes and implementing targeted interventions. Predictive maintenance, enabled by machine learning algorithms that analyze sensor data, can prevent unplanned downtime that contributes to increased energy usage. Optimization algorithms can adjust production parameters in real-time to minimize energy consumption without compromising output quality.

Furthermore, integrating renewable energy sources, such as solar and wind power, into the factory's energy infrastructure can further reduce reliance on fossil fuels and decrease carbon emissions. Innovative grids, which optimize energy distribution within the factory based on real-time demand and availability, can further enhance energy efficiency. Case studies demonstrate 20-30% or more energy savings in innovative factories that have adopted comprehensive energy management strategies. This includes implementing energy-efficient lighting, motor drives, and HVAC systems and optimizing production schedules to align with periods of lower energy costs.

Waste reduction is another crucial aspect of sustainable, innovative manufacturing. Traditional manufacturing often generates significant waste, including material scraps, defective products, and packaging materials. Innovative manufacturing offers several strategies for minimizing waste generation. For instance, advanced process control systems can optimize production parameters to reduce material usage and minimize defects. Real-time quality monitoring enables immediate identification and correction of defects, reducing scrap generation. Predictive maintenance reduces downtime caused by equipment failures, further minimizing material waste. Moreover, data analytics can identify bottlenecks and inefficiencies in the production process, leading to optimized resource allocation and reduced waste. Implementing closed-loop systems, which recycle and reuse materials within the production process, can further minimize waste and reduce the environmental footprint of the manufacturing operation. This can involve incorporating advanced recycling technologies, such as automated sorting and processing systems, to recover valuable materials from production waste. Furthermore, adopting circular economy principles involves designing products for durability, repairability, and recyclability, extending product lifecycles, and reducing the need for new materials. This requires a shift in design thinking, moving away from a linear "take-make-dispose" model towards a circular model that prioritizes resource efficiency and waste minimization.

The environmental impact of manufacturing extends beyond energy consumption and waste generation. Innovative manufacturing can also contribute to reducing emissions of greenhouse gases and other pollutants. Real-time monitoring of emissions from production processes allows for immediate identification and remediation of environmental violations. Predictive maintenance minimizes equipment malfunctions that could lead to increased emissions.

Optimization algorithms can adjust production parameters to minimize emissions without compromising output quality.

Moreover, adopting cleaner production technologies, such as water-efficient processes and less hazardous chemicals, can further reduce the environmental impact of manufacturing. Lifecycle assessment (LCA) tools and data-driven insights from manufacturing systems can help identify environmental hotspots and guide the implementation of targeted sustainability improvements. By comprehensively analyzing the entire product lifecycle, from material extraction to end-of-life disposal, companies can identify areas for improvement and develop strategies for minimizing environmental impact across the value chain. This could involve transitioning to more sustainable materials, optimizing transportation and logistics, and implementing end-of-life recycling or repurposing programs.

Integrating sustainability into innovative manufacturing also involves engaging the entire supply chain. Collaborating with suppliers to adopt sustainable practices, such as using recycled materials and reducing their environmental footprint, is crucial.

Blockchain technology enables transparency and traceability within the supply chain, which can enhance accountability and ensure compliance with sustainability standards. Sharing best practices and knowledge among supply chain partners can promote collective action towards sustainability goals. Furthermore, innovative contracts can automate the implementation of sustainability-related agreements and incentives, ensuring compliance and fostering collaboration. Implementing ethical sourcing strategies and fair labor practices adds another layer of sustainability to the supply chain, ensuring that social and environmental responsibility are considered across the entire production network.

The successful integration of sustainability into innovative manufacturing requires a holistic approach, combining technological advancements with organizational change and cultural shifts. This includes establishing clear sustainability goals, allocating appropriate resources, and engaging employees across all levels of the organization. Adopting appropriate metrics and reporting mechanisms is essential for tracking progress and holding organizations accountable for their sustainability performance. This could include setting targets for energy reduction, waste minimization, emissions control, and water consumption. Regular monitoring and reporting of these metrics are vital for demonstrating progress and driving continuous improvement. Transparency and stakeholder communication are critical for building trust and ensuring that sustainability initiatives align with organizational values and strategic goals.

Furthermore, collaboration and knowledge sharing are essential for accelerating the adoption of sustainable practices in innovative manufacturing. This could involve partnering with universities, research institutions, and industry consortiums to share best practices and collaborate on developing sustainability technologies. Participating in industry forums and conferences can foster the exchange of ideas and promote adopting sustainable practices. Supporting and investing in research and developing sustainable technologies are crucial for long-term progress. This involves investing in new materials, processes, and technologies that minimize environmental impact. This investment can also be seen as an opportunity for innovation and creating new economic opportunities in the green technology sector.

In conclusion, integrating sustainability into innovative manufacturing is not simply a matter of compliance; it's a strategic opportunity to improve efficiency, reduce costs, enhance brand reputation, and contribute to a more sustainable future. By embracing technologies and adopting a holistic approach, manufacturers can transform their operations into more environmentally and socially responsible, creating a win-win scenario for both the environment and the bottom line. The path to sustainable and innovative manufacturing requires ongoing innovation, collaboration, and a commitment to continuous improvement. This is not a destination but an ongoing journey requiring continuous adaptation and refinement as technologies advance and sustainability standards evolve.

IMPLEMENTING GREEN MANUFACTURING PRACTICES

Implementing green manufacturing practices requires a multifaceted approach beyond simple technological adoption to encompass organizational restructuring and a fundamental shift in manufacturing philosophy. The successful implementation hinges on a commitment to continuous improvement, informed by data-driven insights and a collaborative spirit across the entire value chain.

One of the most impactful green manufacturing practices involves harnessing renewable energy sources. While the initial investment in solar panels, wind turbines, or geothermal systems might seem substantial, the long-term environmental and financial benefits are compelling. The reduction in reliance on fossil fuels translates directly into lower carbon emissions and decreased energy costs. Furthermore, integrating renewable energy sources often qualifies companies for various government incentives and tax breaks, further mitigating the initial investment. Effective implementation requires thoroughly assessing the factory's energy needs and the feasibility of different renewable options. This analysis should consider factors such as geographical location, available land area, and energy consumption patterns. Moreover, innovative grid integration allows for dynamic adjustment of energy usage, maximizing the utilization of renewable energy sources and minimizing reliance on the traditional grid during peak demand periods. Real-time monitoring systems can provide valuable energy consumption and generation data, informing operational adjustments and revealing opportunities for further optimization.

Waste reduction is another critical component of green manufacturing. This encompasses a broad spectrum of strategies, beginning with design for disassembly (DfD) and design for recyclability (DfR). DfD focuses on designing products with ease of disassembly in mind, facilitating the recovery and reuse of components at the end of the product's life. DfR, on the other hand, prioritizes the use of recyclable materials and the creation of designs that simplify the recycling process. Implementing these design principles necessitates collaboration with material suppliers and a thorough understanding of the recycling infrastructure available. This holistic approach often necessitates adjustments to the product design itself, which can present significant challenges but yields significant rewards in terms of reduced waste and improved resource efficiency.

Beyond design, several operational practices contribute to waste minimization. Lean manufacturing principles, emphasizing efficiency and waste elimination, are crucial. This includes strategies like just-in-time (JIT) inventory management, reducing the amount of raw materials stored on-site, and minimizing the risk of spoilage or obsolescence. Implementing robust quality control systems, utilizing real-time monitoring and advanced sensors, allows for early detection and correction of defects, preventing the generation of scrap. Predictive maintenance, based on data analytics from connected equipment, minimizes unplanned downtime and the consequent waste associated with production interruptions. Furthermore, optimizing production processes through advanced control systems and machine learning algorithms can significantly reduce material consumption and waste generation.

Sustainable material sourcing is another pillar of green manufacturing. This involves identifying and utilizing environmentally friendly materials and minimizing the environmental impact associated with material extraction, processing, and transportation. This can include using recycled materials, opting for materials with lower embodied carbon footprints, and sourcing materials from sustainably managed forests. Implementing a sustainable material sourcing strategy requires close collaboration with suppliers, ensuring transparency and traceability throughout the supply chain. This often necessitates rigorous auditing of suppliers, ensuring that their manufacturing processes align with the company's sustainability goals. Furthermore, embracing circular economy principles extending product lifecycles through repair, refurbishment, and reuse significantly reduces the demand for new materials and minimizes waste.

The implementation of green manufacturing strategies inevitably presents challenges. The initial investment in new technologies and processes can be substantial. Changes to existing production processes may necessitate retraining employees and altering established workflows. Resistance to change from employees or management can also hinder progress. The lack of standardized metrics for measuring the environmental impact of manufacturing can complicate the evaluation of the effectiveness of green manufacturing initiatives. Furthermore, ensuring the compliance of suppliers with sustainability standards necessitates considerable effort and collaboration.

However, the benefits of adopting green manufacturing practices far outweigh the challenges. Reduced energy consumption and waste generation translate directly into lower operating costs. The adoption of sustainable practices enhances a company's brand image and reputation, attracting environmentally conscious customers and investors. Improved efficiency and reduced waste often lead to increased productivity and profitability. Green manufacturing practices also contribute to a positive social impact, fostering a more sustainable and responsible manufacturing sector. Compliance with increasingly stringent environmental regulations is another key driver, ensuring long-term operational viability.

Successfully implementing green manufacturing practices requires a holistic approach. It necessitates a firm commitment from leadership to integrate sustainability goals into the company's overall strategy. Employees at all levels must be involved, fostering a culture of continuous improvement and environmental stewardship. Regular monitoring and reporting of sustainability metrics are essential for tracking progress and identifying areas for improvement. Transparent communication with stakeholders, including customers, suppliers, and investors, builds trust and fosters collaboration. Continuous learning and knowledge sharing, both internally and externally, are vital for staying abreast of advancements in green manufacturing technologies and best practices. Finally, collaboration with industry partners, research institutions, and government agencies can accelerate the adoption of sustainable practices and facilitate the development of solutions.

The path to sustainable and green manufacturing is a continuous journey, not a destination. It requires ongoing innovation, adaptation, and a commitment to continuous improvement.

However, by embracing the opportunities presented by green manufacturing, companies can not only mitigate their environmental impact but also gain a competitive edge, enhance their profitability, and contribute to a more sustainable future. The future of manufacturing is undeniably intertwined with sustainability, and those who embrace this paradigm shift will be best positioned for long-term success in an increasingly environmentally conscious world. The journey requires proactive engagement, data-driven decision-making, and a collaborative approach that extends beyond the factory floor to encompass the entire supply chain. Only through a holistic, sustained effort can the transformative potential of green manufacturing be fully realized.

THE CIRCULAR ECONOMY AND ITS RELEVANCE TO MANUFACTURING

The circular economy, a radical departure from the traditional linear "take-make-dispose" model, presents a compelling paradigm shift for the manufacturing sector. Instead of viewing resources as finite and destined for disposal, the circular economy envisions a system where materials are kept in use for as long as possible, extracting maximum value before responsibly returning them to the production cycle. This closed-loop system prioritizes resource efficiency, waste reduction, and the minimization of environmental impact. Its relevance to manufacturing is undeniable, offering a pathway towards sustainable growth and reduced reliance on virgin materials.

The core principles of the circular economy revolve around designing out waste and pollution, keeping products and materials in use, and regenerating natural systems. In manufacturing, this translates into a range of strategies, including designing for durability, repairability, and recyclability. Products are conceived not merely as disposable commodities but as valuable assets with a prolonged lifespan, requiring minimal resource input for maintenance and repair. This shift necessitates a fundamental rethink of product design, often demanding interdisciplinary collaboration between engineers, designers, and materials scientists.

Design for disassembly (DfD) plays a critical role in facilitating the recovery and reuse of components at the end of a product's life. By carefully considering the disassembly process during the design phase, manufacturers can optimize the recovery of valuable materials, reducing waste and maximizing the potential for reuse or recycling. This contrasts sharply with the traditional approach, where products are often designed with little consideration for their end-of-life management, resulting in significant quantities of waste ending up in landfills. DfD demands a level of forethought and planning that is not always evident in traditional manufacturing processes.

It necessitates detailed knowledge of the materials used, their properties, and the most effective techniques for disassembly. This often requires investment in specialized tools and equipment, but the long-term benefits in terms of resource recovery and cost savings can be substantial.

Design for recyclability (DfR) complements DfD by focusing on the selection and use of recyclable materials, as well as the creation of product designs that streamline the recycling process. This involves selecting readily recyclable materials, avoiding the use of hazardous substances that complicate the recycling process, and employing design features that make separation and processing easier. For instance, the use of standardized components or easily separable material layers simplifies the recycling operation, improving material recovery rates and reducing contamination.

Implementing DfR requires close collaboration with material suppliers, access to robust recycling infrastructure, and a deep understanding of the materials' end-of-life management. This collaborative approach is essential for ensuring that the design considerations align with the capabilities and limitations of existing recycling processes.

Beyond design, the adoption of manufacturing technologies significantly bolsters the circular economy's implementation. Digital twins, virtual representations of physical assets, can be invaluable in optimizing product lifecycles and improving resource efficiency.

By simulating various scenarios, manufacturers can identify opportunities for enhancing product durability, improving repairability, and optimizing the end-of-life management of products. This data-driven approach enables more informed decision-making, reducing the risk of costly errors and improving the overall efficiency of the circular economy strategy.

Predictive maintenance, enabled by the Internet of Things (IoT) and advanced analytics, significantly contributes to extending product lifespans. By continuously monitoring the operational performance of assets, manufacturers can proactively address potential issues before they escalate into significant failures, reducing downtime and preventing premature disposal. This not only improves the efficiency of production processes but also extends the lifespan of the equipment, promoting the circular economy's principle of keeping products and materials in use for as long as possible.

Additive manufacturing, or 3D printing, offers another promising avenue for enhancing circularity. It allows for the creation of customized parts and components on demand, reducing the need for extensive inventories of spare parts and minimizing waste from obsolete components. Furthermore, 3D printing enables the repair and refurbishment of existing components, extending their lifespan and reducing the demand for new materials. This capability is particularly relevant in industries with high volumes of spare parts, where maintaining stock levels can be costly and environmentally burdensome.

However, transitioning to a fully circular economy model presents significant challenges. The initial investment in new technologies, processes, and infrastructure can be substantial. Changing established business models and fostering collaboration across the entire value chain requires significant effort and commitment. A lack of standardized metrics for measuring circularity can impede progress. Furthermore, achieving widespread adoption necessitates a collaborative approach involving manufacturers, suppliers, consumers, and policymakers.

The successful implementation of circular economy principles requires a holistic approach, encompassing all stages of the product lifecycle. This requires collaboration across the entire value chain, from raw material sourcing to product design, manufacturing, use, and end-of-life management. Manufacturers need to develop strategies for collecting and processing end-of-life products, ensuring the efficient recovery and reuse of valuable materials. This may involve establishing partnerships with recycling companies, developing recycling technologies, and creating closed-loop systems for specific materials.

Furthermore, fostering consumer awareness and engagement is crucial for successful circular economy initiatives. Educating consumers about the benefits of repairing, reusing, and recycling products, as well as promoting sustainable consumption patterns, is essential. This could involve offering extended warranties, promoting repair services, and providing clear information on product recyclability.

Government policies and regulations also play a vital role in shaping the transition towards a circular economy. Incentives for manufacturers to adopt circular economy practices, stricter regulations on waste disposal, and policies promoting the development of recycling infrastructure can significantly accelerate the transition.

In conclusion, the circular economy offers a transformative vision for manufacturing, fostering sustainability and resource efficiency. By integrating manufacturing technologies, embracing design principles that prioritize repairability and recyclability, and fostering collaboration across the value chain, manufacturers can contribute to a more sustainable future. While challenges remain, the potential benefits—reduced waste, enhanced resource efficiency, and increased competitiveness—make the pursuit of a circular economy a worthwhile and ultimately necessary endeavor for the future of manufacturing. The path is complex, requiring investment, innovation, and a fundamental shift in mindset. Yet, the long-term rewards of a more sustainable, resilient, and profitable manufacturing sector make it a journey worth embarking on.

REDUCING CARBON FOOTPRINT IN MANUFACTURING OPERATIONS

The transition to a circular economy necessitates a significant reduction in the environmental impact of manufacturing processes.

A crucial aspect of this is minimizing the carbon footprint, a measure of the total greenhouse gas emissions associated with a product or process. Manufacturing operations, with their energy-intensive processes and reliance on fossil fuels, contribute significantly to global carbon emissions. Reducing this footprint requires a multi-pronged approach involving technological upgrades, operational changes, and strategic partnerships.

One of the most effective strategies is the adoption of energy-efficient equipment and technologies. This includes investing in high-efficiency motors, advanced control systems, and optimized production processes. High-efficiency motors, for instance, can significantly reduce energy consumption compared to older models, leading to substantial reductions in greenhouse gas emissions. These motors often incorporate advanced technologies such as variable speed drives, allowing for precise control of motor speed and power output, minimizing energy waste. Investing in these technologies represents a capital expenditure, but the long-term energy savings often outweigh the initial investment within a relatively short timeframe, leading to both environmental and economic benefits.

Beyond motor efficiency, process optimization plays a crucial role. Analyzing the manufacturing process for energy inefficiencies can identify areas for improvement. This could involve streamlining production flows, minimizing waste heat generation, and optimizing the use of compressed air and other utilities. The use of advanced process control systems, often integrated with supervisory control and data acquisition (SCADA) systems, allows for real-time monitoring and control of energy consumption, providing the data needed to identify and address inefficiencies. Implementing these changes often involves process re-engineering, potentially requiring training for personnel to operate the new systems effectively.

Furthermore, adopting renewable energy sources is paramount in reducing the carbon footprint. This could involve installing on-site renewable energy generation systems, such as solar panels or wind turbines, to power the manufacturing facility. The feasibility of this approach depends on factors such as geographical location, available land area, and energy demand. For facilities with significant energy needs and suitable locations, on-site renewable energy generation can substantially reduce reliance on fossil fuel-based electricity grids, dramatically decreasing carbon emissions. However, implementing such systems requires significant upfront capital investment and may involve navigating complex permitting processes.

Power Purchase Agreements (PPAs) provide an alternative approach. These contracts allow manufacturers to purchase renewable energy from external providers, often wind or solar farms, without the need for on-site generation. This avoids the capital expense of installing and maintaining renewable energy infrastructure, reducing the financial barrier to entry for organizations interested in sourcing renewable energy. However, relying on off-site generation raises concerns about grid reliability and potential transmission losses, which might impact the overall effectiveness of the carbon reduction strategy.

Beyond energy efficiency and renewable energy, manufacturers can explore carbon offsetting initiatives. Carbon offsetting involves investing in projects that reduce greenhouse gas emissions elsewhere to compensate for emissions produced by the manufacturing operation. These projects can include reforestation initiatives, methane capture from landfills, or the development of renewable energy projects. While carbon offsetting shouldn't be viewed as a replacement for direct emission reductions, it can be a valuable supplementary strategy for organizations committed to achieving net-zero emissions targets. The effectiveness of carbon offsetting schemes varies considerably, and selecting reputable and certified projects is crucial to ensure the environmental integrity of the offsetting efforts. Transparency and rigorous verification are essential elements when selecting a suitable carbon offsetting program.

Implementing these carbon reduction measures presents numerous challenges. The initial investment required for new equipment and technologies can be substantial, potentially posing a financial barrier for some manufacturers. Furthermore, integrating new technologies into existing production processes often requires significant changes to operational procedures and workforce training, potentially causing disruptions to production schedules.

Overcoming these challenges requires careful planning, robust financial modeling, and effective change management strategies. It also involves addressing potential resistance to change from employees who may be hesitant to adopt new technologies or processes. Therefore, thorough communication and training are crucial elements of a successful implementation plan.

Despite these challenges, the potential cost savings associated with carbon reduction measures can be considerable. Reduced energy consumption translates directly into lower energy bills, while improved process efficiency can lead to higher productivity and reduced waste. Furthermore, many governments offer financial incentives and tax breaks to companies that implement sustainable practices, further reducing the overall cost of adopting carbon reduction measures. The long-term benefits, both environmental and economic, can significantly outweigh the initial investment costs. In addition, companies with firm sustainability profiles often enjoy enhanced brand reputation and attract environmentally conscious customers, contributing positively to their bottom line.

Moreover, the increasing regulatory pressure on carbon emissions is a significant driver for adopting carbon reduction strategies.

Governments worldwide are enacting stricter regulations to limit greenhouse gas emissions, and manufacturers who fail to comply face hefty fines and reputational damage. These regulations create a compelling business case for investing in carbon reduction measures, turning what was once perceived as a cost into a necessary investment for business continuity and competitiveness. Therefore, a proactive approach to carbon footprint reduction is not simply an environmental responsibility but also a strategic business imperative. By actively addressing their carbon emissions, manufacturers can mitigate risks, improve operational efficiency, enhance their brand image, and secure a more sustainable future. The integration of sustainable practices, therefore, is not a choice but rather a necessity for long-term success in the modern manufacturing landscape.

MEASURING AND REPORTING ON ENVIRONMENTAL PERFORMANCE

Measuring and reporting on environmental performance is paramount for organizations transitioning to a circular economy.

Accurate and transparent data provides a clear picture of a company's environmental impact, enabling informed decision-making, identifying areas for improvement, and demonstrating accountability to stakeholders. In the context of innovative manufacturing, where data collection and analysis are integral, sophisticated environmental performance monitoring becomes increasingly feasible and crucial. This section will explore key metrics, reporting frameworks, and the role of technology in achieving robust and reliable environmental performance measurement.

A comprehensive environmental performance measurement system needs to go beyond simple energy consumption figures. While energy efficiency remains a critical component, it's crucial to consider the broader environmental footprint encompassing resource usage, waste generation, and emissions throughout the entire product lifecycle. This requires a holistic approach, tracking materials from extraction to disposal, considering the embodied carbon in raw materials, and analyzing the impacts of transportation and packaging.

Key performance indicators (KPIs) need to be carefully selected to reflect the specific environmental challenges faced by a particular manufacturing operation. For example, a company heavily reliant on water resources might prioritize water consumption and wastewater generation as primary KPIs, while a manufacturer using significant amounts of hazardous chemicals would focus on chemical usage and waste disposal. For energy, beyond total energy consumption, metrics such as energy intensity (energy consumed per unit of output) and energy efficiency gains year-over-year provide a more nuanced perspective on progress.

Measuring waste generation involves not only quantifying the volume of waste produced but also characterizing its type. This characterization is crucial for optimizing waste management strategies. For example, differentiating between recyclable, compostable, and hazardous waste allows for tailored solutions, maximizing recycling rates and minimizing landfill disposal.

Tracking waste generation per unit of production provides valuable insights into process efficiency and waste reduction opportunities.

Greenhouse gas emissions are a critical focus, especially considering global efforts to mitigate climate change. Measuring emissions requires a comprehensive approach, accounting for direct emissions from energy consumption and indirect emissions embedded in purchased goods and services (Scope 1, 2, and 3 emissions according to the Greenhouse Gas Protocol). Detailed emission inventories, often conducted with the assistance of specialized consultants, are necessary to quantify emissions across all relevant scopes accurately. These inventories should incorporate data on energy use, transportation, raw materials, and waste disposal.

Technological advancements significantly enhance the capabilities for measuring environmental performance. Innovative sensors and IoT devices deployed throughout the manufacturing facility provide real-time data on energy consumption, resource usage, and waste generation. This data, combined with process control systems, allows for continuous monitoring and immediate identification of anomalies or inefficiencies. Advanced analytics techniques, including machine learning and artificial intelligence, can analyze vast datasets to identify trends, predict future performance, and optimize resource utilization to minimize environmental impact.

The implementation of a robust environmental management system (EMS) is essential for effective measurement and reporting. An EMS provides a structured framework for managing environmental aspects, setting targets, implementing control measures, and monitoring progress. ISO 14001 is a widely recognized international standard that provides guidelines for establishing and managing an EMS. Compliance with this standard demonstrates a commitment to environmental responsibility and enhances organizational credibility.

Transparent and accurate environmental reporting is crucial for accountability and stakeholder engagement. Reports should include clear and concise summaries of key environmental performance indicators, along with detailed explanations of the methodologies used for data collection and analysis. The reporting process needs to be consistent and verifiable, allowing for comparisons across different reporting periods and facilitating meaningful assessments of progress. External assurance, such as an independent audit of environmental performance data, can further enhance transparency and build confidence among stakeholders.

The selection of an appropriate reporting framework depends on several factors, including industry-specific requirements, stakeholder expectations, and organizational goals. Several established frameworks, such as the Global Reporting Initiative (GRI) Standards and the Sustainability Accounting Standards Board (SASB) Standards, guide comprehensive environmental reporting. These frameworks offer standardized metrics and reporting protocols, facilitating comparison across organizations and promoting greater transparency.

Beyond regulatory compliance, a strong focus on environmental performance enhances a company's reputation and attracts investors who prioritize sustainability. Consumers are increasingly concerned about the environmental impact of the products they purchase, favoring companies with demonstrably strong environmental performance. Integrating sustainability into corporate strategy can, therefore, attract and retain both customers and talent, providing a competitive advantage in the marketplace.

Furthermore, the transition to a circular economy necessitates a shift in focus from linear production models (take-make-dispose) to circular models that prioritize resource efficiency, waste reduction, and product reuse and recycling. Environmental performance measurement becomes pivotal in monitoring the success of this transition. Metrics should reflect the effectiveness of circularity strategies, including waste diversion rates, material recovery rates, and the reuse of recovered materials in new products.

However, challenges remain in achieving truly comprehensive environmental performance measurement. The complexity of modern manufacturing processes, the diversity of materials and energy sources, and the indirect nature of some environmental impacts can make it challenging to capture the complete environmental footprint fully. Data availability and data quality are also significant concerns. Accurate and reliable data requires robust data collection systems, well-defined measurement methodologies, and effective data management procedures.

Overcoming these challenges necessitates investment in advanced technologies, skilled personnel, and robust data management systems. Continuous improvement in measurement capabilities is crucial as technologies evolve and new environmental concerns emerge. The ongoing development of more sophisticated measurement techniques and reporting frameworks will be vital in enabling organizations to accurately assess and manage their environmental performance in the context of a rapidly evolving circular economy. A commitment to accurate measurement and transparent reporting is not merely a matter of compliance but rather a fundamental component of responsible business practice and a key factor in achieving long-term sustainability. The long-term benefits, including enhanced brand reputation, increased investor confidence, and improved operational efficiency, significantly outweigh the initial investments required for establishing a comprehensive environmental performance monitoring system.

CHAPTER 7
THE FUTURE OF INNOVATIVE
MANUFACTURING

EMERGING TECHNOLOGIES AND TRENDS

The convergence of several influential technological trends is poised to revolutionize innovative manufacturing, pushing its capabilities beyond what was once considered science fiction. This transformation isn't just about incremental improvements; it represents a fundamental shift in how we design, manufacture, and manage products. Let's delve into some of the most impactful emerging technologies and trends shaping the future of this vital sector.

Advanced robotics is leading the charge. No longer limited to repetitive, programmed tasks, robots are becoming increasingly sophisticated, incorporating AI and machine learning to adapt to changing environments and perform more complex operations.

Collaborative robots, or "cobots," are designed to work alongside human workers, enhancing productivity and safety by handling dangerous or strenuous tasks. This collaboration maximizes the strengths of both human ingenuity and robotic precision. The integration of advanced sensors and vision systems provides robots with a higher level of situational awareness, enabling them to interact more effectively with their environment and make real-time adjustments. For example, in a complex assembly line, a cobot equipped with advanced vision can identify and adapt to variations in component placement, ensuring seamless integration despite minor inconsistencies. This level of adaptability minimizes downtime and increases overall efficiency.

Beyond individual robots, we're seeing the emergence of fully automated and highly flexible robotic systems. These systems utilize AI-driven algorithms to optimize workflows and coordinate the actions of multiple robots in a dynamic manufacturing environment. This allows manufacturers to adapt quickly to changing demands and produce customized products efficiently.

Consider a manufacturer producing customized furniture. A traditional approach would involve lengthy setup times and potentially significant waste for smaller batches. With a flexible robotic system, different configurations can be rapidly implemented, minimizing changeover time and maximizing resource utilization. This agility is crucial in today's market, where consumer demand for personalization and customization is constantly growing.

AI-driven process optimization is another game-changer. Through the analysis of massive datasets generated by manufacturing systems, AI algorithms can identify inefficiencies, predict potential failures, and optimize manufacturing processes in real-time. This predictive maintenance aspect significantly reduces downtime, prevents costly breakdowns, and improves overall productivity. By analyzing sensor data from machines, AI can anticipate the need for maintenance before a failure occurs, enabling proactive intervention rather than reactive repairs. This significantly reduces unscheduled downtime, which is often a major contributor to production delays and cost overruns. Beyond maintenance, AI algorithms can analyze production data to identify bottlenecks, optimize resource allocation, and improve overall process flow. This optimization can lead to significant improvements in efficiency, yield, and quality. For instance, AI can identify subtle patterns in production data indicating a gradual decrease in product quality, alerting operators before the issue becomes a significant problem.

The implementation of digital twins – virtual representations of physical assets and processes – is rapidly gaining traction. Digital twins provide a dynamic simulation environment for testing and optimizing manufacturing processes before they are implemented in the real world. This minimizes risk, reduces costs, and accelerates innovation. Imagine designing a new assembly line. Instead of physically building and testing the line, engineers can create a digital twin, simulate its operation, and identify potential bottlenecks or inefficiencies without any physical investment. Once the virtual line is optimized, the physical implementation can proceed with confidence, minimizing the risk of costly errors and rework. Moreover, digital twins allow manufacturers to simulate different scenarios, such as changes in demand or the introduction of new technologies, to anticipate challenges and optimize their strategies proactively.

Blockchain technology, known for its secure and transparent transaction recording capabilities, is finding applications in supply chain management within innovative manufacturing. By providing a tamper-proof record of every step in the supply chain, from raw material sourcing to final product delivery, blockchain enhances traceability, transparency, and accountability. This is crucial for building trust and ensuring product authenticity, especially in industries where counterfeiting is a concern. Consider the pharmaceutical industry, where product authenticity is paramount.

171

Using blockchain, manufacturers can track the journey of each medication from its production to its final destination, ensuring that the product is legitimate and hasn't been tampered with. This enhanced traceability improves patient safety and builds consumer confidence. Furthermore, blockchain can streamline supply chain processes by automating documentation and reducing paperwork, leading to increased efficiency and cost savings.

Additive manufacturing, also known as 3D printing, is transforming prototyping and production. This technology enables the creation of highly customized parts and complex geometries, providing significant design flexibility and reducing lead times. While not entirely new, advancements in materials and process control are expanding the application of additive manufacturing into high-volume production, creating opportunities for on-demand production and reducing reliance on traditional manufacturing techniques. This is particularly beneficial for industries requiring specialized or customized parts, such as aerospace or medical devices. Imagine a manufacturer producing customized implants. Traditional manufacturing methods often necessitate significant upfront investments in tooling and longer production times. With 3D printing, customized implants can be produced efficiently on demand, improving patient outcomes and reducing costs.

The Internet of Things (IoT) is the backbone of innovative manufacturing, connecting machines, sensors, and systems to create a network of interconnected devices. This network generates vast quantities of data, providing valuable insights into production processes and enabling real-time monitoring and control. The combination of IoT data with advanced analytics is crucial for making data-driven decisions, improving efficiency, and optimizing resource utilization. By collecting data from various sensors on the manufacturing floor, manufacturers can gain a granular understanding of their operations. For example, sensors can monitor the temperature, pressure, and vibration levels of machinery, providing early warnings of potential failures and allowing for proactive maintenance.

Predictive analytics leverages historical data and machine learning algorithms to forecast future events, enabling manufacturers to anticipate challenges and adjust their strategies proactively. This proactive approach minimizes disruptions and improves operational efficiency. Predictive analytics is vital for maintaining and optimizing machinery, predicting machine failures, and proactively ensuring the production remains uninterrupted.

Cybersecurity is no longer an afterthought; it's an integral component of innovative manufacturing. With the increasing reliance on interconnected systems and digital data, protecting manufacturing infrastructure from cyber threats is paramount. The risk of cyberattacks disrupting operations, compromising sensitive data, or causing physical damage is real and significant. Implementing robust cybersecurity measures is critical for maintaining business continuity and protecting intellectual property.

The integration of augmented reality (AR) and virtual reality (VR) technologies is enhancing training, maintenance, and collaboration in manufacturing. AR overlays digital information in the real world, providing technicians with real-time instructions and guidance during maintenance or repair tasks. VR creates immersive simulations for training purposes, enabling workers to learn and practice complex procedures in a safe and controlled environment.

The future of innovative manufacturing will also involve a significant emphasis on sustainability. Reducing energy consumption, minimizing waste, and optimizing resource utilization are becoming critical factors in manufacturing competitiveness. Integrating sustainability initiatives into manufacturing systems not only helps the environment but also enhances operational efficiency and reduces costs.

The technologies discussed are not isolated; instead, they are interconnected and mutually reinforcing. The true power of intelligent manufacturing lies in their synergistic integration, creating a holistic, efficient, and sustainable manufacturing ecosystem. The ongoing evolution and convergence of these technologies promise an even more transformative impact on the manufacturing industry in the years to come, offering unprecedented opportunities for innovation, efficiency, and competitiveness. The successful adoption of these technologies requires a multifaceted approach, including investment in advanced technologies, workforce training, and upskilling, as well as strong collaboration across the entire manufacturing ecosystem.

THE IMPACT OF G AND EDGE COMPUTING

The convergence of advanced technologies discussed thus far – AI, robotics, digital twins, and blockchain – lays a strong foundation for the innovative factory. However, the true potential of these technologies is unlocked through robust and responsive communication networks. This is where 5G and edge computing enter the picture, acting as the nervous system of the innovative manufacturing ecosystem. Their impact is profound, transforming data acquisition, processing, and utilization in ways that were previously unimaginable.

5G's ultra-low latency and high bandwidth capabilities are game-changers for real-time data processing in manufacturing environments. Traditional 4G networks, while adequate for many applications, often struggle with the high volume and speed required for the seamless operation of interconnected machines and sensors in an innovative factory. The massive data streams generated by IoT devices, advanced robotics, and machine vision systems can overwhelm 4G networks, leading to delays, dropped connections, and reduced operational efficiency. 5G, with its significantly improved speed and reduced latency, addresses these limitations head-on.

Consider a complex robotic assembly line where multiple robots collaborate to assemble a product. Each robot generates a constant stream of sensor data related to its position, movement, and interaction with the workpiece. In a 4G environment, the transmission and processing of this data might be delayed, potentially leading to synchronization issues and reduced productivity. 5G, however, allows for near-instantaneous data transfer, enabling precise coordination between robots and maximizing overall efficiency. The real-time feedback loop allows for immediate adjustments and corrections, minimizing errors and waste. This level of responsiveness is crucial for complex assembly processes, especially in high-volume manufacturing.

Furthermore, 5G's enhanced bandwidth allows for the seamless transmission of high-resolution images and videos from machine vision systems. These systems play a crucial role in quality control, defect detection, and process optimization. With 5G, real-time image analysis can be performed remotely, enabling prompt identification and resolution of any production issues. For example, a machine vision system could detect a minor defect in a product as it moves along the assembly line. This information is then immediately relayed to the system, allowing for immediate intervention to correct the defect before it impacts further stages of production. Without the speed and reliability of 5G, such real-time analysis would be significantly hampered, leading to potential quality issues and increased waste.

The impact of 5G extends beyond real-time process control. It also enables remote monitoring and maintenance of equipment. With 5G, technicians can remotely access and diagnose problems with machines, reducing downtime and improving overall equipment effectiveness (OEE). This is particularly beneficial in geographically dispersed manufacturing facilities or for equipment located in hazardous environments. Instead of sending a technician to a remote location to troubleshoot a malfunctioning machine, remote diagnostics via 5G can often resolve the issue quickly, saving time and money. High-definition video feeds from the machine enable detailed visual inspection, while remote control capabilities allow technicians to make necessary adjustments or repairs remotely.

However, the sheer volume of data generated in a 5G-enabled innovative factory presents a significant challenge. Processing all this data in a central cloud server can lead to latency issues, particularly given the real-time requirements of many manufacturing processes. This is where edge computing comes into play. Edge computing involves processing data closer to its source – at the "edge" of the network –rather than relying solely on a central cloud server. This decentralized approach significantly reduces latency, enabling faster response times and improved real-time decision-making.

In a manufacturing environment, edge computing devices, such as industrial gateways or specialized servers located on the factory floor, can perform local data processing and analysis. This means that critical decisions, such as adjustments to robot movements or quality control checks, can be made locally without the delay of transmitting data to a central server and waiting for a response. This reduces latency, ensuring a faster and more efficient response to changes in the manufacturing environment. For example, a sensor detecting an anomaly in machine temperature could trigger an immediate shut-down locally, preventing potential damage before it escalates. This capability is impossible with cloud-only processing, given the transmission and processing delays.

The combination of 5G and edge computing creates a powerful synergy, optimizing data flow and processing for enhanced efficiency.

5G provides a high-bandwidth, low-latency network to transmit data quickly and reliably. Edge computing then processes this data locally, reducing latency and ensuring rapid responses.

This integrated approach enables real-time process optimization, predictive maintenance, and improved decision-making, leading to significant improvements in productivity, quality, and cost-effectiveness.

Implementing 5G and edge computing in a manufacturing environment, however, presents significant challenges. The initial investment in upgrading infrastructure and implementing new technologies can be substantial. This includes the cost of 5G network deployment, edge computing devices, and the integration of these technologies into existing manufacturing systems.

Moreover, cybersecurity risks are significantly heightened with increased network connectivity. Protecting sensitive data and manufacturing systems from cyberattacks becomes paramount, requiring robust security measures and ongoing monitoring.

Workforce training and upskilling are also essential for successful implementation. Employees need to be trained to operate and maintain the new technologies, ensuring that the investment in 5G and edge computing translates into tangible benefits. This includes training on data analysis, cybersecurity best practices, and the operation of new software and hardware systems. The change management aspect of transitioning to this new paradigm is not to be underestimated; clear, consistent, and proactive communication with the workforce is crucial.

Furthermore, the standardization of communication protocols and data formats is crucial for the seamless integration of different systems and devices. Different manufacturers often use proprietary technologies, which can create incompatibility issues and hinder the efficient exchange of data. The development of industry-wide standards will foster interoperability and accelerate the adoption of 5G and edge computing in innovative manufacturing. Interoperability between different platforms and systems is key for any successful and long-term implementation of advanced technologies across the manufacturing industry.

Despite the challenges, the potential benefits of 5G and edge computing outweigh the costs. The ability to process data in real-time, optimize manufacturing processes dynamically, and enhance overall efficiency represents a significant step towards the fully realized innovative factory. The resulting improvements in productivity, product quality, and cost-effectiveness will provide manufacturers with a strong competitive advantage in the global marketplace. The ongoing advancements in 5G and edge computing technology, combined with decreasing costs, will make these technologies increasingly accessible to manufacturers of all sizes, furthering the transformation of the manufacturing landscape in the years to come. The future of innovative manufacturing hinges, in no small part, on the successful integration and utilization of these transformative technologies.

DIGITAL TWINS AND THEIR EVOLVING CAPABILITIES

The integration of 5G and edge computing lays the groundwork for a truly responsive and intelligent manufacturing environment, but the evolving capabilities of digital twins further amplify the potential of this interconnected ecosystem. Digital twins, virtual representations of physical assets, processes, or systems, are no longer mere static models. They are dynamic, data-driven entities that are constantly learning and adapting, offering unprecedented insights into manufacturing operations.

Initially conceived as simple virtual replicas, digital twins are rapidly evolving into sophisticated predictive and prescriptive tools. Their enhanced capabilities stem from the convergence of several technologies, including advanced sensor networks, AI-powered analytics, and high-fidelity simulation software. This combination allows digital twins to not only mirror the current state of a physical asset or process but also to predict future behavior and optimize performance proactively.

Consider the application of digital twins in predictive maintenance. Traditional maintenance schedules are often based on fixed time intervals or accumulated operating hours. This approach can lead to unnecessary downtime or, conversely, catastrophic equipment failures due to unforeseen issues. Digital twins, however, can analyze data from various sensors embedded in machinery to monitor its health in real-time. By continuously analyzing vibration patterns, temperature fluctuations, and other relevant parameters, the digital twin can identify subtle anomalies that might indicate an impending failure. This allows for proactive maintenance interventions, minimizing downtime and maximizing equipment lifespan. The predictive capabilities are further enhanced by the incorporation of AI algorithms, which can learn from historical data and identify patterns that might not be apparent to human operators.

This predictive capability extends beyond individual machines. Digital twins can be used to model entire manufacturing lines or even entire factories, enabling holistic performance optimization.

By simulating different scenarios and parameters, manufacturers can identify bottlenecks, optimize production schedules, and improve overall efficiency. For example, a digital twin of an assembly line can simulate the impact of changing the sequence of operations, the speed of individual machines, or the allocation of resources. This allows manufacturers to identify the optimal configuration for maximum throughput and minimal downtime. The ability to conduct such "what-if" analyses without disrupting physical operations is invaluable for improving operations efficiency. Furthermore, the integration of AI enables the digital twin to learn from these simulations, continuously refining its predictive models and becoming more accurate over time.

The enhanced analytical capabilities of digital twins also extend to supply chain optimization. By integrating data from various sources, including suppliers, distributors, and customers, a digital twin of the supply chain can simulate the impact of disruptions, such as unexpected delays or shortages. This allows manufacturers to proactively mitigate risks, ensuring the timely delivery of goods and minimizing disruptions to production. The ability to anticipate and respond to potential disruptions is crucial in today's volatile global supply chains. A more comprehensive digital twin could even encompass logistics networks, simulating transport conditions and identifying points of vulnerability to ensure efficient and reliable delivery of materials and products.

Moreover, the increasing sophistication of digital twin technology allows for the simulation of complex manufacturing processes with unprecedented fidelity. This opens up new possibilities for process optimization and the development of manufacturing techniques. For example, a digital twin of a welding process can simulate the impact of various parameters, such as welding speed, current, and voltage, on the quality of the weld. This detailed simulation allows manufacturers to optimize welding parameters for improved quality and consistency, minimizing defects and maximizing efficiency. Such detailed simulations can save substantial time and resources compared to conducting numerous physical experiments.

The use of digital twins is also transforming the design and development phase of new products and processes. By creating a digital twin of a product before it is physically manufactured, engineers can test and optimize the design in a virtual environment, identifying and resolving potential issues early in the development cycle. This reduces the time and cost associated with physical prototyping and testing. This virtual prototyping allows for rapid design iterations, streamlining the development process and accelerating time-to-market.

Beyond the direct applications mentioned, the future of digital twins lies in their ability to integrate and synthesize information from various

182

sources, creating a holistic view of the manufacturing enterprise. The integration of data from different systems – ERP, MES, PLM, and SCM systems – provides a comprehensive overview of the entire manufacturing process, facilitating better decision-making and improved operational efficiency. This integration requires robust data management systems and interoperability between different software platforms.

Future development trends point towards even more sophisticated digital twins. The incorporation of augmented reality (AR) and virtual reality (VR) technologies will allow engineers and operators to interact with digital twins in more intuitive and immersive ways.

This will facilitate better understanding and control of manufacturing processes and enable more effective collaboration between teams. The use of AR overlays can superimpose information from the digital twin directly onto real-world machinery, providing operators with real-time insights and guidance.

Furthermore, advancements in AI and machine learning will enhance the predictive and prescriptive capabilities of digital twins.

More sophisticated AI algorithms will be able to analyze larger datasets, identifying subtle patterns and anomalies that human operators might miss. This will lead to even more accurate predictions of equipment failures and improved optimization of manufacturing processes. The development of self-learning digital twins, which can adapt and learn from new data autonomously, is a key area of research and development.

The integration of blockchain technology also holds promise for enhancing the security and transparency of digital twins.

Blockchain can ensure the integrity and authenticity of the data used to create and update digital twins, preventing unauthorized modifications and enhancing trust among stakeholders. This is especially important in collaborative environments where multiple parties access and share data related to the digital twin.

However, the widespread adoption of advanced digital twin technologies faces several challenges. The high cost of implementing and maintaining digital twin systems can be a barrier for smaller manufacturers. The requirement for specialized skills and expertise in data analytics, AI, and simulation technologies also presents a challenge. Furthermore, the integration of digital twins with existing manufacturing systems requires careful planning and execution to ensure seamless data flow and interoperability.

Addressing these challenges through strategic investments in infrastructure, training, and standardization will be essential for maximizing the potential of digital twins in the future of innovative manufacturing.

In conclusion, digital twins are evolving from static models to dynamic, data-driven entities that are transforming the way manufacturers design, operate, and optimize their facilities. Their evolving capabilities, fueled by advances in AI, 5G, edge computing, and other technologies, will play a pivotal role in shaping the future of innovative manufacturing, enabling unprecedented levels of efficiency, productivity, and innovation. The journey towards fully realizing the potential of digital twins is ongoing, but the transformative impact is undeniable, paving the way for a more agile, resilient, and data-driven manufacturing landscape.

THE RISE OF AI-DRIVEN AUTONOMOUS FACTORIES

The convergence of advanced robotics, artificial intelligence (AI), and sophisticated data analytics is rapidly ushering in an era of unprecedented automation within the manufacturing sector. We are moving beyond the realm of isolated automated systems towards the vision of fully autonomous factories – self-optimizing, self-regulating production environments that operate with minimal human intervention. This transition promises significant gains in efficiency, productivity, and quality, but it also raises important questions regarding workforce displacement, cybersecurity vulnerabilities, and the ethical implications of increasingly autonomous systems.

The foundation of AI-driven autonomous factories lies in the seamless integration of advanced robotics with sophisticated AI algorithms. Robots are no longer simply programmable machines executing pre-defined tasks; they are becoming increasingly intelligent, capable of adapting to dynamic environments and learning from their experiences. This intelligence is driven by machine learning (ML) algorithms that enable robots to analyze vast amounts of data from various sensors, identify patterns, and make decisions autonomously. For example, a robotic arm in an assembly line can learn to optimize its movements based on real-time feedback from force sensors, minimizing energy consumption and improving efficiency. Furthermore, computer vision systems enable robots to perceive their environment with greater accuracy and precision, allowing them to handle complex tasks that previously required human dexterity and judgment.

Beyond individual robots, AI is transforming the coordination and management of entire robotic systems within a factory. Advanced AI algorithms are being used to optimize the allocation of resources, schedule production tasks, and monitor the overall performance of the factory in real-time. These algorithms can analyze data from various sources – including sensors on robots, machines, and the production line itself – to identify bottlenecks, predict potential failures, and optimize production schedules accordingly. This real-time optimization ensures that the factory operates at peak efficiency, minimizing downtime and maximizing throughput.

The integration of AI also extends to the realm of predictive maintenance. Autonomous factories leverage AI algorithms to analyze data from various machinery sensors to predict potential failures before they occur. This predictive capability allows for proactive maintenance interventions, minimizing costly downtime and extending the lifespan of equipment. Instead of relying on scheduled maintenance based on fixed time intervals, autonomous factories use AI to identify subtle anomalies that might indicate an impending failure, allowing for timely repairs or replacements before they impact production.

Furthermore, AI is revolutionizing quality control in autonomous factories. Computer vision systems, coupled with sophisticated AI algorithms, can inspect products with far greater speed and accuracy than human inspectors. These systems can identify even minute defects that might be missed by human eyes, ensuring that only high-quality products leave the factory. The ability to automate quality control reduces costs, increases efficiency, and enhances the overall quality of the final product.

The concept of a digital twin, discussed in the previous section, becomes particularly critical in the context of autonomous factories. A digital twin of an entire factory, encompassing all its machines, robots, and processes, provides a virtual representation of the physical environment. This virtual model can be used for simulations, allowing engineers to test different scenarios, optimize production parameters, and identify potential problems before they occur in the physical factory. Such simulations are essential for optimizing the performance of an autonomous factory, ensuring seamless operation, and minimizing risks.

However, the transition to autonomous factories is not without its challenges. The initial investment in advanced robotics, AI systems, and sophisticated data infrastructure can be significant, posing a substantial barrier to entry for smaller manufacturers. Furthermore, the implementation and maintenance of these systems require specialized expertise in areas such as robotics, AI, and data analytics, creating a demand for highly skilled technicians and engineers. The integration of these new technologies with existing manufacturing systems can also be complex and time-consuming, requiring careful planning and execution.

A crucial aspect of autonomous factory development is addressing the ethical considerations that arise from the increasing automation of production. One of the most significant concerns is the potential for job displacement. The automation of tasks previously performed by human workers can lead to job losses, necessitating the development of strategies for retraining and reskilling the workforce. This requires

188

proactive collaboration between manufacturers, governments, and educational institutions to ensure a smooth transition and mitigate the negative social impacts of automation.

Cybersecurity also presents a significant concern in the context of autonomous factories. The interconnected nature of these systems makes them vulnerable to cyberattacks, which could have devastating consequences for production, safety, and even national security. Robust cybersecurity measures are therefore critical, encompassing both hardware and software security protocols, as well as comprehensive security training for personnel involved in the operation and maintenance of autonomous factories.

The increasing reliance on AI algorithms also raises ethical questions regarding transparency, accountability, and bias. It is crucial to ensure that AI systems used in autonomous factories are transparent and explainable, allowing humans to understand their decision-making processes. This transparency is essential for maintaining accountability and preventing unintended consequences. Furthermore, AI algorithms must be carefully designed to avoid bias, ensuring that they treat all individuals and groups fairly.

The potential for accidents and safety risks associated with autonomous systems also need careful consideration. Robust safety protocols and fail-safe mechanisms are critical to ensure that autonomous robots and other automated systems operate safely and reliably. This requires stringent testing and verification procedures, as well as ongoing monitoring and oversight.

Looking toward the future, the evolution of AI-driven autonomous factories is likely to be characterized by increasing levels of autonomy, intelligence, and adaptability. AI algorithms will become more sophisticated, enabling robots to handle increasingly complex tasks and make more nuanced decisions. The integration of advanced sensor technologies, including computer vision, force sensors, and other modalities, will further enhance the capabilities of robots and improve their ability to perceive and interact with their environment.

The development of edge computing capabilities will be crucial for enabling real-time decision-making in autonomous factories. By processing data at the edge, closer to the point of origin, latency is minimized, allowing for faster responses and more responsive control systems. This is particularly important for real-time control of robotic systems and for ensuring the safety and efficiency of operations.

The increasing use of digital twins will also play a critical role in the evolution of autonomous factories. More sophisticated digital twins will incorporate greater detail and fidelity, providing an even more accurate virtual representation of the physical factory. This improved accuracy will enhance the predictive capabilities of the digital twin, enabling better optimization of production processes and more accurate predictions of potential failures.

The widespread adoption of AI-driven autonomous factories will inevitably transform the manufacturing landscape, driving innovation and increasing efficiency. However, it is essential to address the ethical and societal implications of this technology, ensuring a just and equitable transition that benefits both industry and society as a whole. Proactive measures to mitigate potential risks, coupled with thoughtful planning and responsible implementation, are critical for ensuring that the future of manufacturing is both prosperous and sustainable. The journey towards fully realizing the potential of autonomous factories is an ongoing process, demanding ongoing research, development, and ethical reflection, but the potential rewards – in terms of increased productivity, efficiency, and quality – are considerable.

CHALLENGES AND OPPORTUNITIES IN THE INNOVATIVE MANUFACTURING LANDSCAPE

The transition to innovative manufacturing presents a complex interplay of challenges and opportunities, demanding a nuanced understanding of the technological, economic, and societal factors at play. While the potential benefits are substantial—increased efficiency, reduced costs, improved product quality, and enhanced flexibility—the path to realizing this potential is fraught with obstacles. Successfully navigating this landscape requires a proactive and multi-faceted approach, encompassing technological innovation, strategic workforce development, robust cybersecurity measures, and a commitment to ethical considerations.

One of the most significant hurdles is the substantial initial investment required for innovative manufacturing adoption. The integration of advanced technologies such as robotics, AI, and IoT necessitates significant capital expenditure for new equipment, software, and infrastructure. This can be particularly challenging for smaller and medium-sized enterprises (SMEs), which may lack the financial resources to compete with larger corporations. This disparity can exacerbate existing inequalities within the manufacturing sector, potentially leading to a consolidation of power in the hands of larger firms better equipped to handle the technological shift. Government initiatives and funding programs aimed at supporting SMEs in their manufacturing journey are crucial to mitigate this risk and promote a more inclusive and equitable transition. These initiatives could include subsidized loans, grants, tax breaks, and training programs designed to equip SMEs with the necessary skills and resources to adopt manufacturing technologies successfully.

Beyond financial constraints, the implementation of manufacturing systems requires a significant amount of expertise.

The integration of complex technologies necessitates specialized skills in areas such as robotics, AI, data analytics, cybersecurity, and cloud computing. The scarcity of qualified personnel poses a significant challenge, particularly given the rapid pace of technological advancements. Bridging this skills gap requires a multifaceted strategy involving collaborations between industry, academia, and government. This includes developing robust educational programs that align with the evolving needs of the manufacturing sector, offering apprenticeships and internships to provide hands-on experience, and facilitating continuous professional development for existing employees. Furthermore, attracting and retaining talent requires competitive salaries and benefits packages, as well as a stimulating and supportive work environment.

The integration of new technologies with legacy systems presents another significant obstacle. Many manufacturing facilities rely on outdated equipment and software, making the seamless integration of advanced technologies a complex undertaking. This often necessitates a phased approach, requiring careful planning and execution to minimize disruption to production while gradually implementing new technologies. A robust digitalization strategy, including a comprehensive assessment of existing infrastructure and a phased implementation plan, is crucial for success. This plan should clearly define objectives, timelines, and resource allocation, ensuring alignment with the overall business strategy.

Cybersecurity is paramount in the context of innovative manufacturing. The interconnected nature of innovative factories makes them vulnerable to cyberattacks, which could have severe consequences ranging from production downtime to data breaches and even physical safety risks. Investing in robust cybersecurity measures, encompassing both hardware and software security protocols, is non-negotiable. This includes implementing multi-factor authentication, intrusion detection systems, firewalls, and regular security audits. Furthermore, employees require comprehensive training in cybersecurity best practices to minimize the risk of human error. A culture of cybersecurity awareness must be fostered throughout the organization, emphasizing the importance of vigilance and proactive security measures. Collaboration with cybersecurity experts and the development of incident response plans are critical for mitigating the potential impact of cyberattacks.

The ethical implications of innovative manufacturing are equally crucial. The automation of tasks previously performed by human workers raises concerns about job displacement. While innovative manufacturing can increase efficiency and productivity, it is essential to address the potential negative impact on the workforce proactively. Retraining and reskilling programs are essential to equip workers with the skills needed for the jobs of the future. This requires collaboration between industry, government, and educational institutions to develop training programs that are relevant to the evolving needs of the manufacturing sector. A just transition to an innovative manufacturing economy requires ensuring that the benefits of automation are shared broadly and that workers are not left behind. This may involve government support for retraining and job placement services, as well as exploring alternative models such as work sharing or guaranteed minimum income.

Data privacy and security are further ethical considerations. Innovative manufacturing relies on the collection and analysis of vast amounts of data, raising concerns about the privacy of individuals and the potential misuse of sensitive information. Robust data governance policies and procedures are essential to ensure compliance with relevant regulations and to protect the privacy of individuals. This includes implementing data encryption, access control mechanisms, and data anonymization techniques. Transparency and accountability in data handling practices are crucial to building trust and ensuring ethical data usage.

Beyond these challenges, significant opportunities exist within the manufacturing landscape. The increased efficiency and productivity afforded by manufacturing technologies can lead to significant cost reductions and improved profitability.

Furthermore, the ability to personalize products and customize manufacturing processes can enhance competitiveness and cater to evolving consumer demands. The integration of advanced analytics can improve decision-making, leading to better resource allocation, optimized production planning, and enhanced supply chain

195

management. Predictive maintenance capabilities can reduce downtime and improve the lifespan of equipment, leading to substantial cost savings. These opportunities extend beyond individual companies, impacting entire supply chains and potentially reshaping global manufacturing ecosystems.

The development of business models is also crucial. Innovative manufacturing technologies can facilitate the development of new business models, such as product-as-a-service, where Manufacturers offer products and services rather than just physical goods. This can lead to new revenue streams and create more sustainable business models. The ability to monitor and track products throughout their lifecycle can improve quality control, enhance customer satisfaction, and create new opportunities for product innovation and service offerings.

The integration of augmented and virtual reality technologies can further transform the manufacturing landscape. Augmented reality (AR) can provide workers with real-time information and guidance during manufacturing processes, improving efficiency and accuracy. Virtual reality (VR) can be used for training and simulation, improving worker safety and reducing training costs.

These technologies can also improve collaboration and communication across geographically dispersed teams. The potential for these technologies to enhance human-machine interaction and optimize manufacturing workflows is vast.

Looking ahead, the future of innovative manufacturing will be shaped by continuous innovation and adaptation. The convergence of technologies such as AI, machine learning, IoT, and cloud computing will create even more sophisticated and interconnected manufacturing systems. The development of advanced robotics and autonomous systems will further automate production processes, increasing efficiency and productivity. The integration of advanced analytics and predictive maintenance capabilities will become increasingly crucial for optimizing operations and mitigating risks.

The successful transition to a manufacturing future demands a concerted effort across industry, academia, and government. This includes promoting research and development in key areas such as AI, robotics, and cybersecurity, investing in education and training programs, and developing supportive policies and regulations.

International collaboration will also be vital to sharing best practices and fostering innovation on a global scale. This collaborative approach will be essential for navigating the complexities of innovative manufacturing and realizing its full potential.

Ultimately, the future of manufacturing will be shaped by those who embrace innovation, adapt to change, and prioritize ethical considerations throughout the journey. The rewards, in terms of economic growth, societal progress, and environmental sustainability, are substantial.

CHAPTER 8
SUPPLY CHAIN MANAGEMENT IN THE AGE OF INNOVATIVE MANUFACTURING

OPTIMIZING SUPPLY CHAINS WITH INNOVATIVE TECHNOLOGIES

The transformative potential of innovative manufacturing extends far beyond the factory floor, profoundly impacting the entire supply chain. Optimizing supply chains with technologies is no longer a futuristic aspiration; it's a necessity for competitiveness in today's dynamic global marketplace. The seamless integration of advanced technologies allows for unprecedented visibility, control, and efficiency across the entire supply chain, from raw material sourcing to final product delivery. This section will delve into the specific ways technologies are revolutionizing supply chain management, focusing on key areas of improvement.

One of the most significant impacts of technologies is the enhanced visibility they provide in the movement of goods. Real-time tracking capabilities, enabled by technologies such as the Internet of Things (IoT), provide a continuous stream of data on the location and status of shipments. RFID tags, GPS tracking devices, and sensor networks embedded within shipping containers and individual products provide granular data, offering unprecedented transparency. This real-time visibility eliminates information silos and reduces uncertainty, allowing for proactive management of potential delays or disruptions. For example, a sudden weather event causing port congestion can be identified instantly, enabling logistics managers to reroute shipments or proactively adjust delivery schedules, minimizing the impact on the entire supply chain. Furthermore, real-time data enables improved coordination between different stakeholders, including suppliers, manufacturers, logistics providers, and retailers. This enhanced communication facilitates smoother collaboration and reduces the likelihood of errors or delays.

Predictive analytics, a powerful application of artificial intelligence (AI) and machine learning (ML), are reshaping demand forecasting.

By analyzing historical sales data, market trends, social media sentiment, and even weather patterns, sophisticated algorithms can predict future demand with greater accuracy than traditional forecasting methods. This improved accuracy reduces the risk of stockouts or overstocking, optimizing inventory levels and minimizing storage costs. The ability to anticipate demand fluctuations allows businesses to proactively adjust production schedules, optimize resource allocation, and ensure that they have the necessary materials and capacity to meet customer demand. In industries with highly seasonal demand, such as apparel or toys, accurate predictive analytics is crucial for managing inventory effectively and avoiding costly surpluses or shortages. This precision also extends to anticipating supply chain disruptions. By analyzing data from various sources, including weather forecasts, geopolitical events, and economic indicators, companies can identify potential risks and develop contingency plans to mitigate their impact.

Beyond demand forecasting, technologies are revolutionizing inventory management. Advanced sensor technologies, combined with data analytics, provide real-time insights into inventory levels at various points in the supply chain. This enables accurate tracking of stock levels, reducing the likelihood of stockouts and minimizing the risk of obsolescence. Automatic replenishment systems, triggered by real-time inventory data, streamline the ordering process, optimizing efficiency and reducing lead times.

Furthermore, warehousing systems utilizing robotics and automated guided vehicles (AGVs) optimize storage space and improve order fulfillment speed. Automated picking and packing systems further streamline the process, reducing labor costs and minimizing errors. For example, a retailer might use AI-powered inventory management systems to optimize stock levels in individual stores based on real-time sales data and anticipated demand. This ensures that popular items are always in stock while minimizing the storage costs associated with slow-moving items.

Blockchain technology, often associated with cryptocurrencies, is emerging as a powerful tool for enhancing supply chain transparency and security. By creating a secure, immutable record of all transactions and movements of goods, blockchain provides a tamper-proof audit trail. This enhanced traceability improves accountability and reduces the risk of counterfeiting or fraud.

Consumers can gain greater confidence in the origin and authenticity of products, while businesses can benefit from increased transparency and reduced risk. For example, in the food industry, blockchain technology can be used to track the journey of a product from farm to table, providing consumers with detailed information about its origin, processing, and handling. This increased transparency can enhance consumer trust and build brand loyalty. Similarly, in the pharmaceutical industry, blockchain can be used to track the movement of drugs, ensuring that they are not counterfeit or diverted.

The integration of advanced analytics enables data-driven decision-making throughout the supply chain. By analyzing large datasets collected from various sources, businesses can identify patterns, trends, and anomalies that might otherwise go unnoticed. This enables the identification of bottlenecks, inefficiencies, and potential risks, allowing for proactive interventions to improve overall performance. For instance, analysis of transportation data might reveal that specific routes are consistently delayed due to traffic congestion or weather patterns. This information can be used to optimize routing, improve delivery times, and reduce transportation costs. Similarly, analysis of supplier performance data can help identify reliable suppliers and mitigate risks associated with supply disruptions.

The optimization of supply chains through technologies is not merely about automating existing processes; it's about fundamentally reshaping how businesses manage their supply chains. It involves creating a more agile, responsive, and resilient supply chain that can adapt to unexpected events and changing market conditions. This involves embracing a holistic approach, integrating advanced technologies with effective change management strategies, and cultivating a data-driven culture within the organization. Continuous monitoring, feedback loops, and iterative improvements are crucial to realizing the full potential of technologies in supply chain optimization. The successful adoption of these technologies requires investment in infrastructure, talent development, and robust cybersecurity measures.

However, the benefits – improved efficiency, reduced costs, enhanced resilience, and increased customer satisfaction – far outweigh the challenges. The future of supply chain management is undeniably intertwined with the intelligent application of technologies. The companies that embrace these technologies proactively will be best positioned to thrive in the increasingly competitive and dynamic global marketplace.

BLOCKCHAIN TECHNOLOGY FOR SUPPLY CHAIN TRANSPARENCY

Blockchain technology, while initially known for its role in cryptocurrencies, presents a transformative solution for enhancing transparency and traceability within complex supply chains. Its decentralized and immutable nature offers a compelling alternative to traditional, centralized systems, which often lack the robustness and security needed to combat counterfeiting, fraud, and inefficient information sharing. The fundamental principle of blockchain lies in its ability to create a shared, secure ledger that records every transaction and movement of goods throughout the supply chain.

This creates a permanent, auditable record that is virtually impossible to tamper with, providing unprecedented levels of transparency and accountability.

One of the most significant benefits of blockchain in supply chain management is its ability to enhance traceability. Each product or shipment can be assigned a unique identifier, which is then recorded on the blockchain along with relevant information such as origin, processing methods, handling, and location. This detailed tracking allows businesses and consumers to easily follow the journey of a product from its source to the final point of sale. This level of transparency is particularly valuable in industries where product authenticity and origin are critical, such as pharmaceuticals, food, and luxury goods. For instance, a consumer can scan a QR code on a package of coffee beans and access a complete history of its production, from the farm where the beans were grown to the roastery where they were processed and packaged, verifying their origin and ensuring quality.

This enhanced traceability directly addresses the challenge of counterfeiting, a pervasive problem that costs businesses billions of dollars annually. By providing an immutable record of a product's journey, blockchain makes it significantly more challenging to introduce counterfeit goods into the supply chain. Any attempt to alter or falsify information on the blockchain would be immediately detectable, alerting stakeholders to potential fraud. This increased security not only protects businesses from financial losses but also safeguards consumers from potentially harmful or substandard products. In the pharmaceutical industry, for example, blockchain can be used to track the movement of drugs, ensuring that they are not counterfeit or diverted. This is crucial for ensuring patient safety and preventing the distribution of potentially harmful medications.

Beyond combating counterfeiting, blockchain improves accountability throughout the supply chain. Each participant in the supply chain—from suppliers to manufacturers, distributors, and retailers—has a record of their actions and responsibilities. This shared transparency fosters greater trust and collaboration among stakeholders, leading to improved efficiency and reduced conflict. For example, if a product is found to be defective, the blockchain record allows for quick identification of the point of failure and the responsible party. This streamlined investigation accelerates problem-solving and minimizes disruption to the supply chain. This level of accountability also extends to environmental and social responsibility. Companies can use blockchain to track the ethical sourcing of materials, ensuring that products are manufactured sustainably and responsibly. This allows businesses to showcase their commitment to sustainability to consumers and strengthens brand reputation.

The implementation of blockchain in supply chain management requires careful consideration of several factors. First, the selection of an appropriate blockchain platform is crucial. Different platforms offer varying levels of scalability, security, and functionality. The choice of platform should be tailored to the specific needs and requirements of the supply chain and the volume of transactions. Second, integration with existing systems is a key challenge.

Companies need to ensure that their blockchain solution seamlessly integrates with their existing enterprise resource planning (ERP) systems and other relevant technologies. This requires careful planning and coordination to avoid disruptions to ongoing operations.

Furthermore, the successful implementation of blockchain requires stakeholder buy-in and collaboration. All participants in the supply chain need to be on board with the new technology and willing to share data transparently. This necessitates a strong communication strategy and effective change management processes. Finally, the security of the blockchain system is paramount. Robust security measures are required to prevent unauthorized access and data breaches. Regular security audits and updates are necessary to maintain the integrity and security of the blockchain network.

The benefits of blockchain extend beyond transparency and accountability. The improved efficiency it brings translates to cost savings across various supply chain activities. Reduced fraud and counterfeiting, faster dispute resolution, and streamlined processes all contribute to significant cost reductions. Additionally, blockchain can facilitate more efficient inventory management by providing real-time visibility into inventory levels across the entire supply chain. This reduces the risk of stockouts and overstocking, optimizes inventory levels, and reduces storage costs. The enhanced traceability and transparency also improve customer satisfaction by giving consumers greater confidence in the products they purchase. Knowing the origin and history of a product increases consumer trust and brand loyalty.

Despite the significant potential of blockchain, its adoption in supply chain management is still in its relatively early stages.

However, the increasing awareness of its benefits and the advancements in blockchain technology are driving its wider adoption. As the technology matures and becomes more accessible, we can expect to see a significant increase in its use in supply chains across various industries. The ability to build trust, enhance transparency, and combat fraud are compelling reasons for businesses to explore the possibilities offered by blockchain. The future of supply chain management is likely to be significantly shaped by this technology, leading to more efficient, resilient, and trustworthy supply chains globally. Early adoption will be a key differentiator for companies seeking a competitive edge in this rapidly evolving landscape. The development of industry standards and interoperability protocols will be crucial for realizing the full potential of blockchain in supply chain management, fostering collaboration, and reducing implementation barriers for businesses of all sizes. The journey towards fully integrated blockchain solutions is ongoing, but the potential rewards are substantial, making it an area of significant investment and innovation for businesses worldwide. The integration of blockchain with other manufacturing technologies further enhances its capabilities, creating a synergistic effect that optimizes the entire value chain. For instance, the combination of blockchain and IoT sensors allows for real-time tracking of goods, providing even greater visibility and control. This combination of technologies creates a brilliant supply chain capable of adapting to disruptions and optimizing efficiency in unprecedented ways. This signifies a paradigm shift in supply chain management, moving away from traditional, opaque systems to a future characterized by transparency, traceability, and resilience.

DIGITALIZATION OF SUPPLY CHAIN PROCESSES

The integration of digital technologies is revolutionizing supply chain management, offering unprecedented levels of efficiency, transparency, and resilience. Central to this transformation is the utilization of cloud-based platforms, which are rapidly becoming the backbone of modern supply chain operations. These platforms provide a centralized repository for all supply chain data, enabling real-time visibility across the entire network, from raw material sourcing to final product delivery. This enhanced visibility empowers businesses to make data-driven decisions, optimize resource allocation, minimize disruptions, and improve overall responsiveness to market demands.

One of the most impactful applications of cloud-based platforms is in logistics management. Traditional logistics processes often rely on manual data entry, paper-based documentation, and disparate systems, leading to delays, errors, and inefficiencies. Cloud-based solutions streamline these processes by automating tasks such as order tracking, shipment scheduling, and route optimization. Real-time tracking capabilities, facilitated by GPS and IoT sensors integrated with the cloud platform, enable companies to monitor the location and status of shipments throughout their journey. This real-time visibility allows for proactive intervention in case of delays or unexpected events, minimizing disruptions and ensuring timely delivery. For example, if a shipment is delayed due to unforeseen circumstances such as inclement weather or traffic congestion, the cloud platform can alert relevant parties, enabling them to take corrective actions, reroute shipments, or notify customers proactively. This not only prevents delays but also strengthens customer relationships by improving transparency and communication.

Beyond logistics, cloud-based platforms are instrumental in facilitating collaboration among various stakeholders in the supply chain. The ability to share data and information seamlessly across the network empowers suppliers, manufacturers, distributors, and retailers to work together more effectively. This improved collaboration fosters greater transparency and trust, leading to reduced lead times, improved inventory management, and enhanced overall efficiency. For instance, suppliers can use the cloud platform to provide real-time updates on inventory levels and production schedules, enabling manufacturers to optimize their production planning and minimize delays. Similarly, distributors can use the platform to track shipments and communicate with retailers regarding delivery schedules, ensuring that products reach their destination on time. This level of collaboration reduces the risk of stockouts, minimizes waste, and enhances customer satisfaction by ensuring product availability.

Furthermore, cloud-based platforms enable comprehensive monitoring of key performance indicators (KPIs) throughout the supply chain. This real-time data analysis provides valuable insights into areas for improvement and allows for data-driven decision-making. By tracking metrics such as order fulfillment rates, delivery times, inventory turnover, and transportation costs, businesses can identify bottlenecks, inefficiencies, and areas for optimization. This data-driven approach allows for proactive interventions to address potential problems, improve overall performance, and reduce costs.

For example, by analyzing delivery times across different transportation modes, companies can identify the most efficient and cost-effective options for their shipments. Similarly, by analyzing inventory turnover rates, businesses can optimize their inventory levels, minimizing storage costs and reducing the risk of stockouts.

The digitalization of supply chain processes also extends to the use of advanced analytics and artificial intelligence (AI). AI-powered systems can analyze vast amounts of data from various sources, identifying patterns and trends that might not be apparent to human analysts. This capability enhances predictive capabilities, allowing businesses to anticipate potential disruptions and take proactive measures to mitigate their impact. For instance, AI-powered systems can analyze historical data on weather patterns, traffic congestion, and geopolitical events to predict potential delays in shipments. This foresight enables businesses to adjust their logistics plans accordingly, minimizing disruptions and ensuring timely delivery. Similarly, AI can be used to optimize inventory levels by predicting future demand based on historical sales data, seasonality, and other relevant factors. This optimization minimizes storage costs and reduces the risk of stockouts.

The implementation of digital technologies in supply chain management necessitates a comprehensive approach that considers various aspects of the organization. Firstly, it requires a robust digital infrastructure, including high-speed internet connectivity, secure data storage, and reliable software applications. Secondly, it requires the integration of various systems, including ERP systems, CRM systems, and transportation management systems, to ensure seamless data flow across the organization. Thirdly, a skilled workforce is required to manage and utilize these technologies effectively. This necessitates investments in training and development to equip employees with the necessary skills and knowledge to work with these new systems and technologies.

Finally, it requires a strong organizational culture that embraces change and innovation. Successfully implementing digital technologies requires buy-in from all levels of the organization, from top management to frontline employees.

The transition to a digitally enabled supply chain is not without its challenges. Data security is a paramount concern, as sensitive data related to shipments, inventory, and customer information needs to be protected from unauthorized access and cyber threats. Robust security measures, including encryption, access controls, and regular security audits, are crucial to mitigate these risks. Another challenge lies in the integration of various systems and technologies, which can be complex and time-consuming. Careful planning and coordination are essential to ensure seamless integration and avoid disruptions to ongoing operations. Moreover, the cost of implementing digital technologies can be significant, requiring substantial investments in hardware, software, and training. However, the long-term benefits of enhanced efficiency, transparency, and resilience often outweigh the initial investment costs.

Despite these challenges, the benefits of digitalizing supply chain processes are undeniable. The increased efficiency and transparency lead to reduced costs, improved customer satisfaction, and enhanced competitiveness. The ability to react swiftly to disruptions and make data-driven decisions enables businesses to remain agile and adapt to changing market conditions. The implementation of digital technologies in supply chain management is not merely a technological upgrade but a strategic imperative for businesses seeking to thrive in the increasingly complex and competitive global marketplace. It represents a paradigm shift toward a more dynamic, responsive, and data-driven approach to managing the flow of goods and services, paving the way for a more efficient and sustainable future. The continuous evolution of digital technologies promises further advancements, leading to even greater levels of optimization, transparency, and resilience in the years to come. The adoption of these technologies marks a significant step towards building more robust, responsive, and sustainable supply chains capable of navigating the complexities of the modern global economy.

BUILDING RESILIENT SUPPLY CHAINS IN A DISRUPTIVE WORLD

The increasing frequency and severity of global disruptions—pandemics, natural disasters, geopolitical instability, and even unexpected shifts in consumer demand—underscore the critical need for resilient supply chains. No longer can businesses rely on traditional, linear supply chain models that prioritize efficiency above all else. The fragility of these models has been painfully exposed in recent years, leading to widespread shortages, production delays, and significant financial losses. Building resilient supply chains is no longer a competitive advantage; it's a prerequisite for survival.

Resilience, in the context of supply chain management, refers to the ability of a supply chain to withstand and recover from disruptions. It encompasses the capacity to anticipate potential risks, mitigate their impact, and adapt quickly to changing circumstances.

Achieving this requires a fundamental shift in thinking, moving away from a purely cost-optimization approach toward a more holistic strategy that considers risk management, diversification, and collaboration as equally crucial elements.

One key strategy for enhancing supply chain resilience is diversification. Over-reliance on a single supplier or a limited geographic region creates a significant vulnerability. A disruption affecting a single supplier can ripple through the entire supply chain, causing widespread shortages. Diversifying sourcing, manufacturing, and logistics networks mitigates this risk. This doesn't simply mean geographically dispersing operations; it involves identifying multiple, reliable suppliers with diverse capabilities and locations. Consider, for example, a company that sources raw materials solely from one country. A political upheaval, a natural disaster, or a pandemic in that country could severely disrupt their operations. By sourcing from multiple countries with different political and economic environments, the company significantly reduces its risk exposure. This diversification strategy extends beyond geographical locations to include supplier types. Relying on a single supplier, even if geographically diversified, can still be risky. Partnering with multiple suppliers with different production processes and capabilities provides a safety net. If one supplier experiences a problem, the others can step in to maintain production.

Another critical element of resilient supply chain management is robust risk management. This involves identifying potential disruptions, assessing their likelihood and impact, and developing mitigation strategies. Several tools and techniques are available to facilitate this process. Scenario planning allows organizations to simulate different disruptions and evaluate their potential consequences. This proactive approach enables businesses to develop contingency plans and allocate resources effectively. For instance, a company could develop a scenario planning exercise to analyze the impact of a major port closure due to a natural disaster.

The exercise would consider alternative transportation routes, potential delays, and the cost implications of each scenario. This allows the company to develop contingency plans, such as using alternative ports or air freight, to minimize the disruption's impact.

Beyond scenario planning, advanced analytics play a significant role in risk management. Data analytics tools can identify patterns and anomalies in supply chain data, providing early warnings of potential problems. For example, a sudden surge in lead times from a particular supplier could indicate an impending disruption.

Similarly, an unexpected spike in transportation costs might signal a looming logistical challenge. Early detection allows businesses to take proactive measures, reducing the severity of any disruption. The integration of advanced analytics with real-time data tracking capabilities allows for proactive decision-making. Companies can actively monitor their suppliers' performance, inventory levels, and transportation routes, enabling them to identify and respond to potential problems before they escalate into significant disruptions.

Furthermore, enhanced visibility and transparency throughout the supply chain are essential for building resilience. This involves implementing systems that provide real-time tracking of goods and materials, allowing businesses to monitor their flow and identify bottlenecks or delays. Blockchain technology, with its secure and transparent ledger, offers a powerful tool for improving supply chain visibility. By tracking materials and products throughout the supply chain on a shared, immutable ledger, businesses can gain real-time insights into their whereabouts and status, fostering greater transparency and accountability. This increased transparency extends to collaboration with suppliers and partners.

Open communication and information sharing are crucial for effective risk management and rapid response to disruptions. This collaborative approach allows businesses to anticipate and address problems collaboratively, mitigating their impact. For example, if a supplier experiences a production delay, they can communicate this promptly to their customers, who can then adjust their production schedules accordingly.

The digitalization of supply chains offers powerful tools for building resilience. The integration of Internet of Things (IoT) devices, cloud computing, and advanced analytics provides real-time visibility into supply chain operations. IoT sensors embedded in goods and transportation vehicles provide real-time tracking data, allowing businesses to monitor shipments and respond to delays or disruptions promptly. Cloud-based platforms provide a centralized repository for all supply chain data, enabling collaboration and efficient decision-making. Advanced analytics tools can identify patterns and anomalies in supply chain data, providing early warnings of potential problems. This integration of digital technologies significantly enhances the ability of companies to anticipate and respond to disruptions, building more resilient supply chains.

However, building a resilient supply chain is not simply a technological challenge; it's also a managerial one. It requires a cultural shift within organizations, prioritizing collaboration, risk management, and adaptability. Leadership needs to champion resilience as a core organizational value, integrating it into strategic planning and decision-making. This involves investing in training and development, empowering employees to identify and address risks, and fostering a culture of open communication and collaboration. Robust internal communication systems and protocols are critical for effective response to disruptions.

Organizations should establish clear communication channels and protocols to ensure that all relevant stakeholders are informed promptly in case of a disruption. This involves both internal and external communications with suppliers, customers, and other stakeholders.

Finally, regulatory compliance and ethical sourcing are increasingly important elements of resilient supply chain management.

Businesses need to ensure that their supply chains comply with relevant regulations, including those related to environmental protection, labor standards, and human rights. Ethical sourcing practices, such as ensuring fair wages and safe working conditions for workers in the supply chain, not only enhance the company's reputation but also contribute to a more stable and resilient supply chain. Unforeseen regulatory changes or ethical lapses can severely disrupt operations. Proactive compliance and ethical sourcing practices mitigate these risks, contributing to long-term stability.

In conclusion, building resilient supply chains is a multifaceted endeavor that requires a holistic approach, encompassing diversification, risk management, enhanced visibility, technological integration, strong leadership, and ethical considerations. It's not simply about minimizing costs; it's about building a supply chain that can withstand and recover from disruptions, ensuring business continuity and long-term success in an increasingly unpredictable world. The journey toward resilience is a continuous process of adaptation and improvement, requiring constant vigilance and a commitment to ongoing learning and innovation. The cost of investing in resilience is undoubtedly significant in the short term, but the long-term benefits—enhanced stability, reduced risk, and improved profitability—far outweigh the initial investment. The future of supply chain management lies in its ability to adapt and thrive in the face of adversity, a future secured not by outdated linear models but by a proactive, resilient, and collaborative approach.

INTEGRATING SUSTAINABLE PRACTICES INTO SUPPLY CHAINS

The imperative for resilient supply chains discussed earlier extends beyond simply withstanding disruptions; it demands a fundamental shift toward sustainability. Integrating sustainable practices isn't merely an ethical consideration; it's a strategic necessity for long-term competitiveness and resilience. A supply chain heavily reliant on unsustainable practices is inherently fragile and vulnerable to resource scarcity, regulatory changes, and shifting consumer preferences. Investors and consumers are increasingly scrutinizing environmental, social, and governance (ESG) factors, which necessitates a proactive approach to sustainability across the entire supply chain.

Reducing carbon emissions presents a significant challenge and opportunity. Transportation accounts for a substantial portion of a typical supply chain's carbon footprint. Optimizing transportation routes, consolidating shipments, and utilizing more fuel-efficient vehicles are crucial steps. Investing in alternative fuels, such as biofuels or hydrogen, offers a longer-term solution, although the infrastructure and technological hurdles remain significant.

Furthermore, the adoption of electric vehicles and the exploration of alternative modes of transportation like rail or inland waterways can significantly diminish environmental impact. Companies should conduct thorough lifecycle assessments of their products, identifying emissions hotspots throughout the entire supply chain, from raw material extraction to end-of-life disposal. This granular analysis allows for targeted interventions, focusing efforts on areas with the most significant potential for emissions reduction.

Minimizing waste is another critical aspect of sustainable supply chain management. This involves reducing material usage during manufacturing, improving packaging efficiency, and promoting recycling and reuse programs. Implementing lean manufacturing principles, which focus on eliminating waste and improving efficiency, plays a significant role. Strategies such as just-in-time inventory management can minimize waste by reducing excess stock and preventing obsolescence. Similarly, the adoption of circular economy models, which emphasize reuse, repair, and recycling, can dramatically reduce the environmental impact of a supply chain. Companies should actively seek out suppliers who share their commitment to waste reduction and partner with them to develop solutions for minimizing environmental impact. This collaborative approach fosters innovation and cost-effectiveness, promoting both sustainability and financial gains.

Ethical sourcing of materials is paramount. This encompasses ensuring fair labor practices, safe working conditions, and responsible resource extraction. Companies should conduct thorough due diligence on their suppliers, verifying their compliance with relevant environmental and social standards.

Transparency is key; companies should strive for complete traceability of their materials, allowing for full accountability and ensuring ethical sourcing practices throughout the entire supply chain. This necessitates the implementation of robust tracking systems, potentially leveraging technologies such as blockchain to provide

221

immutable records of material provenance. Moreover, supporting and investing in sustainable sourcing initiatives, such as responsible forestry or fair-trade practices, further demonstrates commitment to ethical sourcing and environmental stewardship.

Collaboration and transparency are pivotal to integrating sustainable practices effectively. Open communication between suppliers, manufacturers, distributors, and retailers is essential for sharing best practices, identifying areas for improvement, and collectively addressing challenges. The formation of industry partnerships and collaborative initiatives can foster innovation and facilitate the sharing of resources and knowledge. Regularly auditing suppliers' environmental and social performance is crucial for maintaining high ethical standards throughout the supply chain. This continuous monitoring allows for prompt identification and remediation of any lapses in sustainability practices. Companies should adopt standardized reporting frameworks, such as the Global Reporting Initiative (GRI) standards, to provide transparent and consistent information on their environmental and social performance. This promotes accountability and allows stakeholders to assess the company's sustainability initiatives.

Technological advancements play a crucial role in enabling sustainable supply chain management. The Internet of Things (IoT) facilitates real-time monitoring of environmental parameters, such as energy consumption and emissions, providing valuable data for optimizing operational efficiency and reducing waste. Advanced analytics tools can analyze this data to identify patterns and predict potential environmental risks, allowing for proactive mitigation strategies. Blockchain technology, as previously mentioned, offers enhanced traceability of materials, ensuring transparency and accountability throughout the supply chain. Artificial intelligence (AI) can assist in optimizing transportation routes, reducing fuel consumption, improving predictive maintenance, and minimizing downtime and resource waste. The integration of these technologies provides businesses with the data-driven insights necessary for informed decision-making, driving improvements in sustainability performance.

The integration of sustainable practices into supply chains requires a fundamental cultural shift within organizations. Leadership must champion sustainability as a core organizational value, integrating it into strategic planning and decision-making processes. This includes setting ambitious sustainability targets, establishing precise accountability mechanisms, and providing the necessary resources to implement sustainable practices. Employee training and engagement are also crucial; empowering employees to identify and address sustainability-related issues fosters a culture of responsibility and accountability. Internal communication systems should be robust, facilitating the efficient dissemination of sustainability-related information and promoting collaborative efforts across departments. Openly communicating the company's sustainability progress to stakeholders, including investors, customers, and employees, builds trust and enhances the company's reputation.

Furthermore, sustainable supply chain management requires a long-term perspective. While the initial investments in sustainable practices might appear significant, the long-term benefits far outweigh the costs.

Reduced waste, improved efficiency, lower energy consumption, and enhanced brand reputation can lead to significant cost savings and improved profitability. Moreover, aligning with the growing consumer demand for sustainable products strengthens the company's market position, securing its long-term success. The increasing regulatory pressures surrounding environmental and social issues make sustainable supply chain management not merely a responsible choice but a strategic imperative for survival and growth in the long run. Failing to address these issues leaves companies vulnerable to significant financial and reputational risks.

In conclusion, integrating sustainable practices into supply chains is a complex yet crucial undertaking, requiring a multifaceted approach that embraces technological innovation, strategic collaboration, and a commitment to long-term sustainability goals.

It's not simply about adopting isolated green initiatives; it necessitates a systemic overhaul, transforming the entire supply chain to operate efficiently, ethically, and responsibly. The journey towards a sustainable supply chain is an ongoing process of learning, adaptation, and continuous improvement, demanding unwavering commitment from all stakeholders. By proactively integrating sustainability into their supply chain strategies, businesses can build more resilient, responsible, and ultimately more successful operations in the face of an evolving global landscape. This commitment not only benefits the planet but also provides a crucial competitive advantage in the marketplace.

CHAPTER 9

DATA SECURITY AND PRIVACY IN

INNOVATIVE MANUFACTURING

PROTECTING SENSITIVE DATA IN INNOVATIVE FACTORIES

The digital transformation of manufacturing, exemplified by the rise of innovative factories, brings unprecedented opportunities for efficiency and productivity. However, this interconnectedness also introduces significant vulnerabilities, particularly concerning data security and privacy. Innovative factories generate and process vast quantities of sensitive data, encompassing everything from proprietary designs and manufacturing processes to customer information and real-time operational data. Protecting this data is no longer a matter of best practice; it's a fundamental requirement for operational continuity, legal compliance, and maintaining customer trust.

The threat landscape for innovative factories is constantly evolving, with sophisticated cyberattacks becoming increasingly common. These attacks can range from relatively simple denial-of-service attacks, which disrupt operations by overwhelming systems with traffic, to highly targeted intrusions aimed at stealing intellectual property or disrupting critical infrastructure. The consequences of a successful cyberattack can be devastating, resulting in significant financial losses, production downtime, reputational damage, and even legal repercussions.

A robust cybersecurity strategy for an innovative factory must be multi-layered and proactive. It begins with a thorough assessment of the factory's IT infrastructure and its vulnerabilities. This assessment should identify all connected devices, systems, and networks, mapping out potential entry points for attackers. A crucial element of this assessment involves identifying critical assets – those systems and data whose compromise would have the most significant impact on the business. Once vulnerabilities are identified, they must be prioritized based on the risk they pose, allowing for a focused and efficient mitigation strategy. This prioritization considers not only the likelihood of an attack but also the potential consequences should it succeed.

Network security is paramount. Implementing firewalls, intrusion detection and prevention systems (IDS/IPS), and virtual private networks (VPNs) are fundamental steps in protecting the factory's network from unauthorized access. These systems should be regularly updated with the latest security patches to address newly discovered vulnerabilities. Segmentation of the network is also crucial, dividing it into smaller, isolated segments to limit the impact of a successful attack. If one segment is compromised, the damage is contained, preventing attackers from gaining access to the entire network. This also aids in regulatory compliance and minimizes the scope of damage in case of a breach. Regular penetration testing and vulnerability scanning are essential to proactively identifying and addressing weaknesses in the network's security. These simulated attacks expose potential flaws before malicious actors can exploit them.

Device security is equally critical. Innovative factories utilize a vast array of connected devices, from programmable logic controllers (PLCs) and robots to sensors and actuators. These devices often have limited security features and are vulnerable to attack.

Implementing robust authentication and access control mechanisms for each device is crucial, restricting access to authorized personnel only.

Regular firmware updates are also essential, ensuring that devices are running the latest security patches and mitigating known vulnerabilities. The use of secure communication protocols, such as Secure Shell (SSH) and Transport Layer Security (TLS), is vital to protect data transmitted between devices and systems.

Furthermore, the principle of least privilege should be applied, granting devices only the necessary permissions to perform their intended function.

Data security extends beyond network and device protection; it encompasses the secure storage and management of data itself. Data encryption, both in transit and at rest, is critical to protect sensitive information from unauthorized access. Strong encryption algorithms should be used, and encryption keys should be managed securely using a robust key management system. Access control measures should be implemented to restrict access to sensitive data to authorized personnel only, using role-based access control (RBAC) to ensure that individuals only have access to the information necessary to perform their job functions. Data loss prevention (DLP) tools can monitor data movements, identifying and preventing sensitive information from leaving the factory's network without authorization. Regular data backups are essential, providing a means to recover data in the event of a disaster or cyberattack. These backups should be stored securely, ideally in a geographically separate location, to protect against physical damage or theft.

Compliance with relevant data privacy regulations is crucial.

Regulations such as the General Data Protection Regulation (GDPR) in Europe and the California Consumer Privacy Act (CCPA) in the United States impose stringent requirements on how companies collect, process, and store personal data. Innovative factories often collect significant amounts of personal data, such as employee information and customer data. Compliance requires implementing robust data governance policies and procedures, ensuring that data is collected lawfully, processed transparently, and protected securely. This involves appointing a data protection officer (DPO), conducting data protection impact assessments (DPIAs), and implementing procedures for handling data subject access requests (DSARs). Regular audits are needed to ensure continued compliance with these regulations.

Employee training plays a vital role in data security. Employees must be educated about cybersecurity threats and best practices, including safe password management, phishing awareness, and the importance of reporting suspicious activity. Regular security awareness training programs should be conducted, reinforcing the importance of data security and outlining the procedures for handling sensitive information. The creation of a security-conscious culture, where employees are encouraged to report potential security issues without fear of retribution, is essential for an effective security program.

Incident response planning is a critical component of a robust cybersecurity strategy. A well-defined incident response plan outlines the steps to be taken in the event of a security breach or cyberattack. This plan should include procedures for identifying and containing the incident, investigating the cause, mitigating the impact, and recovering from the attack. Regular drills and simulations should be conducted to test the effectiveness of the incident response plan and ensure that employees are familiar with their roles and responsibilities.

In conclusion, protecting sensitive data in innovative factories requires a comprehensive and proactive approach that encompasses network security, device security, data security, regulatory compliance, employee training, and incident response planning. This is not a one-time endeavor but rather an ongoing process requiring continuous monitoring, adaptation, and improvement. The cost of inaction far outweighs the investment in robust security measures; the potential consequences of a data breach – financial losses, reputational damage, and legal penalties – can severely impact a company's viability. A strong cybersecurity posture is not merely a compliance issue; it's a strategic imperative for the long-term success of any factory operation. The integration of robust security measures from the outset of innovative factory implementation is far more efficient and cost-effective than attempting to retrofit security later. A proactive, layered approach to cybersecurity will ensure the resilience and longevity of the digital transformation in manufacturing.

IMPLEMENTING ROBUST CYBERSECURITY MEASURES

Implementing robust cybersecurity measures is paramount to the success and longevity of any innovative factory. While the previous sections outlined the inherent vulnerabilities and the broad strokes of a comprehensive security strategy, this section delves into the specifics of implementation, focusing on practical measures and their integration within the overall operational framework.

Network segmentation is a cornerstone of effective cybersecurity.

Rather than operating as a single, monolithic network, an innovative factory's network should be divided into smaller, isolated segments based on function and sensitivity of data. For example, the production control network, which is responsible for managing real-time operations, should be completely separated from the business network, which handles administrative tasks and customer data. This segmentation limits the impact of a successful breach. If an attacker compromises one segment, they are prevented from accessing other, more critical parts of the network. Implementing robust firewalls between segments is crucial, as well as enforcing strict access control policies and preventing unauthorized lateral movement. This architectural approach significantly reduces the attack surface and limits the potential damage. Careful consideration must be given to the design and implementation of this segmentation, ensuring that the separation of networks does not unduly hinder operational efficiency. The challenge lies in balancing security with the need for seamless data exchange between different operational

231

units. This often necessitates the use of secure communication protocols and gateways to facilitate controlled data transfer between segments.

Access control mechanisms must be rigorously implemented at every level, from network access to individual devices and applications. Strong passwords, multi-factor authentication (MFA), and role-based access control (RBAC) are essential. RBAC ensures that users only have access to the data and functionalities necessary for their roles, minimizing the risk of unauthorized access or data breaches. Regular audits of user accounts and access privileges are necessary to identify and rectify any anomalies or potential security gaps. The principle of least privilege should be strictly adhered to, meaning that users and devices should only be granted the minimum necessary permissions to perform their assigned tasks.

This principle significantly reduces the potential damage from compromised accounts, as even if an account is compromised, the attacker's access is restricted. Furthermore, the regular review of user access rights ensures that former employees or contractors have their access revoked promptly, preventing unauthorized access to sensitive information. This extends to physical access control, with strict protocols managing access to the factory floor and server rooms. Biometric authentication, coupled with video surveillance and access logs, offers an added layer of security.

Intrusion detection and prevention systems (IDS/IPS) are indispensable tools for monitoring network traffic and identifying suspicious activity. IDS passively monitors network traffic, alerting security personnel to potential threats, while IPS actively blocks malicious traffic. These systems should be deployed at strategic points within the network, providing comprehensive coverage. The choice of IDS/IPS depends on the specific needs and the complexity of the network. Next-generation intrusion prevention systems (NGIPS) are often preferred as they combine traditional signature-based detection with more sophisticated behavioral analysis techniques. Real-time threat intelligence feeds can provide an additional layer of protection, enabling the IDS/IPS to detect and block emerging threats quickly. It's crucial to ensure that these systems are configured correctly and regularly updated with the latest signatures and threat intelligence, ensuring their effectiveness against evolving cyber threats. The generated logs from the IDS/IPS need to be carefully analyzed and reviewed regularly to identify any patterns or anomalies that could indicate a security compromise.

Regular security audits and vulnerability assessments are essential for maintaining a strong security posture. These assessments should comprehensively evaluate the entire IT infrastructure, encompassing networks, devices, and applications. Vulnerability scanners can automatically identify known vulnerabilities in software and hardware, providing a prioritized list of remediation tasks. Penetration testing simulates real-world attacks to identify weaknesses in the security defenses. External security experts should conduct these tests to provide an unbiased assessment of the security posture. The results of these assessments should be thoroughly reviewed and prioritized based on the risk level of each vulnerability. A robust remediation plan should be developed and implemented promptly to address identified vulnerabilities. This ensures that any discovered gaps are rapidly patched, reducing the overall security risk. These assessments and subsequent remediation efforts should be documented and tracked, an audit trail that can be used for compliance purposes should be provided, and a proactive security approach should be demonstrated.

Data security in an innovative factory goes beyond network and device security; it encompasses the secure storage and management of data itself. Data encryption, both in transit and at rest, is non-negotiable. Strong encryption algorithms, such as AES-256, should be used to protect sensitive data. Data encryption at rest protects data stored on servers and storage devices. Data encryption in transit protects data as it travels across the network. A robust key management system is crucial for managing encryption keys, ensuring their confidentiality, and preventing unauthorized access. Regular key rotation is also important to minimize the risk of compromise. Data loss prevention (DLP) tools can monitor data movements, preventing sensitive information from leaving the factory's network without authorization. These tools can identify and block data exfiltration attempts through various channels, including email, USB drives, and cloud storage services. Implementing access control measures and role-based access controls (RBAC) limits access to sensitive data to only authorized personnel. This significantly reduces the risk of unauthorized access or data breaches. Regular data backups are crucial, ensuring business continuity in the event of a disaster or cyberattack. These backups should be stored securely, ideally in a geographically separate location, to protect against physical damage or theft. The "3-2-1" backup strategy (three copies of data on two different media, with one copy offsite) is a widely accepted best practice.

Finally, continuous monitoring is critical. Security information and event management (SIEM) systems collect and analyze security logs from various sources, providing a comprehensive view of the security posture. SIEM systems can detect anomalies and potential threats in real-time, alerting security personnel to potential incidents. The use of security orchestration, automation, and response (SOAR) tools can automate many security tasks, such as incident response and threat hunting. This automation improves the efficiency and effectiveness of security operations, enabling faster response times to security incidents. Continuous monitoring, combined with regular security audits and vulnerability assessments, ensures that the security posture remains strong and adapts to the evolving threat landscape.

The implementation of these measures should be seen as an ongoing process requiring constant adaptation and improvement. Regular employee training, emphasizing cybersecurity best practices, is equally essential. This includes awareness of phishing scams, password management, and secure browsing habits. The creation of a security-conscious culture is crucial, where employees are encouraged to report any suspicious activity without fear of retribution. Regular security awareness training sessions should be conducted to reinforce these principles and ensure that everyone understands their role in maintaining the factory's security. A well-defined incident response plan is also crucial, outlining the steps to be taken in the event of a security breach. This plan should include procedures for containing the incident, investigating its cause, mitigating the impact, and recovering from the attack. Regular drills and simulations are needed to ensure that the plan is effective and that personnel are familiar with their roles and responsibilities. The financial and reputational costs of a significant cybersecurity incident are often far greater than the investment required to implement and maintain robust security measures. A proactive, layered approach to cybersecurity is not just a matter of compliance; it is a fundamental requirement for the long-term success and viability of any innovative factory.

COMPLIANCE WITH DATA PRIVACY REGULATIONS

The preceding sections detailed the crucial elements of securing an innovative factory's IT infrastructure. However, robust cybersecurity is only one facet of a comprehensive data management strategy.

Equally critical is compliance with data privacy regulations, a landscape increasingly complex and demanding. Failure to adhere to these regulations can result in substantial financial penalties, reputational damage, and erosion of customer trust – consequences far outweighing the investment in compliance measures. This section explores the complexities of data privacy in the context of innovative manufacturing, focusing on practical steps to ensure conformity with leading regulations such as the General Data Protection Regulation (GDPR) and the California Consumer Privacy Act (CCPA).

GDPR, enacted by the European Union, applies to any organization processing personal data of EU residents, regardless of the organization's location. This broad scope necessitates careful consideration for innovative factories, even those not physically located in the EU if they handle data pertaining to EU citizens. The regulation establishes stringent requirements for data processing, including obtaining explicit consent, ensuring data security, and providing individuals with control over their personal data. Key aspects include the right to access, rectification, erasure ("right to be forgotten"), restriction of processing, data portability, and the right to object. Understanding and implementing these rights is paramount. For example, if an innovative factory collects data from employees within the EU or customers using its products in the EU, stringent compliance with GDPR is mandatory. This extends to data transfer outside the EU; stringent controls, including standard contractual clauses or binding corporate rules, are necessary to ensure the appropriate protection of transferred data. Failure to comply with these provisions can lead to significant fines, potentially reaching millions of euros.

CCPA, California's comprehensive data privacy law, offers a different but equally important model. While geographically confined to California, its influence extends beyond the state's borders, impacting businesses nationwide that process the personal information of California residents. Similar to GDPR, CCPA grants individuals significant rights regarding their personal data, including the right to know what personal information is collected, the right to delete personal information, and the right to opt-out of the sale of personal information. The definition of "sale" under CCPA is broad, encompassing any exchange of personal information for monetary or other valuable consideration. Innovative factories collecting data related to California residents, such as customer feedback through connected devices or employee data from California-based employees, must adhere to CCPA's provisions. This includes establishing a clear privacy policy, providing consumers with notice of their rights, and establishing procedures to respond to consumer requests. Non-compliance results in substantial penalties, potentially reaching millions of dollars.

Beyond GDPR and CCPA, a patchwork of other data privacy regulations exists globally. The Canadian Personal Information

Protection and Electronic Documents Act (PIPEDA), Brazil's General Data Protection Law (LGPD), and numerous other regional and national laws add complexity to the international landscape. An innovative factory operating globally must navigate this diverse legal environment, developing a robust compliance framework that addresses the specific requirements of each jurisdiction. This means not simply checking boxes but understanding the underlying principles and tailoring strategies to the particular nuances of each regulation. This necessitates collaboration between legal, IT, and operational teams to create a holistic and effective data privacy strategy. Ignoring this multifaceted regulatory reality carries severe risks, including legal challenges, financial penalties, and damage to brand reputation.

Implementing data privacy compliance in an innovative factory requires a multi-pronged approach. Firstly, a comprehensive data inventory is crucial. This involves identifying all personal data collected, where it's stored, how it's used, and who has access to it. This inventory provides the foundation for a risk assessment, which helps identify potential vulnerabilities and prioritize compliance efforts. Data minimization is a core principle of both GDPR and CCPA. This principle suggests collecting only necessary data and limiting its retention period. This proactive approach minimizes risks associated with data breaches and simplifies compliance efforts. The use of data anonymization and pseudonymization techniques can further strengthen data protection. Anonymization removes identifying information, while pseudonymization replaces it with pseudonyms, making it more difficult to link data to specific individuals.

Data security mechanisms, as discussed previously, are equally crucial for data privacy. Robust encryption, access controls, and intrusion detection systems help prevent unauthorized access to personal data. Regular security audits and penetration testing identify weaknesses in security infrastructure, allowing for timely remediation and preventing data breaches. Employee training is another critical aspect of data privacy compliance. Employees need to understand their responsibilities in protecting personal data, including following data handling procedures, adhering to access control policies, and reporting any security incidents promptly. A culture of data privacy awareness is essential for a successful compliance program. Regular security awareness training and refresher courses enhance employee understanding of data privacy best practices, fostering a culture of vigilance and responsible data handling.

Incident response planning is paramount. A well-defined incident response plan outlines procedures to be followed in the event of a data breach. This plan should detail steps to contain the breach, investigate its cause, notify affected individuals (as required by regulations), and mitigate its impact. Regular simulations and drills ensure that the plan is effective and that personnel are adequately prepared. A timely and well-executed response minimizes damage, limits legal liabilities, and strengthens customer trust. Post-incident analysis and reporting are crucial to identifying systemic weaknesses and preventing future breaches. These reports are used to improve the organization's data security posture and enhance its overall compliance framework.

Finally, continuous monitoring and improvement are integral parts of an effective data privacy program. Regular reviews of data processing activities, compliance policies, and security measures are necessary to ensure ongoing compliance with evolving regulations and emerging threats. The data privacy landscape is dynamic; regulations are updated, threats change, and best practices evolve. Continuous monitoring enables the timely identification of gaps and proactive implementation of necessary measures to maintain a strong security and compliance posture. This vigilance is key to preventing data breaches and maintaining compliance with the constantly evolving legal landscape. The integration of compliance with operational processes is key, ensuring data privacy is not viewed as a separate function but an integral part of factory operations. This collaborative approach fosters a culture of security and compliance across all levels of the organization.

DATA ENCRYPTION AND SECURE COMMUNICATION PROTOCOLS

Building upon the foundation of robust data privacy practices outlined in the previous sections, we now delve into the crucial aspects of data encryption and secure communication protocols within the manufacturing environment. The interconnected nature of an innovative factory, with its multitude of devices, systems, and networks, necessitates a comprehensive approach to securing the flow of data. This section explores the various encryption techniques and communication protocols that form the bedrock of a secure, innovative factory.

Data encryption, the process of transforming readable data into an unreadable format, is paramount in protecting sensitive information. Several encryption techniques are employed in innovative manufacturing, each suited to different applications and security needs. Symmetric encryption, using the same key for both encryption and decryption, offers high speed and efficiency, making it ideal for encrypting large volumes of data within a controlled environment. Advanced Encryption Standard (AES), a widely adopted symmetric encryption algorithm, is frequently used in factory applications to secure data at rest and in transit. Its strength and flexibility make it a suitable choice for various data types, from production data to sensitive employee records.

However, the secure exchange of the encryption key itself poses a challenge in symmetric encryption.

Asymmetric encryption employs separate keys for encryption and decryption (a public key for encryption and a private key for Decryption) offers a solution to this key exchange problem. This method, also known as public-key cryptography, is commonly used for secure communication and digital signatures. RSA (Rivest-Shamir-Adleman), a widely recognized asymmetric encryption algorithm, is often employed to encrypt smaller pieces of data, such as authentication credentials or digital certificates. The public key can be widely distributed, while the private key must be securely protected. This allows for secure communication without the need for pre-shared secret keys. In an innovative manufacturing context, asymmetric encryption is frequently used to secure communication between different systems and authenticate devices accessing the network.

Hybrid encryption approaches combine the strengths of both symmetric and asymmetric encryption. This method typically uses asymmetric encryption to exchange a symmetric key securely and then employs the symmetric key to encrypt and decrypt large volumes of data efficiently. This combination provides the security benefits of asymmetric encryption for key exchange while maintaining the speed and efficiency of symmetric encryption for data encryption itself. This approach is commonly used in innovative factories to secure communication channels and protect sensitive data transmitted between various devices and systems. For instance, a hybrid encryption approach might be used to encrypt communication between a programmable logic controller (PLC) and a supervisory control and data acquisition (SCADA) system.

The choice of encryption algorithm depends on several factors, including the sensitivity of the data, the computational resources available, and the specific security requirements of the application. AES is a strong choice for securing large volumes of data, while RSA is suitable for smaller pieces of data and digital signatures. The selection process often involves a careful risk assessment, considering the potential impact of a data breach. Proper key management is critical regardless of the encryption method chosen.

Keys must be generated securely, stored safely, and rotated regularly to minimize the risk of compromise.

Beyond encryption, secure communication protocols are crucial for protecting data in transit. These protocols define the rules and procedures for exchanging data over a network, ensuring confidentiality, integrity, and authenticity. Transport Layer Security (TLS), previously known as Secure Sockets Layer (SSL), is a widely used protocol that provides secure communication over a network. TLS encrypts data transmitted between devices, protecting it from eavesdropping and tampering. It also ensures the authenticity of the communicating parties, preventing man-in-the-middle attacks. In a factory environment, TLS is essential for securing communication between different systems, including PLCs, SCADA systems, and enterprise resource planning (ERP) systems.

Secure Shell (SSH) is another secure communication protocol commonly used in innovative manufacturing for remote access and management of devices and systems. SSH encrypts all communication between a client and a server, protecting sensitive information from unauthorized access. It is frequently used by administrators to remotely access and manage PLCs, servers, and other devices within the factory network. The use of SSH contributes significantly to protecting intellectual property and preventing unauthorized access to the factory's control systems.

Message Queuing Telemetry Transport (MQTT) is a lightweight publish-subscribe messaging protocol increasingly used in innovative manufacturing for machine-to-machine (M2M) communication. MQTT's low overhead and efficient use of bandwidth make it ideal for communicating with numerous devices in a resource-constrained environment. When security is paramount, MQTT can be used with TLS/SSL encryption to provide secure communication. This ensures that data exchanged between devices, such as sensor data or control commands, is protected from unauthorized access or modification.

The implementation of these secure communication protocols requires careful consideration of network architecture and security policies. Firewall configurations, intrusion detection systems, and access control mechanisms are crucial for preventing unauthorized access to the factory network and protecting sensitive data. Regular security audits and penetration testing are necessary to identify vulnerabilities and ensure that security measures remain effective. Furthermore, the use of virtual private networks (VPNs) can further enhance security by creating a secure tunnel for communication between remote devices and systems.

The ongoing evolution of cyber threats necessitates a proactive and adaptable approach to data security in innovative manufacturing.

Regular updates to encryption algorithms and security protocols are essential to maintain a robust security posture. The adoption of new technologies, such as blockchain, offers potential benefits for enhancing data security and traceability. The combination of advanced encryption, robust communication protocols, and a comprehensive security architecture creates a resilient environment for manufacturing operations. Investing in comprehensive training for personnel responsible for managing and maintaining these systems is equally crucial. This ensures that the sophisticated security measures implemented are understood, adequately maintained, and utilized effectively. Ultimately, a multi-layered, well-integrated approach to data encryption and secure communication is crucial for the success and security of any manufacturing initiative. Only through a robust, adaptive, and well-understood security architecture can the full potential of innovative manufacturing be realized while mitigating the inherent risks associated with increasingly connected environments. Neglecting these safeguards can lead to significant financial losses, operational disruptions, and reputational damage – far outweighing the initial investment in secure systems and practices.

DEVELOPING A COMPREHENSIVE DATA SECURITY STRATEGY

Building upon the robust encryption and secure communication protocols discussed, the development of a comprehensive data security strategy is paramount for the success of any manufacturing initiative. This strategy must encompass a multifaceted approach, encompassing proactive risk assessment, detailed incident response planning, and comprehensive employee training programs. A reactive approach to security is insufficient; a proactive stance, anticipating and mitigating potential threats before they materialize, is critical.

The first step in developing a robust data security strategy is a thorough risk assessment. This process involves identifying potential vulnerabilities within the manufacturing environment, analyzing the likelihood and potential impact of each threat, and prioritizing them based on their severity. This requires a meticulous examination of all aspects of the system, including hardware, software, network infrastructure, and human factors. For instance, a risk assessment might identify vulnerabilities in legacy systems that haven't been updated with the latest security patches or weak access controls that allow unauthorized access to sensitive data. The assessment should also consider external threats, such as cyberattacks, malware, and physical breaches. Sophisticated tools and methodologies, such as threat modeling and vulnerability scanning, can significantly enhance the accuracy and comprehensiveness of this assessment. The results of the risk assessment should be documented in a comprehensive report, clearly outlining the identified threats, their likelihood and impact, and proposed mitigation strategies.

Following the risk assessment, the next critical component is the development of a comprehensive incident response plan. This plan outlines the procedures to be followed in the event of a security incident, such as a data breach or cyberattack. The plan should detail the roles and responsibilities of different personnel, including IT staff, security personnel, and management. Crucially, it should provide clear steps for containing the incident, eradicating the threat, recovering from the damage, and performing a thorough post-incident analysis to prevent future occurrences. This analysis should identify root causes, implement corrective actions, and update the incident response plan accordingly. Regular drills and simulations are essential to test the effectiveness of the incident response plan and ensure that personnel are adequately trained and prepared to handle real-world scenarios.

Furthermore, the plan should include clear communication protocols to ensure that all stakeholders are informed of the incident and its impact. This may involve notification procedures for customers, regulatory bodies, and other relevant parties. A well-defined communication strategy is critical in managing the reputation and minimizing the long-term consequences of a security incident.

Another cornerstone of a comprehensive data security strategy is the implementation of robust access control mechanisms. This involves limiting access to sensitive data and systems based on the principle of least privilege. Only authorized personnel should have access to specific data and systems, and their access should be carefully monitored and audited. Role-based access control (RBAC) and attribute-based access control (ABAC) are sophisticated techniques that can be employed to manage and control access rights effectively. Multi-factor authentication (MFA) adds an extra layer of security, requiring users to provide multiple forms of authentication, such as passwords, biometric data, or one-time codes, to verify their identity. This significantly reduces the risk of unauthorized access, even if usernames and passwords are compromised. Regular audits of access logs are vital to identify any suspicious activity or potential security breaches. This continuous monitoring and analysis enable proactive detection and response to emerging threats.

Employee training and awareness programs constitute another essential element of a comprehensive data security strategy.

Employees are often the weakest link in any security system, and it is crucial to educate them about data security risks and best practices. Training programs should cover topics such as password security, phishing awareness, and safe internet usage. Employees should also be trained on how to recognize and respond to potential security threats, including suspicious emails, phishing attempts, and malware infections. Regular training sessions and awareness campaigns are essential to reinforce best practices and keep employees updated on the latest security threats and vulnerabilities.

Furthermore, the training should emphasize the importance of reporting security incidents promptly and adhering to the established security policies and procedures. A culture of security awareness within the organization is vital for maintaining a robust security posture.

The ongoing nature of cyber threats necessitates a continuous improvement approach to data security. Regular security audits and penetration testing should be conducted to identify vulnerabilities and assess the effectiveness of security measures. Independent security experts should carry out these assessments to ensure objectivity and thoroughness. The findings of these audits and tests should be used to update and improve security policies, procedures, and technologies. This continuous improvement cycle ensures that the data security strategy remains effective in the face of evolving threats. Keeping abreast of the latest security trends, technologies, and best practices is critical. This necessitates ongoing professional development for security personnel and staying informed about emerging threats and vulnerabilities.

Finally, investment in advanced security technologies is crucial for a robust data security strategy. This includes employing intrusion detection and prevention systems (IDS/IPS), firewalls, and anti-malware software to protect against various cyber threats.

Regular software updates and patching are necessary to address known vulnerabilities and prevent exploitation by attackers.

Consideration should also be given to implementing data loss prevention (DLP) solutions to monitor and prevent sensitive data from leaving the organization's control. The integration of all security technologies into a cohesive security architecture is crucial for ensuring their effectiveness.

In conclusion, developing a comprehensive data security strategy in innovative manufacturing requires a proactive, multifaceted approach that encompasses risk assessment, incident response planning, robust access control, comprehensive employee training, and continuous improvement efforts. Investing in advanced security technologies and maintaining a culture of security awareness is equally critical. Only by addressing all these aspects can organizations ensure the confidentiality, integrity, and availability of their valuable data in the increasingly interconnected world of innovative manufacturing. The cost of inaction far outweighs the investment in a robust and well-maintained security posture.

CHAPTER 10
THE ECONOMIC IMPACT OF
INNOVATIVE MANUFACTURING

RETURN ON INVESTMENT ROI ANALYSIS

The transition to innovative manufacturing represents a significant investment for any organization. Therefore, a rigorous Return on Investment (ROI) analysis is crucial before embarking on such a transformative journey. This analysis shouldn't be a simplistic calculation of immediate cost savings but rather a comprehensive evaluation of both tangible and intangible benefits across the entire lifecycle of the implemented technologies and processes. A robust ROI analysis must encompass a wide range of factors to accurately reflect the true economic impact of innovative manufacturing.

Firstly, let's consider the initial capital expenditures. This includes the cost of acquiring new hardware, such as robots, sensors, and automated guided vehicles (AGVs), as well as the investment in software, including manufacturing execution systems (MES), enterprise resource planning (ERP) systems, and advanced analytics platforms. The cost of integrating these new technologies into existing infrastructure shouldn't be overlooked. This often involves significant system modifications, network upgrades, and potential downtime during implementation. Furthermore, the costs associated with employee training and upskilling are equally important, as the successful adoption of manufacturing technologies relies heavily on a skilled workforce capable of operating and maintaining the new systems. The complexity of the integration process itself can significantly impact the overall cost. For instance, integrating legacy systems, often characterized by disparate and outdated technologies, poses a more significant challenge than implementing new systems in a greenfield environment. The latter allows for greater standardization and simplified integration.

Beyond the initial capital investment, ongoing operational costs must also be factored into the ROI analysis. These include expenses related to software licenses, maintenance contracts, energy consumption, and potential unplanned downtime. The ongoing cost of data storage and management should also be considered, as innovative manufacturing generates massive amounts of data that need to be securely stored, processed, and analyzed. The frequency of software updates and the associated downtime they may cause also adds to the operational costs. In addition, the ongoing cost of employee training and development must be included, as continuous learning and adaptation are essential for maximizing the benefits of innovative manufacturing technologies.

Turning to the benefits, the potential returns are substantial and multifaceted. Increased efficiency is one of the most significant advantages. Innovative manufacturing technologies automate many repetitive tasks, optimizing production processes and reducing cycle times. This leads to higher throughput and increased production output, directly translating into higher revenue. For instance, the implementation of robotic automation can significantly reduce labor costs and enhance overall productivity, while the use of predictive maintenance can minimize costly unplanned downtime and extend the lifespan of equipment. The real-time data analytics capabilities of innovative manufacturing systems enable proactive identification of inefficiencies, bottlenecks, and potential quality issues, enabling timely intervention and minimizing waste.

Reduced costs are another key benefit. Automation reduces labor costs, optimizes resource utilization, and minimizes material waste.

Predictive maintenance, powered by data analytics, minimizes unplanned downtime and associated repair costs. Improved supply chain management, facilitated by real-time data visibility, enhances efficiency and reduces inventory holding costs. The benefits extend beyond immediate cost reduction. By streamlining processes and enhancing productivity, innovative manufacturing can improve profitability and free up resources for further investment in innovation and growth. A detailed analysis of production costs before and after implementation is critical for quantifying these savings. This involves a comparison of labor costs, material costs, energy costs, and other relevant expenses.

Enhanced product quality is another substantial benefit. Innovative manufacturing technologies enable greater precision and consistency in manufacturing processes, leading to fewer defects and higher product quality. Real-time data monitoring allows for immediate detection and correction of quality issues, reducing waste and improving customer satisfaction. This improved quality often translates into reduced warranty claims and enhanced brand reputation, contributing positively to long-term profitability. A robust quality control system integrated with innovative manufacturing technologies can significantly reduce the incidence of defects, leading to measurable improvements in yield rates and customer satisfaction.

Improved product traceability is another significant advantage.

Innovative manufacturing systems allow for complete and accurate tracking of products throughout the entire manufacturing process. This enhances transparency and accountability, facilitates efficient recall management in case of defects, and provides valuable data for continuous improvement. Improved traceability helps comply with regulatory requirements and build trust with customers, fostering brand loyalty and potentially commanding premium pricing.

Data-driven decision-making is a crucial aspect of the ROI analysis. Innovative manufacturing systems generate vast amounts of data that can be used to make informed business decisions. Advanced analytics tools provide insights into production processes, supply chains, and customer behavior, enabling companies to optimize operations, improve efficiency, and develop new products and services that better meet market demands. This data-driven approach contributes to a more agile and responsive business model, enhancing the organization's ability to adapt to changing market conditions.

Finally, the long-term strategic benefits of innovative manufacturing should be considered. The improved efficiency, reduced costs, and enhanced product quality all contribute to a more decisive competitive advantage. The increased agility and responsiveness fostered by innovative manufacturing enable companies to adapt more quickly to changing market demands and capitalize on new opportunities. This improved competitiveness can translate into higher market share, increased profitability, and enhanced long-term sustainability.

In conclusion, a comprehensive ROI analysis of innovative manufacturing initiatives requires a holistic approach that considers both the initial investment and ongoing operational costs, alongside the tangible and intangible benefits across the entire lifecycle. By meticulously assessing the potential return in increased efficiency, reduced costs, enhanced product quality, improved traceability, data-driven decision-making, and long-term strategic advantages, organizations can make informed decisions about their investment in innovative manufacturing technologies and maximize the economic impact of this transformative journey. The analysis should not only focus on financial metrics but also include qualitative factors such as improved employee satisfaction, enhanced brand reputation, and enhanced risk mitigation. A well-executed ROI analysis is vital for justifying the investment and demonstrating the long-term value proposition of innovative manufacturing. Regular monitoring and assessment after implementation are essential to track performance, identify areas for improvement, and ensure the continued realization of the projected ROI.

INCREASED PRODUCTIVITY AND EFFICIENCY GAINS

Increased productivity and efficiency are cornerstones of the economic benefits derived from innovative manufacturing. The integration of advanced technologies fundamentally reshapes manufacturing processes, leading to quantifiable improvements across numerous operational aspects. Let's delve into the specific ways innovative manufacturing achieves these gains.

One of the most significant contributions of innovative manufacturing is the dramatic reduction in downtime. Traditional manufacturing often suffers from unpredictable and costly downtime caused by equipment malfunctions, unexpected maintenance needs, or supply chain disruptions. Innovative manufacturing mitigates these issues through predictive maintenance. By leveraging real-time data from sensors embedded within machinery, sophisticated algorithms can identify patterns and anomalies indicative of impending failures.

This allows for proactive maintenance, scheduling repairs and replacements before they lead to production halts. The ability to anticipate and prevent breakdowns minimizes costly emergency repairs, reduces lost production time, and extends the lifespan of expensive equipment. For example, a manufacturer of automotive parts might deploy sensors on their injection molding machines to monitor temperature, pressure, and vibration. Anomalies detected by the system can trigger an alert, allowing maintenance personnel to address a potential issue before it results in a production stoppage that could cost thousands of dollars per hour.

Beyond predictive maintenance, innovative manufacturing optimizes production processes by leveraging automation and data analytics. Robotics and automated guided vehicles (AGVs) handle repetitive and physically demanding tasks with more incredible speed, precision, and consistency than human workers. This frees up human employees to focus on higher-value activities such as process improvement, quality control, and innovation. Moreover, real-time data visualization dashboards provide a comprehensive overview of the entire production process, highlighting bottlenecks, inefficiencies, and potential areas for improvement. For instance, a textile manufacturer could use data analytics to identify slowdowns at specific stages of the production line, revealing opportunities to rebalance workloads, improve material flow, or optimize machine settings. This granular level of process visibility is simply unavailable in traditional manufacturing environments.

The optimization extends to resource utilization. Innovative manufacturing systems enable precise control over energy consumption, material usage, and waste generation. Data analytics can pinpoint areas of excess energy consumption, allowing for targeted adjustments to reduce operational costs and minimize environmental impact. Similarly, real-time monitoring of material usage can identify instances of waste or inefficient utilization, enabling manufacturers to make adjustments to their processes and reduce material costs. Consider a food processing plant using innovative manufacturing technologies to monitor energy use across different stages of production. By identifying peak energy consumption periods, the plant can implement strategies such as load shifting or energy storage to reduce overall energy costs and their carbon footprint. The precision of these resource allocation strategies vastly surpasses the capabilities of traditional methods.

Improved supply chain management is another significant area where innovative manufacturing contributes to increased efficiency.

Real-time visibility into the supply chain, facilitated by sensors, RFID tags, and connected systems, provides accurate information on inventory levels, order status, and delivery times. This enhanced transparency minimizes disruptions due to unexpected delays or shortages, ensuring a consistent flow of materials and products. For example, a pharmaceutical manufacturer can use real-time tracking to monitor the temperature and humidity of its drug shipments, preventing spoilage and ensuring product quality. This level of visibility reduces the risk of recalls and ensures compliance with stringent regulatory requirements. Furthermore, predictive analytics can forecast demand fluctuations, allowing manufacturers to optimize inventory levels and prevent stockouts or excess inventory holding costs. This streamlined supply chain management directly contributes to a leaner and more efficient operation.

Furthermore, the improvements in efficiency are not limited to production floors. Innovative manufacturing systems enhance the effectiveness of administrative and support functions. Data analytics can streamline processes such as order fulfillment, logistics management, and customer service. The automation of tasks like data entry and report generation frees up administrative staff to focus on higher-level tasks that require human judgment and strategic thinking. For example, an electronics manufacturer might use automated systems to process customer orders, manage inventory, and track shipments, freeing up employees to focus on addressing customer inquiries and building relationships. The efficiency gains across the entire organization, not just the production floor, significantly impact the bottom line.

The economic benefits are not merely confined to cost reduction. Innovative manufacturing enhances product quality and consistency. By automating processes and incorporating real-time quality control measures, manufacturers can reduce defects and improve overall product quality. This reduces the cost of rework, scrap, and warranty claims. The enhanced product quality strengthens the company's reputation and allows for premium pricing, further boosting profitability. For example, a precision engineering firm might use robotic systems to perform highly accurate assembly tasks, eliminating human error and ensuring consistent product quality. This precision translates directly into improved customer satisfaction and a stronger competitive advantage.

Moreover, the increased efficiency and productivity contribute to improved employee satisfaction and retention. Automation of repetitive and physically demanding tasks reduces employee fatigue and improves workplace safety. This can lead to higher job satisfaction and reduced employee turnover, saving the company the costs associated with recruiting, training, and onboarding new employees. Investing in employee upskilling programs to equip them with the skills needed to operate and maintain innovative manufacturing systems ensures that the workforce is equipped to leverage the technologies fully and contributes to a more engaged and skilled workforce.

Finally, the data generated by innovative manufacturing systems provides invaluable insights into business operations, enabling data-driven decision-making. This enhances the agility and responsiveness of the organization, allowing it to quickly adapt to changing market conditions and capitalize on new opportunities. The ability to proactively identify and address potential challenges, such as supply chain disruptions or changes in customer demand, gives the organization a significant competitive advantage. The insights gained allow for informed strategic decisions, leading to optimized resource allocation, improved profitability, and sustainable long-term growth. In summary, the increased productivity and efficiency gains from innovative manufacturing represent a significant economic advantage, impacting not only the production floor but the entire organization's operational efficiency, profitability, and competitiveness. The benefits extend beyond immediate cost savings to encompass enhanced product quality, improved employee satisfaction, and data-driven strategic decision-making, paving the way for long-term sustainable growth and market leadership.

COST REDUCTION STRATEGIES THROUGH AUTOMATION

The transformative impact of innovative manufacturing extends far beyond increased productivity; it delivers substantial cost reductions across various operational facets. This section will delve into the specific cost-saving strategies enabled by automation within the innovative manufacturing paradigm. These strategies are not isolated initiatives but interconnected elements that contribute to a holistic reduction in operational expenditure.

One of the most immediate and significant cost reductions stems from optimized labor utilization. While the fear of widespread job displacement due to automation is often raised, the reality in innovative manufacturing is more nuanced. Automation doesn't replace human workers entirely; it reshapes their roles. Repetitive, physically demanding, and error-prone tasks are automated, freeing human employees to focus on higher-value activities such as process improvement, quality control, complex problem-solving, and innovation. This shift in responsibilities not only increases overall productivity but also leads to significant cost savings by reducing labor costs associated with these low-value tasks. For instance, a large automotive assembly plant might automate the welding of car body parts, significantly reducing the number of welders required while enhancing the speed and consistency of the welding process.

The savings are realized not only in reduced wages but also in lower healthcare costs and worker's compensation premiums associated with a reduced workforce engaged in physically strenuous activities. Furthermore, improved safety resulting from automated handling of hazardous materials directly lowers insurance premiums and reduces potential costs from workplace injuries.

Beyond labor cost reduction, automation plays a crucial role in minimizing material waste. Traditional manufacturing processes often involve a degree of material waste due to imperfections, inaccuracies, and inefficient resource allocation. Innovative manufacturing employs sophisticated sensors, data analytics, and automated systems to control material usage, reducing scrap and rework precisely. Real-time monitoring allows manufacturers to identify and address material inefficiencies proactively, optimizing material flow and minimizing waste generation. Consider a textile manufacturer using automated cutting machines guided by precise digital patterns. These machines minimize fabric waste by cutting precisely to the pattern, reducing material costs and environmental impact simultaneously. Similarly, in a food processing plant, automated sorting systems can identify and remove defective products before they enter the packaging process, significantly reducing waste and improving overall product quality. The precision and accuracy of automated systems greatly surpass the capabilities of manual processes, leading to tangible cost savings. Moreover, the ability to track and analyze material usage in real-time allows for continuous optimization of material sourcing and inventory management, further reducing waste and storage costs.

Energy consumption represents another significant area where innovative manufacturing delivers considerable cost savings. Traditional manufacturing plants often operate with less-optimized energy usage. Innovative manufacturing integrates advanced energy management systems that leverage real-time data and analytics to optimize energy consumption throughout the production process.

These systems identify inefficiencies in energy usage, allowing manufacturers to implement targeted adjustments to reduce operational costs and minimize their environmental impact. For example, in a chemical processing plant, intelligent control systems can optimize the operation of reactors and other energy-intensive equipment, minimizing energy consumption without impacting production output. This could involve adjusting operational parameters based on real-time feedback, predicting energy needs based on historical data, and integrating renewable energy sources into the plant's energy supply. Similarly, innovative lighting systems that adjust brightness and occupancy according to real-time needs can lead to substantial reductions in energy costs. The data-driven nature of these optimization strategies ensures that energy savings are maximized without compromising production efficiency or product quality. These savings translate directly into a lower carbon footprint, potentially qualifying the company for government incentives and improved brand reputation.

Furthermore, the automation of logistics and supply chain management contributes significantly to cost reduction. Traditional supply chain management often involves inefficiencies in inventory management, transportation, and warehousing. Innovative manufacturing systems leverage real-time tracking, predictive analytics, and automated processes to optimize these aspects of the supply chain.

Real-time visibility into inventory levels enables manufacturers to avoid stockouts or overstocking, minimizing storage costs and preventing potential production stoppages due to material shortages. Automated guided vehicles (AGVs) and robotic systems can streamline material handling within the factory, reducing labor costs and improving efficiency. Moreover, advanced predictive analytics can forecast demand fluctuations, allowing manufacturers to optimize production schedules and adjust inventory levels accordingly. This minimizes transportation costs, reduces lead times, and enhances overall supply chain agility. Consider a pharmaceutical company that uses real-time tracking of drug shipments to ensure temperature and humidity are within specified ranges. This helps prevent spoilage and reduces the risk of recalls, significantly reducing associated costs. The enhanced transparency and efficiency within the supply chain directly translate into a more lean and cost-effective operation.

Beyond these core areas, automation contributes to cost reductions in numerous ancillary ways. For example, the automation of routine administrative tasks, such as data entry and report generation, frees up human employees to focus on more strategic activities. This can lead to increased efficiency and productivity in administrative functions, reducing labor costs and freeing resources for investment in innovation. Automated quality control systems can significantly reduce the costs associated with defects, rework, and warranty claims, leading to considerable savings in the long run. The automated detection and prevention of equipment failures through predictive maintenance minimize downtime and repair costs, ensuring continuous production and maximizing output.

Furthermore, improved product quality and consistency, resulting from the precision and repeatability of automated processes, can lead to reduced customer returns and warranty claims, contributing to further cost reduction.

The implementation of innovative manufacturing technologies requires an upfront investment. However, the long-term cost savings and efficiency gains far outweigh these initial expenditures. A comprehensive cost-benefit analysis, considering the total cost of ownership, operational expenses, and potential revenue increases, is crucial for justifying the investment in automation technologies.

This analysis should account for factors such as equipment costs, software licensing, employee training, and integration with existing systems. However, the potential for significant and sustained cost reductions in labor, materials, energy, logistics, and waste makes innovative manufacturing a compelling strategy for enhancing profitability and competitiveness in today's rapidly evolving industrial landscape. The data-driven nature of innovative manufacturing also allows for continuous optimization and refinement of processes, further amplifying the long-term cost-saving benefits. The continuous improvements and adaptations make innovative manufacturing a truly transformative strategy for achieving sustainable cost reductions and ensuring long-term economic viability.

IMPACT ON EMPLOYMENT AND JOB CREATION

The transition to innovative manufacturing, while promising significant economic benefits, inevitably raises concerns about its impact on employment. The narrative often revolves around the fear of widespread job displacement due to automation. However, the reality is far more nuanced and multifaceted. While some jobs will undoubtedly be automated, leading to workforce reductions in specific sectors, innovative manufacturing simultaneously creates new job opportunities, reshapes existing roles, and enhances overall economic productivity. This section will delve into this complex interplay, examining both the potential job displacement and the significant job creation spurred by the adoption of innovative manufacturing technologies.

One of the key aspects to understand is that automation in innovative manufacturing primarily targets repetitive, physically demanding, or hazardous tasks. These are the jobs most susceptible to automation, leading to potential job displacement in the short term.

Consider, for instance, the automotive industry, where robotic welding systems have already replaced many human welders.

Similar trends are evident in manufacturing plants across various industries, where automated assembly lines, robotic material handling systems, and automated quality control mechanisms reduce the need for manual labor in routine tasks. However, this displacement is not necessarily a negative outcome. These automated systems often work alongside human operators, enhancing efficiency, productivity, and safety. They do not eliminate human involvement but instead restructure the roles and responsibilities within the manufacturing environment.

A significant rise in demand for skilled labor in new and evolving roles accompanies the displacement of workers in routine tasks. Innovative manufacturing relies heavily on data analysis, artificial intelligence, and robotics, creating a surge in demand for professionals with expertise in these areas. Data scientists, AI specialists, robotics engineers, and cybersecurity experts are increasingly in demand to design, implement, maintain, and optimize innovative manufacturing systems. These professionals are essential for ensuring the smooth operation and continuous improvement of these advanced systems. The expertise required to manage, troubleshoot, and program complex automated systems requires a highly specialized skill set, leading to higher wages and greater job security for these specialized professionals.

Furthermore, the increasing complexity of innovative manufacturing systems requires a skilled workforce for tasks such as system integration, programming, maintenance, and troubleshooting. The seamless integration of various technologies, including sensors, actuators, software, and cloud platforms, necessitates individuals with a deep understanding of these systems. This demand for skilled technicians and engineers goes beyond the initial implementation phase; it extends to ongoing maintenance, upgrades, and operational optimization. This sustained demand for specialized skills ensures a continuous flow of job opportunities in the innovative manufacturing ecosystem.

Beyond the technical roles, innovative manufacturing creates opportunities in areas such as process optimization, quality control, and supply chain management. The data generated by innovative manufacturing systems provides rich insights into operational efficiencies, allowing companies to optimize their production processes and reduce waste. This requires analytical skills to interpret the data and make informed decisions about process improvements. This shift from manual labor to data-driven decision-making necessitates analytical and managerial expertise.

Professionals with expertise in statistical process control, lean manufacturing principles, and data-driven decision-making are crucial for leveraging the full potential of innovative manufacturing technologies.

The shift towards innovative manufacturing also leads to the creation of jobs in areas related to system integration, cybersecurity, and data management. Integrating various systems and technologies requires specialized expertise in software engineering, network management, and cybersecurity. The secure operation of these systems is crucial to avoid potential disruptions, data breaches, and financial losses.

This necessitates a strong focus on cybersecurity and data protection, leading to the creation of new jobs in this critical area.

Furthermore, the large volumes of data generated by innovative manufacturing systems require effective data management and storage solutions. This creates new opportunities for professionals with expertise in data warehousing, data analytics, and cloud computing.

Another crucial factor is the creation of new services and industries supporting innovative manufacturing. The development, implementation, and maintenance of innovative manufacturing systems necessitate the emergence of specialized service providers. These providers offer consulting, training, and support services to businesses implementing these technologies. This includes services such as system integration, software development, cybersecurity consulting, and technical training. The growth of this supporting ecosystem creates a significant number of jobs across a range of skill levels.

It's also important to note that the impact of innovative manufacturing on employment varies significantly across different industries and regions. Industries with a high concentration of repetitive tasks, such as automotive manufacturing, electronics assembly, and food processing, will likely see a more significant shift in labor demand. Conversely, industries requiring specialized skills and craftsmanship may experience less disruption and potentially even an increase in employment. Similarly, the geographic location of manufacturing facilities plays a role, with regions with more substantial technological infrastructure and skilled workforce potentially attracting more investment and job creation in innovative manufacturing.

The transition to innovative manufacturing necessitates a proactive approach to workforce development and reskilling initiatives.

Governments and educational institutions play a vital role in preparing the workforce for the new job opportunities created by this technological shift. Investment in education and training programs focused on STEM fields (Science, Technology, Engineering, and

Mathematics) is crucial to equip individuals with the skills needed for high-demand jobs in innovative manufacturing. Reskilling programs for displaced workers can help them transition into new roles, minimizing the negative impact of automation and fostering a smoother transition to the new economic landscape.

These programs are not merely reactive measures; they are crucial investments in ensuring a resilient and adaptable workforce capable of harnessing the full potential of innovative manufacturing.

Furthermore, the overall economic impact of innovative manufacturing should be considered holistically. While job displacement in specific sectors is unavoidable, the increased productivity and efficiency gains lead to overall economic growth. This growth translates into the creation of new industries, new services, and new markets, potentially leading to higher overall employment levels in the long term. The increased competitiveness of industries adopting innovative manufacturing also stimulates economic growth, potentially attracting further investment and leading to even more incredible job creation in other sectors. The long-term economic benefits significantly outweigh the short-term challenges associated with job displacement, highlighting the importance of strategic planning and proactive workforce development measures.

Finally, the discussion around employment impact needs to extend beyond simply counting jobs. The quality of jobs created by innovative manufacturing is equally, if not more, important. The new roles created often involve higher wages, greater job satisfaction, and increased opportunities for career advancement. The shift from repetitive, physically demanding work to more intellectually stimulating and challenging roles contributes to a more skilled and engaged workforce. This positive shift in job quality contributes to a more prosperous and inclusive society, maximizing the potential of human capital within an innovative manufacturing ecosystem. The overall impact is a shift toward higher-skilled, higher-paying jobs, contributing to improved societal well-being. The successful transition to an innovative manufacturing economy requires a proactive and multifaceted approach that addresses both the challenges and opportunities presented by this transformative shift.

ECONOMIC GROWTH AND COMPETITIVENESS ENHANCEMENT

The transition to innovative manufacturing offers a powerful catalyst for economic growth and enhanced international competitiveness. This isn't merely about increased productivity within existing industries; it's about the creation of entirely new sectors, the enhancement of existing product lines, and the unlocking of previously inaccessible markets. The data-driven insights and automated processes inherent in innovative manufacturing enable businesses to optimize their operations, leading to significant cost reductions and improved efficiency. These efficiencies directly translate to higher profit margins, allowing companies to reinvest in research and development, further fueling innovation and growth.

One of the most immediate impacts of innovative manufacturing is the development of new products and services. The ability to gather and analyze vast amounts of real-time data allows manufacturers to gain a deeper understanding of customer preferences, enabling them to tailor their offerings to meet specific demands. This data-driven approach to product development leads to the creation of highly customized, high-value products that command premium prices in the market. For example, the automotive industry's use of innovative manufacturing has enabled the development of highly sophisticated vehicles with advanced driver-assistance systems, autonomous driving capabilities, and personalized comfort features, significantly expanding market potential and driving revenue growth.

Beyond the creation of new products, innovative manufacturing significantly enhances the quality and consistency of existing offerings. Automated quality control systems, utilizing advanced sensors and machine vision, identify defects and inconsistencies with unprecedented accuracy, reducing waste and improving overall product quality. This improvement in quality directly impacts customer satisfaction, leading to increased brand loyalty and repeat business. The ability to deliver consistently high-quality products, combined with the capacity for agile, personalized production runs, enhances a company's reputation and gives it a clear competitive edge in the global marketplace.

The increased efficiency and productivity afforded by innovative manufacturing technologies lead to significant gains in export competitiveness. By reducing production costs and improving product quality, manufacturers can offer more competitive pricing in international markets, expanding their reach and boosting export revenues. This is incredibly impactful for businesses operating in sectors with intense global competition, where even minor improvements in efficiency and cost reduction can significantly impact market share. The ability to rapidly adjust production to meet fluctuating international demand, facilitated by the flexibility of innovative manufacturing systems, provides a further edge in global commerce.

The attractiveness of innovative manufacturing extends beyond the realm of export competitiveness; it also serves as a significant magnet for foreign direct investment (FDI). Countries and regions embracing innovative manufacturing strategies are increasingly attractive destinations for multinational corporations seeking to establish or expand their manufacturing operations. The availability of a skilled workforce, advanced technological infrastructure, and supportive government policies attract significant investment, creating high-paying jobs and stimulating local economic growth. The concentration of technologically advanced industries and the resulting innovation ecosystem fosters a virtuous cycle of further investment and growth. This attraction of FDI is pivotal for nations seeking to diversify their economies and enhance their long-term economic prospects.

The adoption of innovative manufacturing also presents opportunities for significant improvements in supply chain efficiency. The real-time data generated by connected devices and automated systems provides unprecedented visibility into the supply chain, enabling manufacturers to optimize inventory management, predict potential disruptions, and proactively address supply chain bottlenecks. This improved supply chain efficiency reduces lead times, minimizes inventory costs, and improves overall responsiveness to market demands. The use of blockchain technology, integrated within innovative manufacturing ecosystems, further enhances transparency and traceability within the supply chain, fostering trust and collaboration among stakeholders.

Moreover, the move toward innovative manufacturing is not confined to the traditional manufacturing sector. The principles of data-driven optimization, automation, and connectivity are increasingly being adopted in other sectors such as agriculture, healthcare, and logistics. In agriculture, innovative farming technologies utilizing sensors, drones, and AI-powered analytics improve crop yields, optimize resource allocation, and enhance overall farm productivity. In healthcare, innovative manufacturing principles are contributing to the development of advanced medical devices and personalized medicine, improving patient outcomes and driving innovation. The widespread adoption of innovative manufacturing principles across various sectors generates a ripple effect, boosting overall economic productivity and enhancing national competitiveness.

Furthermore, the implementation of innovative manufacturing necessitates a significant investment in infrastructure and human capital. The development of high-speed internet connectivity, robust cybersecurity systems, and advanced training programs are crucial for successful adoption. Government investment in these areas not only supports the transition to innovative manufacturing but also contributes to the broader development of a knowledge-based economy. This investment in infrastructure and human capital is a long-term strategy with substantial payoffs in terms of economic growth and improved living standards. This requires coordinated efforts between government, industry, and educational institutions to ensure a skilled workforce equipped to operate and maintain advanced innovative manufacturing systems.

The economic benefits of innovative manufacturing are not limited to tangible economic indicators like GDP growth and export revenues.

They also include intangible benefits such as improved working conditions and increased job satisfaction. The automation of hazardous and repetitive tasks leads to a safer and more fulfilling work environment for employees, contributing to a more productive and engaged workforce. This positive impact on the workforce creates a ripple effect, leading to increased innovation, higher-quality output, and overall improved economic outcomes. The investment in worker training and upskilling is a crucial aspect of successful innovative manufacturing implementation, creating a virtuous cycle of improved employee capabilities and enhanced economic performance.

However, it's crucial to acknowledge the potential challenges associated with the transition to innovative manufacturing. The initial investment costs can be substantial, requiring businesses to carefully assess the financial implications and develop a phased implementation strategy. Furthermore, the need for skilled labor and the potential for job displacement in specific sectors necessitates proactive workforce development initiatives to ensure a smooth transition and minimize disruption. Careful consideration of these challenges, coupled with proactive planning and strategic investment, will maximize the positive economic impacts of innovative manufacturing while mitigating any potential negative consequences. This requires collaboration between governments, industry, and educational institutions to develop effective workforce training programs and support measures for workers affected by automation.

In conclusion, the economic impact of innovative manufacturing is multifaceted and profound. It fosters economic growth through increased productivity, the creation of new products and services, enhanced export competitiveness, and attraction of foreign investment. While challenges exist, the long-term benefits of innovative manufacturing significantly outweigh the short-term hurdles. By embracing this transformative technology and investing in the necessary infrastructure and human capital, nations can unlock significant economic growth, enhance their global competitiveness, and improve the lives of their citizens. The key to success lies in a proactive, holistic approach that addresses both the opportunities and challenges presented by this technological revolution. This requires ongoing dialogue, collaboration, and adaptation to ensure a successful transition to an innovative manufacturing-driven economy.

CHAPTER 11
ETHICAL CONSIDERATIONS IN
INNOVATIVE MANUFACTURING

ADDRESSING ALGORITHMIC BIAS IN AI SYSTEMS

The transformative potential of AI in innovative manufacturing is undeniable, offering unprecedented levels of efficiency, optimization, and innovation. However, the deployment of AI systems also introduces significant ethical considerations, particularly concerning algorithmic bias. Algorithmic bias, stemming from flaws in the data used to train AI models or inherent biases in the algorithms themselves, can lead to unfair or discriminatory outcomes in manufacturing processes. This section will delve into the multifaceted nature of algorithmic bias within innovative manufacturing contexts, exploring its sources, manifestations, and critically essential mitigation strategies.

One primary source of bias lies in the data used to train AI models.

If the training data reflects existing societal biases, the AI system will inevitably learn and perpetuate those biases. For instance, if an AI system designed to optimize workforce scheduling is trained on historical data that reflects gender or racial biases in hiring or promotion practices, it might inadvertently reinforce these inequalities by scheduling female or minority workers for less desirable shifts or assigning them fewer opportunities for skill development. This isn't malicious intent; it's a direct consequence of the data reflecting past discriminatory practices. Similarly, AI systems used for quality control, if trained on data predominantly from a specific geographic region or manufacturing facility, might overlook defects or variations common in products from other regions or facilities, leading to inconsistencies in product quality and potentially impacting customer satisfaction in specific markets.

Beyond the training data, the design of the algorithms themselves can contribute to bias. The choices made by developers—such as feature selection, model architecture, or the choice of optimization algorithms—can inadvertently introduce biases. For example, an algorithm designed to predict equipment failures might prioritize certain types of failures based on historical data, potentially neglecting less frequently occurring but equally critical failures. This could lead to inadequate maintenance strategies and an increased risk of catastrophic equipment malfunctions. Moreover, the choice of performance metrics can also inadvertently amplify existing biases. If an AI system is optimized solely for maximizing throughput, it might neglect other important factors, such as worker safety or environmental impact, leading to potentially harmful consequences.

The manifestations of algorithmic bias in innovative manufacturing can be diverse and subtle. It might lead to unfair resource allocation, skewed production priorities, discriminatory hiring or promotion practices, or even unsafe working conditions. Consider an AI system controlling robotic arms in an assembly line. If the system is biased, it might assign more demanding tasks to certain workers consistently, leading to physical strain and potentially work-related injuries. Similarly, an AI-powered supply chain management system might prioritize suppliers from specific regions, potentially disadvantaging suppliers from disadvantaged or less connected areas. These seemingly minor biases can accumulate and have significant long-term consequences on individuals, communities, and the overall sustainability of manufacturing operations.

Addressing algorithmic bias requires a multi-pronged approach, starting with careful data curation and preprocessing. This involves rigorously auditing datasets for biases, employing techniques like data augmentation to balance underrepresented groups, and using advanced statistical methods to identify and mitigate potential sources of bias. It's crucial to ensure that the training data is representative of the diverse populations and contexts the AI system will encounter. For instance, if an AI is being developed to predict maintenance needs for equipment across diverse manufacturing sites, the training data needs to encompass data from all sites, including those with different operational conditions and equipment age profiles. Ignoring this can lead to inaccuracies and potential bias against specific sites.

Beyond data, the algorithmic design itself requires careful consideration. Utilizing transparent and explainable AI (XAI) techniques allows developers to understand how the model arrives at its decisions, thus revealing potential sources of bias. This might involve techniques like LIME (Local Interpretable Model-agnostic Explanations) or SHAP (SHapley Additive exPlanations) to investigate the contribution of different features in model predictions. Furthermore, incorporating fairness constraints into the algorithm's design can proactively mitigate bias. Fairness constraints can be designed to ensure that the AI system treats different groups equitably, irrespective of protected characteristics like gender, race, or ethnicity. This might involve adjusting the model's weights or thresholds to minimize disparities in outcomes for different groups.

Furthermore, robust testing and validation are critical to identify and rectify biases. This involves evaluating the AI system's performance on diverse datasets and considering various metrics beyond accuracy, such as fairness metrics like equal opportunity or demographic parity. Regular audits and monitoring of the AI system's performance in real-world deployments are also necessary to detect and address emerging biases over time. These audits should involve not only technical experts but also stakeholders from diverse backgrounds who can offer valuable insights and perspectives on the potential impacts of the AI system. For example, including representatives from worker unions in the testing and validation phase could reveal biases that might not be readily apparent to technical experts alone.

The legal and regulatory landscape surrounding AI bias is also evolving rapidly. Manufacturers must stay abreast of emerging regulations and standards related to AI ethics and fairness. This includes understanding data privacy regulations, such as GDPR, and potentially emerging sector-specific regulations concerning AI deployment in manufacturing. Compliance with these regulations is not only essential for avoiding legal penalties but also demonstrates a commitment to responsible AI development and deployment. Proactive engagement with regulators and industry bodies can help shape future policies and standards, ensuring that the regulatory framework supports ethical AI innovation in manufacturing.

Finally, cultivating a culture of ethical AI development within manufacturing organizations is paramount. This involves providing training for developers on bias awareness and mitigation techniques, establishing clear ethical guidelines for AI development and deployment, and promoting transparency and accountability in the use of AI systems. The commitment to ethical AI needs to be embedded within the organization's culture, reflected in its values, and integrated into its operational processes. Regular ethical reviews of AI projects involving diverse stakeholders can help ensure that the organization's AI systems align with its ethical values and avoid perpetuating biases. The fostering of a diverse and inclusive workforce, both in terms of skills and background, can also contribute to developing and deploying more equitable AI systems in manufacturing.

In conclusion, while AI holds immense promise for revolutionizing innovative manufacturing, addressing algorithmic bias is crucial for ensuring fairness, equity, and the responsible use of this powerful technology. A proactive approach that encompasses careful data handling, bias-aware algorithm design, rigorous testing and validation, legal and regulatory compliance, and a strong organizational commitment to ethical AI is indispensable. By prioritizing these considerations, manufacturers can harness the full potential of AI while mitigating the risks of algorithmic bias and fostering a more just and sustainable future for their operations and the wider society.

ENSURING DATA PRIVACY AND SECURITY

The transformative power of AI in innovative manufacturing hinges not only on its ability to optimize processes but also on its ethical implementation. A critical aspect of this ethical framework revolves around data privacy and security. Innovative manufacturing generates vast quantities of data, much of which is sensitive – encompassing details about employees, customers, intellectual property, and operational processes. The responsible handling of this data, therefore, is paramount, demanding a robust and ethically sound approach to data collection, storage, processing, and usage.

The sheer volume and variety of data collected in innovative manufacturing environments pose unique challenges. Consider the data streams emanating from connected machines, sensors, and robotic systems. These systems continuously collect information on production parameters, equipment performance, and even employee activity within the manufacturing space. This wealth of data provides unprecedented opportunities for optimization and predictive maintenance; however, it also presents a significant risk if not handled appropriately. A single data breach could expose confidential information, leading to financial losses, reputational damage, and legal repercussions.

Moreover, the interconnected nature of innovative manufacturing systems increases the attack surface for cyber threats. A vulnerability in one system could cascade across the entire network, compromising the integrity and confidentiality of vast quantities of sensitive data. This interconnectedness also necessitates a holistic approach to security, one that considers the entire ecosystem of devices, networks, and software involved in the manufacturing process. A siloed approach, where security measures are implemented independently for individual systems, would be insufficient to safeguard the entire operation from threats.

The ethical implications of data collection extend beyond the mere prevention of data breaches. The very act of collecting data raises concerns about transparency and informed consent. Employees may not be fully aware of the extent to which their activity is being monitored or the purposes for which their data is being used. This lack of transparency can undermine trust and create a sense of unease within the workforce. Therefore, manufacturers must establish clear and transparent data collection policies, ensuring that employees understand what data is being collected, how it will be used, and the measures in place to protect their privacy. Obtaining explicit consent for data collection, particularly for sensitive personal data, is essential. This consent should not be implied or inferred but explicitly provided by the individuals concerned.

Furthermore, the use of data analytics in innovative manufacturing raises concerns about potential biases and discrimination. If AI algorithms are trained on biased data, they might perpetuate or even amplify existing inequalities. For example, an AI system used for recruitment might inadvertently discriminate against certain demographic groups if the training data reflects past biases in hiring practices. Similarly, an AI system used for performance evaluation could unfairly penalize employees based on subjective or incomplete data. To mitigate these risks, it is crucial to ensure that the data used to train AI algorithms is representative and unbiased. Regular audits and evaluations should be conducted to identify and correct potential biases in the algorithms themselves.

The ethical implications of data security extend to the protection of intellectual property. Innovative manufacturing systems often collect and process sensitive information relating to product designs, manufacturing processes, and supply chain operations. The unauthorized access or disclosure of this information could cause significant financial losses and compromise the manufacturer's competitive advantage. Therefore, robust security measures must be put in place to protect intellectual property from unauthorized access or disclosure. This includes measures such as access control, encryption, and data loss prevention technologies. Regular security audits and penetration testing are crucial to identify and address vulnerabilities in the system.

Beyond technological safeguards, a strong ethical framework necessitates clear guidelines and policies related to data governance. This includes establishing clear roles and responsibilities for data management, defining data retention policies, and specifying procedures for data access and disclosure.

These policies should align with relevant legal and regulatory frameworks, such as GDPR and CCPA. Compliance with these regulations is not merely a legal obligation but a demonstration of ethical commitment to data privacy and security. Regular training programs for employees on data privacy and security best practices are essential to foster a culture of responsible data handling throughout the organization.

The development and implementation of data privacy and security protocols should be a collaborative effort involving not only technical experts but also legal counsel, ethics officers, and stakeholders from different parts of the organization. A holistic approach, considering all aspects of the data lifecycle, is essential. This includes robust data governance frameworks, comprehensive security measures, and clear communication with all stakeholders.

The increasing sophistication of cyberattacks necessitates a proactive and adaptive approach to data security. Continuous monitoring, threat intelligence, and regular security updates are essential to keep pace with evolving threats. Investment in advanced security technologies, such as intrusion detection and prevention systems, is vital for maintaining a secure, innovative manufacturing environment. Moreover, a robust incident response plan should be in place to effectively handle any security breaches or data leaks. This plan should encompass clear procedures for containment, investigation, and remediation, as well as communication strategies for informing affected stakeholders.

Finally, the ethical considerations surrounding data privacy and security extend beyond the organization itself. Manufacturers have a responsibility to consider the impact of their data practices on the broader community and the environment. This includes minimizing data collection to only what is necessary, ensuring data minimization principles are adhered to, and adopting sustainable practices in data storage and processing. A commitment to ethical data handling not only protects the organization from potential risks and liabilities but also fosters trust among employees, customers, and partners, contributing to a more responsible and sustainable manufacturing ecosystem. Transparency, accountability, and a proactive approach to data privacy and security are essential for navigating the complex ethical landscape of innovative manufacturing.

THE IMPACT OF AUTOMATION ON WORKFORCE DISPLACEMENT

The transition to innovative manufacturing, driven by automation and AI, presents a significant ethical challenge: the potential for widespread workforce displacement. While automation promises increased efficiency and productivity, it simultaneously threatens the livelihoods of countless individuals whose jobs have become obsolete due to technological advancements. This displacement isn't merely an economic issue; it carries profound ethical implications, demanding a thoughtful and proactive response from businesses, governments, and society as a whole.

The ethical dimension of workforce displacement stems from the fundamental human right to work and the inherent dignity it provides. Employment offers not only financial security but also a sense of purpose, social connection, and personal fulfillment. The sudden loss of a job due to automation can lead to severe economic hardship, emotional distress, and social isolation. The impact extends beyond the individual worker, affecting families, communities, and the broader social fabric. Therefore, the ethical imperative is to minimize the negative consequences of automation and to ensure a just transition for affected workers.

This is not to argue against technological progress. Automation offers immense potential for economic growth, improved working conditions, and the creation of new, higher-skilled jobs. However, the benefits of automation should not come at the expense of human well-being. A responsible approach requires careful planning, proactive mitigation strategies, and a commitment to ethical principles throughout the implementation process.

One critical aspect of a responsible approach is the need for transparency and open communication. Companies implementing automation should not keep workers in the dark. A proactive dialogue, including the early engagement of unions and employee representatives, is essential to address concerns and anxieties. This transparency builds trust and allows for collaborative problem-solving, fostering a sense of shared responsibility in navigating the transition. Workers should be informed well in advance about potential job losses, the reasons for these losses, and the support available to them. Such open communication is crucial for managing expectations and preventing the spread of misinformation and fear.

Furthermore, proactive reskilling and upskilling initiatives are vital to mitigating the negative impacts of automation. Companies should invest in training programs that equip workers with the skills needed to thrive in the new job market. This might involve providing opportunities for learning new technologies, acquiring advanced digital literacy, and developing transferable skills that are applicable across various industries. This investment is not just ethically sound but also strategically crucial. A workforce equipped with the skills to adapt to technological change is a more productive and competitive workforce. Collaboration with educational institutions and government agencies is essential to create comprehensive and practical reskilling and upskilling programs that meet the evolving needs of the job market.

Beyond individual-level training, the transition also necessitates broader societal initiatives. Governments have a role to play in providing social safety nets for workers displaced by automation.

This could include expanded unemployment benefits, income support programs, and initiatives that facilitate career transitions. Investment in infrastructure development and the creation of new industries can also create job opportunities and mitigate the negative economic consequences of automation. Such governmental interventions are not just acts of social welfare; they are essential for maintaining social stability and ensuring that the benefits of technological progress are shared broadly within society.

The ethical considerations extend to the design of the automation itself. Instead of simply replacing human workers, automation should be designed to augment human capabilities and enhance productivity. This necessitates a shift in mindset from viewing automation as a purely cost-cutting measure to recognizing its potential to create new opportunities and enhance human-machine collaboration. The focus should be on creating a collaborative work environment where human expertise and machine intelligence complement each other. This requires designing automation systems that are flexible, adaptable, and able to work alongside human workers rather than replacing them entirely.

The implementation of automation should also consider the potential for increased inequality. While automation may lead to the creation of new, higher-skilled jobs, it may also exacerbate existing inequalities if those displaced workers lack the education and resources to access these new opportunities. This underscores the importance of policies aimed at promoting equal opportunity and access to education and training. Targeted support for disadvantaged groups is essential to ensure that the benefits of automation are shared equitably. This commitment to inclusivity is not just morally right; it's essential for a stable and prosperous society.

Furthermore, it's crucial to consider the long-term implications of widespread automation on society. The potential for mass unemployment, coupled with the concentration of economic power in the hands of a few, presents a profound challenge to social cohesion and democratic values. The discussion must extend beyond the immediate impacts on individual workers to address the broader systemic risks. This necessitates a proactive and forward-looking approach, engaging economists, sociologists, policymakers, and technology experts to anticipate and manage the potential societal transformations brought about by widespread automation.

Addressing the ethical challenges of workforce displacement requires a multi-pronged strategy that involves businesses, governments, and individuals alike. Businesses must prioritize transparency, invest in reskilling and upskilling programs, and adopt ethical design principles in the implementation of automation technologies. Governments should implement supportive policies, including social safety nets and targeted investments in education and infrastructure. Individuals should actively participate in lifelong learning and adapt to the changing demands of the job market. Only through a concerted and ethical approach can we harness the potential of automation while ensuring a just and equitable transition for all members of society. The failure to do so risks not only widespread social unrest but also a missed opportunity to build a more prosperous and inclusive future for all. The moral imperative demands that we prioritize the human element in this technological revolution, ensuring that the progress we make does not come at the cost of human dignity and well-being.

RESPONSIBLE USE OF AI AND ROBOTICS

The ethical considerations surrounding AI and robotics in innovative manufacturing extend far beyond the issue of workforce displacement. While job displacement is a critical concern demanding immediate attention, the responsible deployment of these powerful technologies necessitates a comprehensive ethical framework addressing safety, transparency, and accountability throughout the entire lifecycle – from design and implementation to operation and eventual decommissioning.

Safety is paramount. AI and robotics systems, particularly those operating in complex manufacturing environments, present inherent risks. Malfunctions, unforeseen interactions, or even malicious attacks could lead to accidents, causing injury or damage. Therefore, rigorous safety protocols and robust testing procedures are essential. This includes comprehensive risk assessments that identify potential hazards and implement mitigation strategies.

Furthermore, the design of these systems must prioritize fail-safe mechanisms, redundancy, and emergency shutdown capabilities.

Regular maintenance and updates are also crucial to ensure continued safety and prevent the degradation of performance over time. The ethical imperative extends to the responsibility of manufacturers to provide adequate training to workers interacting with these systems, enabling them to safely and effectively operate within their parameters. Clear safety guidelines and emergency response plans should be readily accessible and regularly practiced. Negligence in safety measures is not only morally reprehensible but also carries significant legal ramifications.

Transparency in the development and deployment of AI and robotics systems is equally critical. Proprietary algorithms and opaque decision-making processes can lead to mistrust and hinder accountability. Ethical AI development demands transparency in the data used to train AI models, the algorithms employed, and the decision-making logic. This transparency enables scrutiny, allowing for the identification and correction of biases, inaccuracies, and potential harms. Moreover, it facilitates trust between workers, management, and stakeholders. Openness about the capabilities and limitations of these systems empowers workers to understand their roles in the new collaborative workplace, fostering a sense of security rather than fear of job displacement. The lack of transparency not only undermines trust but also inhibits independent verification of safety and fairness, creating a breeding ground for potential future problems.

Accountability forms the cornerstone of responsible AI and robotics implementation. When AI systems make decisions that have far-reaching consequences, it is crucial to establish clear lines of responsibility. Who is accountable when an AI-powered robot malfunctions and causes an accident? Who is responsible for the data used to train an AI system that perpetuates bias? These are critical questions requiring clear answers. Establishing precise accountability mechanisms might involve the development of specific regulatory frameworks, the establishment of independent oversight boards, or the implementation of robust auditing protocols. Regardless of the specific mechanisms chosen, the principle of accountability must be enshrined in the design and implementation of these technologies. This is not merely an ethical imperative; it is also a necessary step to build public trust and ensure the widespread adoption of these technologies.

Beyond these core principles, ethical considerations extend to the broader societal impact of AI and robotics in manufacturing. The potential for automation to exacerbate existing inequalities requires careful consideration. The creation of new, high-skilled jobs alongside the elimination of lower-skilled ones might disproportionately impact underprivileged communities lacking access to training and education. Therefore, proactive measures must be implemented to ensure that the benefits of technological advancement are shared equitably. This might involve targeted support for disadvantaged communities, initiatives promoting reskilling and upskilling, and the development of policies designed to bridge the digital divide. The transition to an innovative manufacturing environment should not deepen existing socioeconomic disparities but rather catalyze social mobility and economic inclusion. This requires a comprehensive and collaborative approach involving governments, educational institutions, industry leaders, and community organizations.

Furthermore, the environmental impact of AI and robotics should be considered. The production, operation, and eventual disposal of these advanced technologies have environmental consequences. The energy consumption associated with training complex AI models and the manufacturing of robots represents a substantial environmental footprint.

298

The ethical use of AI and robotics requires a commitment to sustainable practices throughout the lifecycle of these technologies, including the use of renewable energy sources, the optimization of energy efficiency, and the responsible disposal and recycling of components. The development of energy-efficient algorithms and the design of modular, easily repairable robots are crucial steps in minimizing the environmental impact of this technological transformation. This eco-conscious approach is not just ethically sound; it is also essential for building a truly sustainable future.

The responsible use of AI and robotics in innovative manufacturing demands a continuous dialogue involving stakeholders from across the technological, societal, and regulatory landscapes. This continuous evaluation of ethical implications is critical to anticipate and adapt to the evolving challenges presented by these rapidly advancing technologies. The engagement of ethicists, social scientists, policymakers, and technology experts is crucial in developing ethical guidelines, regulatory frameworks, and educational programs that promote the responsible use of these technologies. Furthermore, continuous monitoring and evaluation of the impact of these technologies is essential to identify and address potential ethical issues proactively, ensuring a future where automation serves humanity's interests rather than threatening its well-being. This ongoing conversation is essential to navigating the complexities of a technologically advanced world and harnessing the potential benefits of AI and robotics while safeguarding ethical principles and promoting a just and sustainable future for all. The journey towards responsible automation is a continuous process of learning, adaptation, and commitment to ethical principles – a journey that demands our unwavering attention and engagement.

PROMOTING TRANSPARENCY AND ACCOUNTABILITY IN INNOVATIVE MANUFACTURING

The ethical deployment of innovative manufacturing technologies hinges critically on fostering transparency and accountability across all operational levels. This goes beyond simply meeting regulatory compliance; it demands a proactive and demonstrable commitment to ethical practices that build trust among employees, customers, investors, and the wider public. Without this commitment, the potential benefits of innovative manufacturing – increased efficiency, improved quality, and enhanced innovation – risk being overshadowed by concerns about data privacy violations, algorithmic bias, and a lack of responsibility for potential negative consequences.

Transparency begins with data. Innovative manufacturing systems generate vast amounts of data, encompassing everything from production processes and equipment performance to employee productivity and customer preferences. This data is the lifeblood of the system, driving optimization and informed decision-making.

However, the collection, use, and storage of this data must be conducted with utmost transparency. Companies must establish clear data governance policies that outline how data is collected, what it's used for, who has access to it, and how it's protected. These policies must be readily accessible to all stakeholders, and their implementation should be regularly audited for compliance.

Crucially, transparency extends beyond mere data governance. It also necessitates open communication about the algorithms and AI models that underpin innovative manufacturing systems. While proprietary algorithms are understandably protected intellectual property, the underlying logic and decision-making processes should be explainable to a reasonable degree. This "explainable AI"(XAI) is vital for building trust and accountability. If an AI system makes a decision that has significant consequences, such as rejecting a product or adjusting a production line, stakeholders need to understand why that decision was made. This understanding allows for the identification and correction of potential biases, errors, or unintended consequences. Techniques such as decision tree visualizations, feature importance analysis, and counterfactual explanations can be used to shed light on the workings of complex AI systems, making them more transparent and understandable.

Accountability is the other critical pillar of ethical, innovative manufacturing. It's not enough to implement transparent processes; there must be precise mechanisms to address potential failures or ethical breaches. This requires establishing a robust framework for responsibility and identifying who is accountable for different aspects of the system. For instance, is the manufacturer responsible for malfunctions in the AI-powered robots? Is the software developer accountable for flaws in the algorithms? Is management responsible for ensuring the ethical use of employee data? These questions need unambiguous answers.

Implementing accountability mechanisms demands a multi-faceted approach. Internal oversight committees, comprised of individuals from diverse backgrounds and expertise, can play a crucial role in reviewing and auditing the ethical practices of innovative manufacturing systems. External audits conducted by independent third-party organizations can provide an additional layer of scrutiny and assurance. Furthermore, robust reporting mechanisms should be in place to allow for the timely identification and resolution of ethical concerns. Employees should feel empowered to raise ethical concerns without fear of reprisal. This necessitates a culture of open communication and feedback, where concerns are addressed promptly and effectively.

The legal landscape also plays a significant role in accountability.

Data privacy regulations, such as GDPR in Europe and CCPA in California, are increasingly stringent. Compliance with these regulations is not simply a matter of avoiding legal penalties; it's a fundamental aspect of ethical data handling. Beyond legal compliance, however, companies should consider implementing internal standards that exceed minimum legal requirements, demonstrating a commitment to responsible data practices that build trust and enhance their reputation.

Building trust, ultimately, is the overarching goal of promoting transparency and accountability in innovative manufacturing. Trust is not simply a byproduct of ethical practices; it's an active process that requires continuous engagement and dialogue with stakeholders. This involves proactively communicating with employees about the potential impacts of innovative manufacturing technologies, addressing concerns about job displacement, and providing opportunities for retraining and upskilling. It also means engaging with customers to ensure they understand how their data is being used and protected. Transparency and accountability are not only ethical imperatives; they are essential for building a positive and sustainable relationship between innovative manufacturing companies and the stakeholders who depend on them.

Moreover, the development of industry-wide ethical guidelines and best practices can significantly contribute to the promotion of transparency and accountability. Industry associations and professional organizations can play a pivotal role in developing and disseminating these guidelines, providing a framework for companies to follow and promoting a shared understanding of ethical responsibilities. These guidelines could cover topics such as data privacy, algorithm transparency, and accountability mechanisms, offering a common standard for ethical conduct within the innovative manufacturing sector. This collective effort can help to harmonize approaches and foster a more ethical and responsible industry landscape.

The adoption of standardized auditing procedures can further enhance accountability. Consistent auditing processes using pre-defined criteria and metrics can provide a transparent assessment of a company's adherence to ethical guidelines and regulations. This not only improves accountability but also enhances the credibility of the company's ethical commitments, fostering greater trust among stakeholders. The results of these audits could be publicly disclosed, enhancing transparency and promoting a culture of continuous improvement in ethical practices.

Furthermore, the training and education of employees are crucial aspects of building transparency and accountability. Employees must

304

understand the ethical implications of their work, including the proper handling of data and the responsible use of innovative manufacturing technologies. Comprehensive training programs tailored to the specific roles and responsibilities of employees can ensure that they are equipped with the knowledge and skills needed to promote ethical practices throughout the organization. These programs should cover topics such as data privacy, algorithmic bias, and the importance of reporting potential ethical breaches.

Finally, it's essential to acknowledge that the technological landscape is continuously evolving, demanding a dynamic and adaptable approach to ethical considerations. Innovative manufacturing systems are becoming increasingly sophisticated, introducing new ethical challenges that require continuous evaluation and adaptation of strategies. This ongoing process of learning and adaptation demands continuous engagement with experts in ethics, technology, and law to anticipate and address emerging challenges proactively. This forward-looking perspective is vital for maintaining the ethical integrity of innovative manufacturing and ensuring its responsible development and deployment. The journey towards a genuinely ethical and accountable innovative manufacturing ecosystem is an ongoing process, requiring constant vigilance, collaboration, and a deep commitment to responsible innovation.

CHAPTER 12
GOVERNMENT POLICIES AND REGULATIONS

GOVERNMENT INITIATIVES TO PROMOTE INNOVATIVE MANUFACTURING

Government support plays a crucial role in accelerating the adoption of innovative manufacturing technologies. Numerous countries have implemented comprehensive strategies combining financial incentives, regulatory reforms, and public-private partnerships to foster innovation and competitiveness in this rapidly evolving sector. These initiatives recognize that innovative manufacturing is not merely a technological advancement but a strategic imperative for economic growth and national security.

One of the most common approaches is direct financial support through government grants and subsidies. These programs often target small and medium-sized enterprises (SMEs), which may lack the resources to invest in advanced technologies independently. For example, the European Union's Horizon Europe program allocates significant funding to research and development projects in innovative manufacturing, with a particular focus on supporting the digitalization of industrial processes. Similar initiatives exist in the United States, such as the Manufacturing USA network, which brings together government, industry, and academia to address key manufacturing challenges through collaborative research and development projects. These programs typically provide funding for the purchase and implementation of innovative manufacturing technologies, including robotics, automation systems, and data analytics platforms. They often include requirements for technology demonstration and knowledge transfer, ensuring that the funded projects have a lasting impact on the broader manufacturing landscape.

Beyond direct funding, governments utilize tax incentives to encourage investment in innovative manufacturing. These incentives can take many forms, including tax credits for investments in advanced technologies, accelerated depreciation allowances, and reduced corporate tax rates for companies engaged in innovative manufacturing activities. Such tax incentives lower the financial burden of adopting new technologies, making it more attractive for companies to invest in modernization and innovation. For instance, many countries offer tax breaks for investments in energy-efficient equipment, aligning innovative manufacturing initiatives with broader sustainability goals. These tax strategies often incorporate specific criteria, such as the level of automation achieved or the environmental impact reduction demonstrated, to ensure that the incentives are targeted effectively. The design of these tax policies needs careful consideration to prevent unintended consequences and ensure equitable access to benefits across different businesses.

The effectiveness of these incentives is often evaluated through rigorous econometric analyses to measure their impact on investment and economic growth.

Regulatory frameworks play a critical role in facilitating the responsible adoption of innovative manufacturing technologies. While regulations can sometimes be perceived as barriers to innovation, well-designed regulatory frameworks can create a level playing field, fostering trust and ensuring the safe and ethical deployment of these technologies. This includes establishing clear standards for data security and privacy, addressing cybersecurity concerns, and promoting interoperability between different systems. For example, the establishment of standard data formats and communication protocols can facilitate the seamless integration of different innovative manufacturing technologies from various vendors. This approach reduces the complexity and cost of implementation, accelerating the widespread adoption of innovative manufacturing solutions.

In the context of data security and privacy, governments are developing robust frameworks to protect sensitive information generated by innovative manufacturing systems. This involves establishing clear guidelines for data collection, storage, and use, ensuring compliance with relevant privacy regulations such as GDPR and CCPA. It also necessitates robust cybersecurity measures to prevent data breaches and protect against malicious attacks. These regulations are vital for maintaining public trust and ensuring the responsible use of data generated in innovative manufacturing environments.

Furthermore, governments are actively promoting the development of workforce skills to support the transition to innovative manufacturing.

The adoption of advanced technologies necessitates a workforce equipped with the knowledge and skills to operate, maintain, and develop these systems. Government initiatives often include funding for training programs, apprenticeships, and reskilling initiatives to equip workers with the necessary digital literacy and technical expertise. These programs focus on bridging the skills gap, addressing potential job displacement concerns, and ensuring a smooth transition to an innovative manufacturing-based economy. The success of these workforce development programs depends on close collaboration between educational institutions, industry stakeholders, and government agencies, ensuring that training programs are aligned with the evolving needs of the innovative manufacturing sector.

In addition to direct intervention, governments are actively fostering public-private partnerships to promote innovative manufacturing innovation. These partnerships often involve collaboration between government agencies, research institutions, and industrial companies to develop and deploy new technologies.

This collaborative approach leverages the expertise of different stakeholders, combining government funding and policy support with the industry's practical experience and market insights. These partnerships can range from collaborative research projects to the establishment of dedicated, innovative manufacturing innovation hubs, providing a centralized platform for collaboration and knowledge sharing. The effectiveness of these partnerships depends on clear communication, shared goals, and a well-defined framework for intellectual property rights and technology transfer.

The impact of government initiatives is multifaceted and requires comprehensive evaluation. While increased investment in research and development, fostered by financial incentives and regulatory clarity, fuels innovation, the long-term effects on economic growth, employment, and competitiveness need careful study. This requires developing robust metrics to track the impact of these programs on various indicators, including job creation, productivity gains, and export growth. Economic modeling and econometric analysis provide crucial tools for assessing the cost-effectiveness and broader societal impact of different policies.

Governments are increasingly recognizing the importance of fostering a supportive ecosystem for innovative manufacturing. This includes not only financial incentives and regulatory frameworks but also the development of appropriate infrastructure, including high-speed internet connectivity and advanced digital networks.

Reliable and robust infrastructure is critical for the seamless operation of innovative manufacturing systems, which rely heavily on real-time data exchange and communication. Investments in infrastructure are, therefore, crucial for creating a competitive environment and attracting investment in innovative manufacturing technologies. The sustainability of these infrastructure investments requires careful planning and long-term vision, recognizing the evolving needs of the sector. Strategic partnerships between government, industry, and telecommunication providers are crucial to ensure the appropriate development and deployment of infrastructure supporting innovative manufacturing.

Furthermore, governments play a vital role in promoting international collaboration in innovative manufacturing. This involves engaging with other countries to share best practices, coordinate research efforts, and develop common standards. International collaboration is critical for addressing global challenges and promoting the widespread adoption of innovative manufacturing technologies. This can involve participation in international organizations, the establishment of bilateral agreements, and the facilitation of technology transfer between countries. These collaborative efforts contribute to a more robust and competitive global innovative manufacturing ecosystem.

In conclusion, government initiatives are pivotal to the success of innovative manufacturing adoption. By strategically combining financial incentives, regulatory frameworks, skills development programs, and fostering public-private partnerships, governments create the conditions necessary for innovation and widespread implementation of these technologies. However, the effectiveness of these initiatives hinges on continuous monitoring, evaluation, and adaptation to the ever-evolving technological and economic landscape. A holistic approach, encompassing research, development, deployment, and workforce development, is crucial for realizing the full potential of innovative manufacturing and securing a competitive advantage in the global economy. The ongoing evolution of innovative manufacturing necessitates a dynamic and responsive policy environment, adapting to new technological developments and economic realities.

REGULATORY LANDSCAPE FOR INNOVATIVE MANUFACTURING TECHNOLOGIES

The proliferation of innovative manufacturing technologies necessitates a robust and adaptable regulatory framework. While fostering innovation is paramount, it's equally crucial to address the potential risks associated with these advanced systems. This regulatory landscape encompasses several key areas, demanding a nuanced approach that balances technological advancement with societal well-being and economic stability.

One of the most significant areas is data privacy. Innovative manufacturing generates vast amounts of data, encompassing operational parameters, product specifications, and even potentially sensitive employee information. Regulations like the General Data Protection Regulation (GDPR) in Europe and the California Consumer Privacy Act (CCPA) in the United States establish stringent standards for data handling, storage, and usage. These regulations dictate how companies collect, process, and protect personal data, demanding transparency and user consent.

Compliance necessitates significant investment in data security infrastructure, robust data governance policies, and employee training. For innovative manufacturing organizations, this translates to implementing data anonymization techniques, employing encryption protocols, and establishing precise data access control mechanisms.

Failure to comply can result in hefty fines and reputational damage, underscoring the importance of proactive regulatory adherence. Furthermore, international harmonization of data privacy regulations remains a crucial goal, aiming to streamline cross-border data flows and foster global collaboration in the innovative manufacturing sector. The complexities involved in navigating multiple jurisdictions with varying regulatory standards necessitate a deep understanding of legal frameworks and the development of flexible, adaptable compliance strategies.

Cybersecurity forms another critical aspect of the regulatory landscape. Innovative manufacturing systems are inherently interconnected, relying on networks and cloud-based platforms for data exchange and operational control. This interconnectedness creates vulnerabilities to cyberattacks, potentially leading to production disruptions, data breaches, and even physical damage to equipment. Regulatory bodies worldwide are increasingly addressing cybersecurity risks through standards, guidelines, and mandates. The National Institute of Standards and Technology (NIST) in the US, for instance, provides cybersecurity frameworks tailored to various industries, including manufacturing. These frameworks offer a structured approach to identifying, assessing, and mitigating cybersecurity risks. Regulations often mandate the implementation of robust security measures, such as intrusion detection systems, firewalls, and regular security audits. Moreover, the increasing reliance on artificial intelligence and machine learning in innovative manufacturing necessitates the development of specific cybersecurity protocols for these technologies, addressing the unique challenges posed by AI-driven systems. The regulatory focus extends beyond basic security measures to encompass incident response plans, data breach notification protocols, and continuous security monitoring and improvement. The evolving nature of cyber threats demands a proactive and dynamic approach to cybersecurity, with continuous adaptation to emerging vulnerabilities and attack vectors. This includes staying abreast of the latest security standards and technologies, investing in employee training, and conducting regular security assessments to ensure compliance.

Environmental protection regulations are also becoming increasingly relevant in the context of innovative manufacturing. The adoption of innovative technologies presents opportunities for enhancing energy efficiency, reducing waste, and minimizing environmental impact. However, the production and disposal of advanced technologies also pose environmental challenges. Regulations related to emissions, waste management, and resource efficiency are, therefore, crucial in shaping the sustainable development of innovative manufacturing. This includes compliance with regulations concerning the use of hazardous materials, the proper disposal of electronic waste, and the reduction of carbon emissions throughout the manufacturing lifecycle. Innovative manufacturing technologies can contribute positively to environmental sustainability through optimized energy consumption, reduced material usage, and improved process control. Regulatory frameworks should incentivize these positive impacts through tax incentives, grants, and other financial mechanisms. Moreover, the development of life-cycle assessment (LCA) methodologies tailored to innovative manufacturing technologies can help assess their environmental footprint and guide the development of more sustainable solutions.

Transparency and traceability throughout the supply chain are critical, requiring robust data collection and reporting mechanisms to ensure accountability and facilitate the continuous improvement of environmental performance. The integration of environmental considerations into the design, operation, and disposal phases of innovative manufacturing technologies is crucial for ensuring their long-term sustainability and minimizing their environmental footprint.

Beyond data privacy, cybersecurity, and environmental protection, the regulatory landscape also encompasses intellectual property rights, product liability, and worker safety. Protecting intellectual property is crucial for encouraging innovation, requiring clear regulatory frameworks for patent protection, trade secrets, and licensing agreements. Product liability laws address the responsibility of manufacturers for defects in their products, emphasizing the need for rigorous quality control and product safety measures in the innovative manufacturing environment. Worker safety regulations must adapt to the new risks posed by automated systems and robotics, ensuring appropriate training, safety protocols, and risk assessment procedures. The dynamic interplay between technological advancement and regulatory frameworks necessitates continuous adaptation and collaboration between stakeholders, including manufacturers, regulators, and academic institutions.

The evolution of the regulatory landscape for innovative manufacturing is continuous. As technologies advance and new

316

challenges emerge, regulatory frameworks must adapt to ensure responsible innovation and mitigate potential risks. This requires close collaboration between governments, industry, and research institutions, fostering a dialogue that balances the need for technological progress with the imperative to protect societal interests. A proactive and adaptive approach to regulation is crucial for realizing the full potential of innovative manufacturing while mitigating the associated risks. This involves ongoing monitoring of technological developments, regular evaluation of regulatory effectiveness, and flexible adaptation to emerging challenges. The ultimate goal is to create a regulatory environment that fosters innovation, ensures responsible technology deployment, and promotes a sustainable and equitable future for innovative manufacturing.

INDUSTRY POLICIES AND THEIR IMPLEMENTATION

Industry 4.0, with its promise of increased efficiency, productivity, and competitiveness, has spurred governments worldwide to formulate and implement supportive policies. These policies, however, vary significantly in their approach, scope, and effectiveness. A common thread, however, is the recognition that successful Industry 4.0 adoption requires a multifaceted strategy going beyond simple financial incentives.

Germany, a pioneer in Industry 4.0, has adopted a strategy focused on collaborative partnerships between industry, academia, and government. Initiatives like "Industrie 4.0" aim to foster innovation and technology development through research funding, standardization efforts, and the creation of platforms for knowledge sharing. The government's emphasis on establishing common standards and protocols simplifies integration across different systems and manufacturers, reducing implementation barriers for companies of all sizes. This collaborative approach, while effective in generating technological advancements, also highlights the importance of widespread industry buy-in and a commitment to long-term strategic alignment. Challenges remain, however, in ensuring that the benefits of Industry 4.0 are distributed equitably across all sectors and regions, preventing a widening gap between technologically advanced firms and those lagging behind.

In contrast, China's approach to Industry 4.0, often termed "Made in China 2025," is characterized by a more centralized and directive approach. The government has outlined ambitious goals for technological self-reliance and global competitiveness, emphasizing the development of key strategic industries. This strategy involves substantial government investment in research and development, infrastructure development, and the creation of industrial clusters.

While this centralized approach can accelerate technological adoption in specific sectors, it also carries potential risks. Over-reliance on government-directed investments can lead to market distortions and stifle innovation outside of prioritized areas.

Furthermore, concerns about intellectual property rights and the potential for state-sponsored industrial espionage remain significant considerations. The success of China's Industry 4.0 strategy hinges on its ability to balance its centralized approach with market-driven innovation and create a level playing field for all participating businesses.

The United States, on the other hand, has pursued a more decentralized approach, relying on market forces and private sector investment to drive the adoption of innovative manufacturing technologies. While government initiatives exist, including funding for research and development and tax incentives for investment in advanced technologies, the emphasis is on creating an enabling environment that fosters competition and innovation. This approach has the advantage of promoting agility and adaptability, allowing the market to identify and prioritize the most promising technologies. However, it can also lead to a slower rate of adoption, particularly in smaller businesses lacking the resources to invest in advanced technologies. The lack of a cohesive national strategy can also result in fragmentation and inefficiency as different regions and industries adopt different technologies and standards. A coordinated national strategy might facilitate the sharing of best practices and address common challenges more efficiently.

The policies of various countries also differ in their focus on specific aspects of Industry 4.0. Some countries prioritize the development of specific enabling technologies such as artificial intelligence, robotics, and advanced sensors. Others focus on the development of supporting infrastructure, including high-speed internet access, data centers, and secure communication networks. Still, others emphasize the need for workforce development, providing training and education programs to equip workers with the skills necessary to operate and maintain advanced manufacturing systems. The effectiveness of these policies often depends on their alignment with the specific needs and priorities of the country's industrial sector. A successful strategy requires a careful assessment of a country's strengths and weaknesses, taking into account its industrial structure, technological capabilities, and the skills of its workforce.

The implementation of Industry 4.0 policies often involves a range of challenges. These challenges include securing funding, navigating regulatory complexities, overcoming resistance to change within businesses, and fostering collaboration between different stakeholders. Securing sufficient funding for research, development, and infrastructure investments is often a significant hurdle, especially for countries with limited resources. Navigating regulatory complexities, such as data privacy regulations and cybersecurity standards, can be challenging, requiring significant expertise and investment in compliance. Overcoming resistance to change within businesses can be difficult, as many companies are hesitant to adopt new technologies that may disrupt their existing operations.

Fostering collaboration between government, industry, and academia is essential for successful implementation, requiring effective communication channels and mechanisms for shared decision-making.

Successful implementation often requires a phased approach, starting with pilot projects and gradually scaling up adoption across different sectors. This iterative approach allows for continuous improvement and adaptation based on lessons learned. Regular evaluation and monitoring are crucial to assess the effectiveness of the policies and to identify areas for improvement. The participation of multiple stakeholders, including government agencies, industry representatives, academics, and labor unions, is critical. Effective communication and collaboration among these stakeholders are essential to ensure that the policies are aligned with the needs and priorities of all parties involved.

Transparency and accountability are also essential, as they provide stakeholders with clear information on the progress of the policies and the outcomes achieved.

Beyond national-level strategies, the role of regional and local initiatives should not be underestimated. Regional clusters focused on specific industries can leverage synergies, sharing expertise and resources to facilitate the adoption of Industry 4.0 technologies.

Local initiatives can address specific needs and challenges in particular communities, bridging the digital divide and ensuring that the benefits of innovative manufacturing are accessible to all. The effectiveness of such initiatives often hinges on the creation of strong networks and collaborations between businesses, research institutions, and local government bodies.

In conclusion, the success of Industry 4.0 policies hinges on a number of factors. These include a clear understanding of national priorities, a robust implementation strategy that accounts for the specific needs and circumstances of different industries and regions, effective collaboration between stakeholders, and a commitment to continuous monitoring and evaluation. While the approaches may differ, a common thread among successful strategies is a recognition that Industry 4.0 is not just about technological advancement; it is about a fundamental transformation of manufacturing processes, business models, and the broader economic landscape. This requires a holistic approach that addresses technological, organizational, and societal aspects of the transformation, as well as the continuous adaptation to an ever-evolving technological and economic environment. The continuous evolution of technology demands flexibility and adaptability in policymaking, ensuring that regulations remain relevant and supportive of responsible innovation. Only through a dynamic interplay of government support, private sector investment, and collaborative efforts can the full potential of Industry 4.0 be unlocked, delivering tangible benefits for businesses, workers, and society as a whole.

INTERNATIONAL STANDARDS AND BEST PRACTICES

The global adoption of innovative manufacturing necessitates a degree of harmonization and standardization to ensure seamless interoperability between different systems, devices, and platforms. Without common standards, the diverse array of technologies and protocols employed by various manufacturers can create significant barriers to integration and data exchange, hindering the realization of the full potential of Industry 4.0. This is where international standards and best practices play a crucial role. These standards provide a common framework for communication, data exchange, and security, facilitating the development and deployment of interoperable systems across diverse industrial settings.

Several international organizations are actively involved in developing and promoting standards for innovative manufacturing. The International Organization for Standardization (ISO) plays a central role, with numerous standards addressing various aspects of innovative manufacturing, including data management, cybersecurity, and industrial automation. ISO 9001, while not explicitly focused on Industry 4.0, serves as a foundational standard for quality management systems and provides a framework for businesses to implement robust processes for managing the risks and complexities associated with the adoption of new technologies. ISO/IEC 27001, concerning information security management systems, is critical in establishing cybersecurity protocols that are crucial in the context of connected systems vulnerable to cyber threats. This standard ensures that data exchanged between devices and systems in an innovative manufacturing environment remains secure and protected from unauthorized access and data breaches. The lack of robust cybersecurity measures can lead to production downtime, financial losses, and reputational damage.

Furthermore, the IEC (International Electrotechnical Commission) contributes significantly through standards relevant to industrial communication networks and protocols such as PROFINET, EtherNet/IP, and OPC UA. These protocols govern how devices and systems communicate and exchange data within an innovative manufacturing environment. The importance of standardization in this context cannot be overstated, as it prevents vendor lock-in and facilitates the seamless integration of equipment from different manufacturers. Without standard communication protocols, integrating equipment from different suppliers becomes a complex and costly undertaking, hindering the flexibility and scalability that are hallmarks of innovative manufacturing. OPC UA (Open Platform Communications Unified Architecture) stands out as a key enabler of interoperability, acting as a universal translator between different devices and systems, allowing for communication irrespective of underlying protocols.

Beyond ISO and IEC, organizations such as the International Data Spaces Association (IDSA) are actively developing standards and frameworks for secure and controlled data sharing in industrial environments. The IDSA focuses on the establishment of data spaces, allowing various stakeholders to securely share and exchange data while maintaining control over their data assets. This is particularly relevant in the context of Industry 4.0, where large volumes of data are generated and shared across different systems and organizations, necessitating robust mechanisms for data governance and access control. The IDSA's efforts are crucial in addressing concerns related to data privacy and security, promoting trust and collaboration within the industrial ecosystem.

The adoption of international standards offers numerous benefits. Firstly, it fosters interoperability, allowing businesses to integrate equipment and systems from various suppliers seamlessly. This reduces the complexity and costs associated with system integration and enhances the flexibility of innovative manufacturing systems.

Secondly, it improves efficiency and productivity by optimizing data exchange and facilitating real-time monitoring and control. Improved data sharing leads to more informed decision-making and helps optimize manufacturing processes. Thirdly, it enhances cybersecurity by establishing secure communication protocols and data management practices. The standardization of cybersecurity practices minimizes the risks associated with cyber threats and protects sensitive data. Fourthly, it reduces risks associated with vendor lock-in, giving businesses the freedom to choose equipment and systems from different suppliers without compromising interoperability. This fosters competition and innovation within the innovative manufacturing market. Finally, it promotes global collaboration and knowledge sharing, allowing businesses to learn from each other's experiences and best practices.

However, challenges remain in the widespread adoption of these standards. One key challenge is the sheer number and diversity of standards available, which can make it difficult for businesses to determine which standards are most relevant to their needs. Many businesses lack the expertise to navigate the complexities of different standards and their implications for system integration. Moreover, the implementation of standards can require significant investment in time, resources, and expertise. The initial cost of adopting and implementing new standards can be a barrier for many businesses, especially small and medium-sized enterprises (SMEs). Furthermore, resistance to change within organizations can impede the adoption of new standards and associated technologies. Many companies are reluctant to disrupt their existing operations to implement new standards, even if those standards offer significant long-term benefits.

To overcome these challenges, several strategies are essential.

Firstly, a simplified and consolidated framework for standards is needed to help businesses better understand and implement them.

Secondly, practical training and education programs should be developed to equip businesses with the necessary expertise. Thirdly, government support and incentives can help reduce the financial burden associated with standard adoption. This support might come in the form of grants, tax breaks, or subsidies to offset the investment cost of adopting standards. Fourthly, fostering collaboration among stakeholders, including standards organizations, government agencies, and industry players, is crucial to promote the widespread adoption of best practices. Collaborative efforts can simplify the process, share expertise, and ensure a unified approach.

International best practices in innovative manufacturing go beyond standards and encompass organizational strategies and cultural shifts. This includes adopting a data-driven culture, where decisions are made based on real-time data insights rather than gut feelings or traditional experience. It necessitates a workforce capable of utilizing and interpreting this data effectively, necessitating investments in education and training programs that equip workers with the necessary skills. Furthermore, agile methodologies are increasingly important, allowing companies to quickly adapt to changing market conditions and technological advancements. This involves iterative development cycles and rapid prototyping, promoting responsiveness and adaptability. Finally, cybersecurity best practices, including robust security protocols and regular vulnerability assessments, are essential to protect the integrity and confidentiality of sensitive data.

Successful implementation of Industry 4.0 requires a holistic approach that addresses technological, organizational, and societal aspects. It necessitates collaborative efforts between governments, industry players, and research institutions, fostering innovation and knowledge sharing. A strong regulatory framework is needed to protect data privacy and security, ensuring a safe and secure environment for data exchange. International collaboration plays a critical role in creating a global ecosystem for innovative manufacturing, enabling efficient information exchange and knowledge dissemination. By actively participating in the development and implementation of international standards and by embracing best practices in innovative manufacturing, businesses can unlock the full potential of Industry 4.0 and gain a competitive advantage in the global marketplace. The ongoing evolution of technology requires a continuous review and adaptation of standards and best practices, ensuring a dynamic and relevant framework for the advancement of innovative manufacturing technologies. This dynamic interplay of international cooperation, technological innovation, and responsible regulatory frameworks will pave the way for a more efficient, sustainable, and competitive global industrial landscape.

POLICY RECOMMENDATIONS FOR FOSTERING INNOVATIVE MANUFACTURING GROWTH

Policy recommendations to stimulate innovative manufacturing growth must be multifaceted, addressing the technological, economic, and societal challenges simultaneously. A comprehensive strategy necessitates a coordinated effort involving governments, industry, academia, and standardization bodies. Investing strategically in research and development (R&D) is paramount. This shouldn't be limited to incremental improvements in existing technologies but should focus on pioneering advancements in areas like artificial intelligence (AI) for predictive maintenance, advanced robotics for flexible automation, and the development of secure and interoperable data platforms. Public-private partnerships can leverage the expertise of both sectors, fostering innovation and accelerating the deployment of cutting-edge technologies. Funding mechanisms should prioritize projects with a clear path to commercialization and demonstrable societal benefits. This necessitates a robust evaluation process to ensure that public funds are allocated effectively and efficiently, maximizing the return on investment. Furthermore, it is crucial to encourage collaborative R&D initiatives, fostering the sharing of knowledge and resources amongst competing firms to avoid redundant efforts and maximize the potential for breakthroughs.

Workforce development is another critical area requiring significant attention. The transition to innovative manufacturing necessitates a workforce equipped with the skills to operate, maintain, and innovate within this new paradigm. This calls for a multi-pronged approach, encompassing initiatives at all educational levels. At the secondary education level, emphasis should be placed on STEM (Science, Technology, Engineering, and Mathematics) education, fostering an early interest in technology and providing foundational knowledge crucial for future careers in innovative manufacturing. At the tertiary level, universities and colleges must adapt their curricula to reflect the evolving needs of the industry, offering specialized programs in areas like mechatronics, data analytics, cybersecurity, and AI. Furthermore, robust apprenticeship programs and vocational training initiatives are needed to bridge the skills gap and provide practical, hands-on experience to the workforce. These programs should be designed in close collaboration with industry to ensure relevance and alignment with evolving job requirements.

Continuous professional development is equally important, providing ongoing opportunities for upskilling and reskilling to keep pace with the rapid technological advancements characterizing the sector. Government support for these initiatives should include funding for education programs, grants for companies investing in employee training, and tax incentives for companies that prioritize skills development.

Creating a favorable regulatory environment is equally crucial for fostering innovative manufacturing growth. This entails developing clear, consistent, and predictable regulations that encourage innovation while protecting worker safety, data privacy, and environmental sustainability. A streamlined regulatory process is essential to minimize bureaucratic hurdles and reduce the time and cost associated with implementing new technologies. Regulations should be technology-neutral, focusing on outcomes rather than specific technologies, to encourage innovation and avoid stifling technological advancements. Furthermore, regulatory bodies should collaborate with industry stakeholders to ensure that regulations are practical, feasible, and aligned with the evolving needs of the sector.

Regular reviews and updates of regulations are necessary to keep pace with rapid technological changes and avoid becoming overly restrictive. Transparency and public consultation in the development of regulations are also essential to foster trust and ensure that all stakeholders have a voice in the process.

Tax incentives and subsidies can play a significant role in encouraging the adoption of innovative manufacturing technologies.

Targeted tax breaks for businesses investing in automation equipment, software, and digital technologies can significantly reduce the initial cost of adoption. These incentives should be designed to prioritize small and medium-sized enterprises (SMEs), which often lack the financial resources of larger corporations. Subsidies for workforce training and reskilling programs can further incentivize companies to invest in their employees, improving their skills and competitiveness. Government-backed loan programs can provide access to capital for companies looking to invest in innovative manufacturing technologies.

These programs should offer attractive interest rates and flexible repayment terms, reducing the financial burden on businesses. Furthermore, the government can support the development of shared facilities and infrastructure, such as collaborative research labs and testbeds, making cutting-edge technologies more accessible to smaller firms.

International cooperation is vital for fostering global innovative manufacturing growth. Harmonizing standards and regulations across different countries can reduce trade barriers and promote the seamless flow of goods and services. Collaboration on research and development can accelerate technological advancements and ensure that the benefits of innovative manufacturing are shared globally.

International forums and partnerships can provide a platform for exchanging best practices and learning from each other's successes and challenges. This collaboration should encompass not just governments but also industry bodies, research institutions, and standardization organizations. The sharing of best practices, particularly regarding cybersecurity and data privacy, is particularly crucial in ensuring the secure and reliable functioning of globally interconnected innovative manufacturing systems. Joint initiatives to promote skills development and workforce training can help create a globally skilled workforce capable of supporting the global innovative manufacturing industry.

Finally, fostering a culture of innovation and collaboration is crucial for the success of innovative manufacturing. Government policies should support the creation of innovation hubs and clusters, bringing together businesses, researchers, and entrepreneurs to foster collaboration and the exchange of ideas. Incentives for collaborative projects and joint ventures can stimulate innovation and encourage the development of new technologies and business models. Public awareness campaigns can educate the public about the benefits of innovative manufacturing and dispel any misconceptions or concerns. This includes addressing issues relating to job displacement due to automation and emphasizing the need for retraining and upskilling programs to ensure a smooth transition for affected workers.

Promoting a culture of lifelong learning will be crucial to ensure that the workforce remains adaptable and resilient in the face of rapid technological changes. By addressing these challenges proactively and collaboratively, governments can help to ensure that innovative manufacturing delivers its full potential, benefiting both industry and society. The ongoing evolution of this field demands a dynamic and adaptive policy environment, one that fosters innovation while mitigating risks and ensuring responsible and equitable growth.

CHAPTER 13

EDUCATION AND TRAINING FOR THE INNOVATIVE MANUFACTURING WORKFORCE

DEVELOPING CURRICULUM FOR INNOVATIVE MANUFACTURING PROGRAMS

Developing robust curricula for innovative manufacturing programs requires a departure from traditional engineering and technology-focused approaches. The successful implementation of innovative manufacturing hinges on a multidisciplinary workforce possessing a blend of technical expertise, business acumen, and a deep understanding of the socio-economic implications of advanced technologies. Therefore, curriculum design must move beyond siloed learning and embrace an integrated model that fosters holistic understanding.

A core component of any effective, innovative manufacturing program should be a strong foundation in engineering principles. This includes, but is not limited to, mechatronics, robotics, automation systems, and industrial control systems. Students need a solid grasp of the underlying physical processes within a manufacturing environment, the principles of automation, and the capabilities of various technologies. However, this foundational engineering knowledge must be augmented with a comprehensive understanding of the digital technologies underpinning innovative manufacturing.

This necessitates incorporating courses on data analytics, machine learning, artificial intelligence, and the Internet of Things (IoT). Students should develop the skills to collect, analyze, and interpret large datasets generated by innovative manufacturing systems. They should learn how to use machine learning algorithms to identify patterns, predict equipment failures, and optimize production processes. Furthermore, a deep understanding of the security implications of interconnected systems is critical. Courses focused on cybersecurity and data privacy are essential to ensure the robustness and resilience of innovative manufacturing operations.

Beyond the technical skills, the curriculum must also address the business aspects of innovative manufacturing. This includes topics such as supply chain management, operations management, project management, and financial modeling. Students must understand how to integrate innovative manufacturing technologies within the broader business context, aligning technological advancements with strategic organizational objectives. Understanding financial metrics, return on investment calculations, and the economic impact of innovative manufacturing technologies are crucial skills for professionals in this field.

The human element is equally critical. A significant portion of the curriculum should focus on the human-machine interface, human factors engineering, and the impact of automation on the workforce. Students should explore the ethical implications of increasingly autonomous systems, considering issues such as job displacement, worker retraining, and the need for a just transition.

Furthermore, understanding the importance of teamwork, communication, and collaboration in the context of complex, innovative manufacturing systems is vital. Interdisciplinary projects and collaborative learning activities can foster these skills effectively.

Effective curriculum design should also consider the pedagogical approaches used. Traditional lecture-based learning should be supplemented with hands-on laboratory experiences, simulations, and real-world case studies. This active learning approach enables students to apply their knowledge in practical scenarios, solidifying their understanding and preparing them for the challenges of the real world. Access to advanced manufacturing facilities and simulation environments is essential for providing realistic training opportunities. Furthermore, industry partnerships and collaborations can provide valuable insights and perspectives, making the curriculum more relevant and engaging.

The integration of industry-relevant projects is crucial. Students should have the opportunity to work on real-world problems posed by industry partners, allowing them to apply their knowledge and skills in a practical setting. These projects can range from developing algorithms for predictive maintenance to designing and implementing new automation systems. This hands-on experience provides invaluable practical skills and strengthens the connection between academia and industry, preparing students for a seamless transition into the professional world. Furthermore, this collaborative approach fosters networking opportunities and can lead to valuable career prospects.

Furthermore, the curriculum must be adaptable and responsive to the rapid pace of technological advancements within innovative manufacturing. Regular updates and revisions are crucial to ensure the relevance and currency of the curriculum. This requires ongoing collaboration with industry experts, tracking technological trends, and incorporating new developments into the course content. It's equally crucial to involve alums in the curriculum review process to gain insights into the evolving needs of the industry and to ensure the curriculum remains aligned with market demands.

The assessment methods within the curriculum should reflect the multifaceted nature of innovative manufacturing education. Traditional exams should be complemented with project-based assessments, presentations, and portfolio reviews. This holistic assessment approach accurately captures students' understanding of the technical, business, and human aspects of innovative manufacturing. The emphasis should be on assessing problem-solving skills, critical thinking, and the ability to apply knowledge in real-world contexts.

Finally, the development of an innovative manufacturing curriculum should be guided by a clearly defined set of learning outcomes.

These outcomes should articulate the knowledge, skills, and competencies students are expected to acquire upon completion of the program. They should be measurable, attainable, relevant, and time-bound (SMART). The learning outcomes should serve as a guide for curriculum design, instructional strategies, and assessment methods, ensuring a coherent and purposeful learning experience.

These outcomes must align with the needs of the industry, ensuring graduates are prepared for immediate contribution upon entering the workforce.

International collaboration is another vital aspect. Innovative manufacturing is a global phenomenon, and programs should incorporate global perspectives, best practices, and technologies.

Including case studies from different countries, fostering collaborations with international universities, and inviting guest lecturers from overseas can enrich the learning experience and expose students to diverse approaches and challenges. Furthermore, exposure to international standards and regulations in innovative manufacturing is crucial for graduates who may work in multinational companies or on international projects.

In summary, the development of effective curricula for innovative manufacturing programs demands a comprehensive and holistic approach. The curriculum must not only equip students with technical skills but also foster their business acumen, ethical awareness, and collaborative spirit. A strong emphasis on hands-on learning, industry partnerships, and continuous curriculum updates is crucial to ensure graduates are well-prepared to lead the future of innovative manufacturing. Through strategic curriculum design, institutions can play a pivotal role in fostering a skilled and adaptable workforce capable of driving innovation and growth in this rapidly evolving field. The successful implementation of this type of program requires significant investment in infrastructure, faculty development, and technology acquisition. Securing adequate funding through government grants, industry partnerships, and philanthropic contributions is therefore essential.

UPSKILLING AND RESKILLING INITIATIVES FOR EXISTING WORKERS

The transition to innovative manufacturing presents significant challenges and opportunities for the existing workforce. While automation and advanced technologies offer increased productivity and efficiency, they also necessitate a shift in skills and competencies required for many manufacturing roles. This necessitates a robust and multifaceted approach to upskilling and reskilling initiatives to ensure a smooth transition and prevent job displacement. Ignoring this crucial aspect risks creating a skills gap, hindering the successful implementation of innovative manufacturing strategies.

A successful upskilling and reskilling program must be tailored to the specific needs of the existing workforce and the demands of innovative manufacturing technologies. This requires a thorough assessment of current skill sets and a detailed analysis of the future skills required. This assessment should go beyond simply identifying technical skills gaps. It should also consider the soft skills necessary for success in a collaborative, data-driven environment, such as problem-solving, critical thinking, communication, and teamwork.

Detailed competency models should be developed, specifying the knowledge, skills, and behaviors required for each role within the innovative manufacturing ecosystem.

The reskilling efforts shouldn't be a one-size-fits-all approach.

Different workers require different levels and types of training. Experienced machinists, for example, might need training in data analytics and predictive maintenance to oversee and interpret data from sophisticated sensors and machine learning algorithms monitoring their equipment. Similarly, line supervisors might require training in managing autonomous systems and optimizing production schedules based on real-time data analysis. Office staff may need to understand how data flows across the entire innovative factory system, learn about data visualization, and be able to contribute to the development and utilization of new business intelligence dashboards. Furthermore, even high-level management roles will require a deeper understanding of the technical aspects of innovative manufacturing to make informed strategic decisions.

The delivery method of training is equally crucial. Traditional classroom-based training can be supplemented and, in some cases, replaced by more engaging and accessible methods. Online learning platforms, virtual reality simulations, and microlearning modules can offer flexible and personalized learning experiences catering to different learning styles and schedules. The use of gamification techniques can make the learning process more enjoyable and increase engagement, leading to better knowledge retention. The use of online simulations, particularly in the context of complex machinery, can mitigate risks associated with hands-on training and allow for the exploration of a broader range of scenarios.

Industry 4.0 technologies, such as augmented reality (AR) and virtual reality (VR), offer promising avenues for upskilling. AR overlays digital information in the real world, providing workers with real-time guidance and support during complex tasks. VR, on the other hand, creates immersive simulations of manufacturing environments, allowing workers to practice new skills in a safe and controlled setting without the risk of equipment damage or injury. These technologies can be particularly effective in training workers to operate complex new equipment or to perform intricate maintenance procedures.

Effective upskilling and reskilling initiatives also require a strong commitment from management and a supportive work environment. Workers must be provided with adequate time and resources to participate in training programs without fear of job insecurity. Creating a culture of continuous learning and improvement is essential, encouraging workers to actively seek out opportunities for professional development. Open communication and transparency about the changes brought about by innovative manufacturing are crucial to alleviating anxieties and building trust.

Regular feedback and mentorship programs can further support workers as they navigate the transition to new roles and responsibilities.

Successful upskilling programs often involve collaboration between employers, educational institutions, and government agencies. This collaboration can leverage the expertise and resources of each stakeholder, ensuring that training programs are aligned with industry needs and accessible to the workforce. Government initiatives can provide financial support for training programs, while educational institutions can develop and deliver customized training curricula based on industry demands. Employers, in turn, can provide access to their

342

facilities and equipment for practical training, and they can ensure that the training is directly relevant to the tasks and responsibilities of the workers.

The measurement of success in upskilling and reskilling programs is also crucial. Key performance indicators (KPIs) should be established to track the effectiveness of the training and to identify areas for improvement. These KPIs might include improvements in worker productivity, reduction in error rates, increased job satisfaction, and improved retention rates. Regular evaluations and feedback from workers, supervisors, and managers can provide valuable insights into the strengths and weaknesses of the programs, enabling continuous improvement.

Furthermore, the success of upskilling and reskilling initiatives can be significantly enhanced through the development of strong partnerships with industry associations and professional organizations. These partnerships can offer valuable industry insights, access to best practices, and opportunities for networking and collaboration. They can also facilitate the development of standardized training curricula and certifications, enhancing the credibility and value of the training programs. These organizations can play a crucial role in disseminating information about available training opportunities and promoting the importance of upskilling for workers in the innovative manufacturing sector.

The economic benefits of upskilling and reskilling initiatives are substantial. Improved worker productivity, reduced error rates, and increased job satisfaction all contribute to a more efficient and profitable manufacturing operation. A skilled and adaptable workforce is also better positioned to embrace new technologies and drive innovation, giving companies a competitive edge in the global marketplace. This leads to increased profitability and overall economic growth. Moreover, investing in the workforce through upskilling and reskilling initiatives is also a responsible approach to mitigating potential job displacement caused by automation, ensuring a just transition for workers and contributing to social equity. These programs can also foster a culture of continuous improvement, leading to increased innovation and competitiveness for the company as a whole. This investment demonstrates a commitment to the well-being of the employees, fostering loyalty and improving morale within the organization.

In conclusion, upskilling and reskilling initiatives are not merely an optional add-on but a crucial strategic imperative for the successful implementation of innovative manufacturing. A multifaceted approach, encompassing tailored training programs, delivery methods, supportive work environments, and strong collaborations between stakeholders, is essential to ensure the successful transition of the existing workforce into the age of innovative manufacturing. By proactively addressing the skills gap and investing in the development of its workforce, the industry can unlock the full potential of innovative manufacturing, creating a more productive, efficient, and competitive manufacturing sector while ensuring a just and equitable transition for all involved. The long-term economic and social benefits of a well-trained and adaptable workforce far outweigh the initial investment required in upskilling and reskilling initiatives. A failure to act decisively in this area risks hindering the progress of innovative manufacturing and creating significant social and economic challenges.

PARTNERSHIPS BETWEEN ACADEMIA AND INDUSTRY

The successful implementation of innovative manufacturing strategies hinges not only on technological advancements but also on a workforce equipped with the necessary skills and knowledge. While the previous section highlighted the crucial role of upskilling and reskilling initiatives within individual companies, a broader perspective reveals the vital contribution of partnerships between academia and industry in addressing the evolving needs of the innovative manufacturing workforce. These collaborative efforts are essential for bridging the gap between theoretical knowledge and practical application, ensuring that training programs remain relevant and adaptable to the rapid pace of technological change.

This synergy leverages the strengths of both sectors: academia's expertise in research, curriculum development, and pedagogical innovation, industry's practical experience, access to real-world equipment, and understanding of current market demands.

One of the most significant benefits of these partnerships is the development of customized training programs tailored to the specific needs of individual industries and companies. Traditional academic programs, while providing a solid foundation in engineering and management principles, often lack the specific, hands-on training required for navigating the complexities of innovative manufacturing technologies. By collaborating with industry partners, educational institutions can gain valuable insights into the current and future skill requirements within specific sectors, allowing them to design curricula that directly address those needs. This collaborative approach ensures that graduates possess not just theoretical knowledge but also the practical skills and experience demanded by employers, facilitating a smoother transition into the workforce. For instance, a partnership between a university's engineering department and a leading automotive manufacturer could result in a specialized program focusing on the application of robotics, AI, and data analytics within the context of automotive assembly lines. Such a program would equip graduates with the specific skills required for roles in this industry, significantly enhancing their employability and providing the manufacturer with a readily available pool of skilled workers.

Furthermore, industry partnerships provide access to cutting-edge technologies and equipment that are often unavailable in academic settings. Many innovative manufacturing technologies, such as advanced robotics systems, industrial IoT platforms, and sophisticated data analytics software, are expensive and require specialized infrastructure. Academic institutions may struggle to invest in these technologies due to budgetary constraints or lack of space.

However, through partnerships with industry, universities and colleges can provide students with hands-on experience with these technologies, enhancing their learning and preparing them for real-world scenarios. This access to state-of-the-art equipment allows for more realistic simulations and practical exercises, making the learning process more engaging and effective. Imagine a partnership between a university's computer science department and a semiconductor manufacturer: students could gain experience working with advanced fabrication equipment, learning firsthand about the challenges and intricacies of modern chip manufacturing.

Beyond access to technology, industry partnerships also offer invaluable opportunities for mentorship and networking. Industry professionals can act as mentors, providing students with guidance on career development, sharing industry best practices, and offering insights into the latest trends and technological advancements. This mentorship extends beyond formal classroom settings, creating ongoing relationships that benefit both the students and the industry partners. Networking opportunities provided by these partnerships are equally valuable, allowing students to connect with potential employers and industry leaders, enhancing their career prospects and providing them with a valuable professional network.

Career fairs, guest lectures, and site visits are all examples of activities that facilitate these invaluable networking opportunities.

These partnerships also play a crucial role in the development and implementation of continuing education and professional development programs for existing employees. As technologies evolve, the skills required to operate and maintain innovative manufacturing systems are constantly changing. Industry-academia partnerships can create tailored upskilling and reskilling programs that address these evolving needs, providing opportunities for experienced workers to adapt to new technologies and maintain their competitiveness in the job market. For example, a collaboration between a community college and a local manufacturing plant might offer a short-course on the use of predictive maintenance software, enabling technicians to proactively identify and address equipment malfunctions, improving efficiency and reducing downtime. This targeted training is far more effective than generic professional development programs, directly impacting worker productivity and overall business performance.

The financial benefits of these partnerships also extend beyond direct cost savings. By collaborating with universities, companies can access a pipeline of highly skilled graduates, reducing the need for costly recruitment and training efforts. The investment in university research projects can lead to the development of technologies and solutions that can be directly applied to the industry, offering a significant return on investment.

Furthermore, these collaborations enhance the company's brand image and reputation, attracting top talent and fostering a positive relationship with the local community. For example, a company sponsoring a university's robotics lab not only gains access to cutting-edge research but also enhances its image as an innovator and employer of choice, attracting highly qualified engineering graduates.

However, building and maintaining successful industry-academia partnerships requires careful planning and a commitment from both sides. Clear communication and well-defined objectives are essential. Both partners must have a shared understanding of the goals of the partnership, the responsibilities of each party, and the metrics used to measure success. Clear agreements on intellectual property rights, data-sharing protocols, and confidentiality are also critical. Without these clear agreements, potential conflicts can arise, hindering the collaboration's effectiveness. Furthermore, ongoing communication and feedback mechanisms are crucial for ensuring that the partnership remains aligned with the evolving needs of both partners.

The establishment of formal structures and mechanisms is essential for facilitating these partnerships. Joint steering committees or advisory boards composed of representatives from both academia and industry can provide guidance and oversight, ensuring that the partnership remains on track and addresses the needs of both partners. Regular meetings and communication channels must be established to facilitate information exchange and resolve any emerging conflicts. Funding mechanisms are also crucial, with both industry and government potentially providing financial support for research projects, curriculum development, and training programs.

In conclusion, partnerships between academia and industry are not merely beneficial; they are indispensable for developing a skilled and adaptable workforce capable of driving the successful implementation of innovative manufacturing. By leveraging the combined expertise and resources of both sectors, these collaborations ensure that training programs remain relevant, accessible, and responsive to the evolving needs of the industry. The benefits extend beyond immediate skill development, fostering innovation, promoting economic growth, and enhancing the competitive edge of both academic institutions and industry partners in the global marketplace. Investing in these partnerships is not merely an investment in education and training; it is also an investment in the future of innovative manufacturing itself. The long-term economic and social returns far outweigh the initial investment required, securing a skilled and adaptable workforce ready to embrace the challenges and opportunities of this transformative era.

INVESTING IN STEM EDUCATION TO SUPPORT INNOVATIVE MANUFACTURING GROWTH

The preceding discussion underscored the critical role of industry-academia partnerships in cultivating a skilled, innovative manufacturing workforce. However, the foundation for this success rests upon a robust and sustained investment in Science, Technology, Engineering, and Mathematics (STEM) education at all levels. A thriving, innovative manufacturing sector demands a pipeline of talent—from entry-level technicians to advanced researchers—equipped with the fundamental knowledge and skills necessary to navigate the complexities of this rapidly evolving field. Without a strong STEM foundation, the sophisticated technologies driving innovative manufacturing will remain underutilized, hindering the potential for increased productivity, innovation, and global competitiveness.

The current landscape reveals a concerning gap between the demand for STEM professionals in innovative manufacturing and the supply of qualified graduates. Many industries report difficulties in recruiting and retaining individuals with the necessary skills in areas such as robotics, data analytics, AI, and cybersecurity. This skills shortage is not simply a matter of filling vacant positions; it represents a fundamental constraint on the growth and competitiveness of the entire sector. Investing in STEM education is not merely a desirable option; it is a strategic imperative for ensuring the continued expansion and success of innovative manufacturing.

This investment must be multifaceted, encompassing improvements at all levels of the educational system. At the K-12 level, the focus should be on fostering a love of STEM subjects from an early age. This involves engaging and inspiring young learners, often through hands-on activities, project-based learning, and exposure to real-world applications of STEM principles. Encouraging participation in STEM competitions, robotics clubs, and science fairs can spark a passion for these fields, laying the groundwork for future success in STEM careers. Furthermore, ensuring equitable access to quality STEM education for all students, regardless of socioeconomic background or geographical location, is crucial. Targeted programs and initiatives can help to address systemic inequalities that often limit access to STEM education for underrepresented groups.

At the post-secondary level, investment in STEM education needs to go beyond simply increasing the number of graduates. The curriculum itself must be modernized and aligned with the evolving needs of the innovative manufacturing sector. This means integrating cutting-edge technologies and methodologies into the curriculum, providing students with hands-on experience with the tools and techniques they will encounter in the workplace. Collaboration with industry partners, as discussed earlier, is essential in this regard, ensuring that academic programs remain relevant and responsive to the demands of the marketplace. This partnership extends beyond simply providing access to equipment and expertise; it involves co-developing curricula, incorporating industry-relevant case studies, and creating internships and apprenticeships that allow students to gain practical experience.

Investment in advanced research and development within universities is another crucial component. Universities serve as incubators for innovation, driving advancements in areas such as AI, machine learning, robotics, and industrial IoT. This research not only expands the boundaries of knowledge but also provides a fertile ground for developing new technologies and solutions that can be directly applied to innovative manufacturing processes. Funding for research projects, graduate fellowships, and postdoctoral positions is essential for maintaining this critical pipeline of innovation. This research should focus on addressing the specific challenges faced by the innovative manufacturing sector, such as improving the efficiency and reliability of manufacturing processes, enhancing cybersecurity measures, and developing more sustainable and environmentally friendly manufacturing practices.

The investment should also extend to the development of specialized training programs focused on specific aspects of innovative manufacturing. These programs can target both recent graduates seeking entry-level positions and experienced workers requiring upskilling or reskilling to adapt to new technologies. These programs can take various forms, including short courses, certificates, and specialized master's degree programs, focusing on areas such as predictive maintenance, digital twins, cybersecurity for industrial control systems, and advanced data analytics techniques. These programs should be designed in close collaboration with industry partners to ensure they address real-world needs and provide graduates with the necessary skills for immediate employment.

The role of government in fostering STEM education for innovative manufacturing cannot be overstated. Government funding plays a vital role in supporting research, curriculum development, and the training of future generations of STEM professionals. Targeted initiatives focused on supporting STEM education at all levels, including financial aid for students pursuing STEM degrees, grants for universities to develop and implement cutting-edge programs, and tax incentives for companies investing in STEM education, are crucial elements of a comprehensive strategy. Moreover, the government can play a crucial role in promoting collaboration between academia and industry, establishing frameworks and incentives for partnerships, and fostering a national conversation on the importance of STEM education for future economic competitiveness.

Beyond financial investment, a strong commitment to STEM education requires a broader cultural shift. This includes promoting STEM careers to young people, particularly underrepresented groups, and highlighting the societal impact of STEM fields.

Encouraging female participation in STEM is particularly critical, as the lack of women in these fields represents a significant untapped potential for innovation and growth. A multifaceted approach that incorporates mentorship programs, outreach initiatives, and targeted recruitment efforts can help to overcome barriers to entry and create a more diverse and inclusive STEM workforce.

Furthermore, continuous evaluation and improvement of STEM education programs are essential. Regular assessments of program effectiveness, including student outcomes, graduate employment rates, and industry feedback, are crucial for ensuring that educational institutions are meeting the needs of the innovative manufacturing sector. This ongoing evaluation allows for adjustments to the curriculum, training programs, and research priorities, ensuring that they remain aligned with the ever-evolving technological landscape. This iterative process of refinement ensures the continued relevance and efficacy of the investments made in STEM education.

In conclusion, investing in STEM education is not simply an expense; it is a strategic investment in the future of innovative manufacturing and the broader economy. A robust pipeline of skilled STEM professionals is essential for driving innovation, competitiveness, and economic growth. This investment must be comprehensive, encompassing support at all educational levels, fostering collaboration between academia and industry, and promoting a cultural shift that values and celebrates STEM careers.

The long-term benefits of a well-educated and adaptable STEM workforce far outweigh the initial costs, ensuring a sustainable and prosperous future for the innovative manufacturing sector and the nation as a whole. The commitment to a robust STEM educational system is not just an investment in education; it's an investment in the future prosperity of our nations. It is a critical element in ensuring global competitiveness in the increasingly technology-driven world. The rewards of such an investment are not just economic; a skilled workforce contributes to overall societal well-being and strengthens a nation's standing on the world stage.

DEVELOPING A SKILLED WORKFORCE FOR FUTURE INNOVATIVE FACTORIES

Building a workforce capable of thriving in the innovative factories of tomorrow requires a multifaceted approach that goes beyond simply increasing the number of STEM graduates. It demands a commitment to continuous learning, adaptability, and a proactive response to the ever-evolving technological landscape. This involves a shift in educational philosophy, emphasizing practical skills alongside theoretical knowledge and fostering a culture of lifelong learning within the manufacturing sector.

One crucial aspect is the integration of advanced technologies and methodologies into existing vocational and apprenticeship programs. Traditional training models often lag behind technological advancements, leaving workers unprepared for the complexities of modern innovative factories. Curriculum reform is vital, incorporating hands-on training with cutting-edge technologies like robotics, AI-powered systems, and advanced data analytics tools.

This requires substantial investment in updated equipment and facilities within vocational schools and training centers, ideally in partnership with leading manufacturing companies. These partnerships can provide access to state-of-the-art equipment, real-world case studies, and mentorship opportunities, bridging the gap between theoretical learning and practical application. For example, a collaboration between a local community college and a major automotive manufacturer could allow students to work on actual assembly lines, learning to program and maintain robotic systems while simultaneously contributing to the manufacturer's production goals.

Furthermore, the focus should shift from imparting static knowledge to cultivating critical thinking and problem-solving skills. The rapid pace of technological change means that the specific technologies used in innovative factories will inevitably evolve.

Therefore, the emphasis must be on equipping workers with the adaptability and analytical skills needed to learn and master new technologies throughout their careers. This can be achieved through project-based learning, simulations, and real-world problem-solving exercises. For instance, trainees could be tasked with diagnosing and resolving simulated malfunctions in a robotic arm using diagnostic software and data analysis techniques. Such exercises build not only technical proficiency but also critical thinking and troubleshooting skills—essential attributes in a dynamic, innovative factory environment.

The upskilling and reskilling of the existing workforce are equally critical. Many experienced workers possess valuable practical knowledge and expertise that can be leveraged in the transition to innovative manufacturing. However, they often lack the knowledge of advanced technologies. Targeted training programs designed to bridge this gap are essential. These programs should be modular and flexible, allowing workers to acquire specific skills relevant to their roles and career aspirations. For example, a program could focus on training machine operators on the use of predictive maintenance software to anticipate equipment failures and reduce downtime, or it could focus on empowering quality control inspectors with advanced data analytics tools to identify patterns and root causes of defects more effectively. These upskilling initiatives should be accessible, affordable, and offered through various formats – from short online courses to intensive workshops.

The role of industry-sponsored training programs and apprenticeships cannot be overstated. Companies must invest in training their employees not only to ensure a skilled workforce but also to retain valuable talent. These programs should be integrated into a broader talent development strategy, providing clear pathways for career advancement and skill enhancement. This investment can range from sending employees to external training courses and workshops to establishing in-house training academies that offer specialized skills development in areas such as programming industrial robots, cybersecurity, or advanced data analytics. The financial benefits of such investment are readily apparent: a better-trained and more adaptable workforce leads to increased productivity, reduced errors, and higher-quality products, ultimately boosting profitability.

A crucial aspect often overlooked is the integration of soft skills training. While technical skills are essential, effective collaboration, communication, and problem-solving are equally critical in an innovative factory setting, where teams often work across different disciplines and geographical locations. Training programs should incorporate elements that focus on teamwork, communication, and leadership development. Role-playing exercises, team-building activities, and conflict-resolution training can enhance these essential soft skills.

Moreover, the ability to adapt to change and embrace new technologies requires a growth mindset, fostering a culture of continuous learning.

Beyond formal training programs, fostering a culture of lifelong learning within the manufacturing sector is essential. Companies can achieve this through various initiatives, including access to online learning platforms, mentoring programs, and internal knowledge-sharing networks. These platforms can provide employees with opportunities to learn new technologies at their own pace, broadening their skillset and adapting to the demands of the changing workplace. Furthermore, encouraging employees to participate in industry events, conferences, and workshops keeps them updated on the latest advancements and allows them to network with colleagues and experts from across the sector.

Government policies play a crucial role in supporting workforce development. Financial incentives for companies that invest in training programs, tax credits for tuition reimbursement, and funding for vocational schools and training centers are some examples of policy interventions that can incentivize investment in skills development. Moreover, government initiatives can foster collaboration between academia, industry, and training providers, ensuring that training programs are aligned with the needs of the innovative manufacturing sector and are accessible to all. Furthermore, targeted programs can assist underrepresented groups in accessing these training opportunities, ensuring a diverse and inclusive workforce.

Finally, the effective development of a skilled workforce requires a continuous feedback loop. Regular assessments of training programs' effectiveness, including employee feedback, industry needs, and technological advancements, are crucial. This feedback mechanism ensures that training remains relevant, responsive, and effective in equipping individuals with the skills needed to thrive in the dynamic environment of future innovative factories. This constant monitoring and adaptation of training programs is crucial to address the ongoing changes in technology and industry demands.

By embracing this iterative approach, we can ensure that the investment in skills development consistently produces the desired outcome: a robust and adaptable workforce prepared for the exciting and challenging future of innovative manufacturing. This ongoing evaluation allows for continuous improvement, ensuring that educational initiatives remain aligned with industry needs and that the resulting workforce possesses the skills required for success in this technologically advanced field. The development of a skilled workforce is not a one-time undertaking but rather an ongoing process requiring continuous investment, adaptation, and evaluation.

CHAPTER 14

GLOBAL PERSPECTIVES ON INNOVATIVE MANUFACTURING

INNOVATIVE MANUFACTURING ADOPTION IN DIFFERENT COUNTRIES

The global landscape of innovative manufacturing adoption reveals a fascinating tapestry of progress, challenges, and diverse approaches.

While the overarching goal is similar—to leverage digital technologies for enhanced efficiency, productivity, and competitiveness—the pace and trajectory of implementation vary significantly across countries. This divergence stems from a complex interplay of factors, including existing industrial infrastructure, government policies, technological capabilities, workforce skills, and cultural influences.

Consider the case of Germany, a nation long renowned for its manufacturing prowess, particularly in the automotive and machinery sectors. Germany has embraced Industrie 4.0, a national initiative focused on integrating cyber-physical systems, the internet of things (IoT), and cloud computing into manufacturing processes. This commitment has resulted in a high density of highly automated factories, particularly among large enterprises. However, the transition has not been without its hurdles. The prevalence of highly specialized, often family-owned, small and medium-sized enterprises (SMEs) presents a unique challenge, as many lack the resources and expertise to implement comprehensive, innovative manufacturing solutions. Government support programs aimed at assisting SMEs in their digital transformation are crucial in bridging this gap. Furthermore, while Germany boasts a highly skilled workforce, the rapid pace of technological change necessitates continuous upskilling and reskilling initiatives to keep pace with evolving demands. The integration of advanced robotics and AI necessitates training programs that equip workers with the skills to operate, maintain, and program these sophisticated systems.

In contrast, China's approach to innovative manufacturing is marked by a different dynamic. Driven by a national strategy to become a global manufacturing powerhouse, China is investing heavily in advanced technologies, fostering the growth of domestic technology companies, and aggressively promoting the adoption of Industry 4.0 principles. China's sheer scale and its centralized planning capabilities offer significant advantages. Massive investments in infrastructure, including high-speed internet access and advanced communication networks, provide a strong foundation for innovative manufacturing initiatives. However, challenges remain. Addressing concerns about data security and intellectual property protection is paramount.

Furthermore, bridging the skills gap within a vast and diverse workforce requires considerable resources and well-planned training programs. The emphasis on fostering innovation through supportive government policies and research funding is critical for China's long-term success in this arena. The focus on collaboration between industry, academia, and government is equally important.

The United States, with its strong technology sector and a long history of automation, is also actively pursuing innovative manufacturing initiatives. However, the U.S. approach differs from

Germany and China in its more decentralized and market-driven nature. While government initiatives provide support, the emphasis is mainly on private-sector investment and innovation. The U.S. boasts a strong foundation of engineering and technological expertise, but the fragmentation of the manufacturing sector poses challenges in achieving widespread adoption of innovative manufacturing practices. Differences in industry structures and company sizes contribute to uneven adoption rates, and bridging this gap requires a multi-faceted approach involving public-private partnerships and effective workforce development initiatives.

Moreover, addressing the digital divide and ensuring equitable access to technology and training are crucial aspects of achieving broader adoption within diverse communities.

Japan, another manufacturing powerhouse, presents a unique case study. Long a leader in automation, Japan is now focusing on the integration of advanced robotics, AI, and big data analytics to enhance efficiency and competitiveness. The emphasis on precision engineering and high-quality products aligns naturally with the principles of innovative manufacturing. However, concerns regarding the aging workforce and the need to attract young talent into manufacturing necessitate workforce development strategies. Japan's commitment to continuous improvement and its embrace of lean manufacturing principles provide a solid foundation for the smooth integration of innovative manufacturing technologies.

South Korea exhibits a remarkable pace of innovative manufacturing adoption, driven by a strong focus on technology development and a highly skilled workforce. South Korea's success in the electronics and semiconductor industries provides a strong foundation for expanding innovative manufacturing principles across other sectors. Government-led initiatives provide strong support for research and development, creating an environment conducive to innovation.

However, like other nations, South Korea faces the challenge of maintaining a skilled workforce capable of adapting to rapidly evolving technologies. The commitment to education and training is essential for continued success.

Looking at the broader picture, a comparative analysis reveals several recurring themes. The availability of high-speed internet and robust digital infrastructure is crucial for seamless data exchange and communication within innovative factories. Government policies play a significant role in fostering innovation and supporting SMEs in their digital transformation journeys. The skills and adaptability of the workforce are paramount, requiring substantial investments in education and training initiatives. Furthermore, the development of robust cybersecurity measures to protect sensitive data and systems is essential for the successful implementation of innovative manufacturing technologies.

Furthermore, cultural factors can influence the adoption of innovative manufacturing technologies. In some cultures, a reluctance to embrace change or a preference for traditional methods might impede the adoption of new technologies. In others, a strong emphasis on collaboration and knowledge sharing can facilitate a faster and more effective transition to innovative manufacturing.

Understanding these cultural nuances is critical for tailoring effective implementation strategies.

Beyond the national level, regional disparities within individual countries also warrant attention. Rural areas, for instance, may lack the infrastructure or skilled workforce necessary to support the adoption of advanced technologies. Bridging this digital divide requires targeted investment and policies that promote regional economic development.

The global race towards innovative manufacturing is not a zero-sum game. International collaboration, the sharing of best practices, and the development of common standards can significantly accelerate progress for all nations. Joint research initiatives, collaborative projects, and the free exchange of knowledge are essential for maximizing the benefits of innovative manufacturing across the globe. This collaborative approach can lead to the development of more affordable and accessible technologies, ensuring broader and more equitable access to the benefits of the innovative manufacturing revolution.

In conclusion, the diverse approaches to innovative manufacturing adoption across countries highlight the complex interplay of technological, economic, and social factors. While the ultimate goal of enhanced efficiency and competitiveness is shared, the paths taken vary considerably. Understanding these diverse experiences and fostering international collaboration is crucial for ensuring a globally equitable and successful transition to a future defined by innovative manufacturing practices. Continuous monitoring, adaptation, and sharing of best practices will be essential to address the ever-evolving challenges and opportunities presented by this transformative technological shift. The journey towards a genuinely innovative and globally connected manufacturing sector is a dynamic and ongoing process that demands continuous innovation, collaboration, and adaptability.

EMERGING INNOVATIVE MANUFACTURING HUBS AROUND THE WORLD

The emergence of innovative manufacturing is not confined to a few established industrial powerhouses; it's a global phenomenon, with numerous regions rapidly developing into significant hubs of innovation and technological advancement. These emerging hubs are characterized by a confluence of factors: supportive government policies, readily available skilled labor, robust infrastructure, and a burgeoning ecosystem of technology providers and research institutions. Understanding their unique strengths and challenges provides valuable insights into the future trajectory of innovative manufacturing.

One prominent example is the rapidly evolving innovative manufacturing landscape in Southeast Asia. Countries like Singapore, Malaysia, and Vietnam are actively investing in advanced technologies, attracting significant foreign direct investment, and fostering a culture of innovation. Singapore, with its highly developed infrastructure, skilled workforce, and government support for digitalization, has positioned itself as a leading innovative manufacturing hub in the region. The country's commitment to Industry 4.0 principles, coupled with its strategic location and access to global markets, has attracted numerous multinational corporations to establish advanced manufacturing facilities. Similarly, Malaysia is leveraging its existing strengths in electronics and automotive manufacturing to integrate innovative manufacturing technologies, focusing on areas such as robotics, automation, and data analytics. Vietnam, with its growing manufacturing sector and a large, relatively low-cost workforce, is also witnessing significant growth in innovative manufacturing, attracting companies seeking to diversify their supply chains and tap into the region's potential. However, these Southeast Asian nations face challenges, including the need for continuous upskilling and reskilling initiatives to meet the demands of advanced technologies, as well as the development of robust cybersecurity frameworks to protect sensitive data within increasingly interconnected systems.

The growth of innovative manufacturing in India presents a compelling narrative of potential and challenges. India's vast manufacturing sector, combined with a large pool of skilled engineers and IT professionals, provides a fertile ground for the adoption of innovative manufacturing technologies. The government's "Make in India" initiative is driving investment in advanced manufacturing and digitalization, while initiatives focused on skill development and technological education are aimed at bridging the skills gap.

However, addressing challenges related to infrastructure development, particularly in rural areas, remains critical for ensuring widespread adoption. Furthermore, fostering a culture of innovation and collaboration between industry, academia, and government is essential for realizing India's innovative manufacturing aspirations. The country's diverse manufacturing base, ranging from textiles and pharmaceuticals to automobiles and aerospace, presents both opportunities and complexities for implementing innovative manufacturing solutions effectively. Tailoring strategies to the specific needs of different industries is crucial for achieving widespread adoption and maximizing benefits.

Moving to Latin America, countries like Mexico and Brazil are emerging as significant players in the global innovative manufacturing landscape. Mexico's proximity to the United States and its established automotive industry provide a strong foundation for the adoption of innovative manufacturing technologies. Foreign direct investment in the automotive sector has driven technological advancements, and the government's support for industrial development is creating a favorable environment for innovation.

Similarly, Brazil, with its large and diversified manufacturing sector, is also investing in innovative manufacturing, focusing on sectors such as aerospace, agriculture, and energy. However, challenges remain, including improving infrastructure, reducing bureaucratic hurdles, and enhancing the skills of the workforce. Addressing these challenges is critical for maximizing the potential of innovative manufacturing in these dynamic economies. Moreover, fostering innovation within local technology companies and supporting the development of a vibrant ecosystem of technology providers is essential for long-term growth.

In Africa, while the adoption of innovative manufacturing is still in its nascent stages, several countries are demonstrating significant potential. Countries like South Africa, Egypt, and Morocco are making strides in developing their manufacturing sectors and adopting innovative manufacturing technologies. These countries possess strong educational institutions and a growing pool of skilled engineers and technicians, and they are taking steps to upgrade their infrastructure. However, they face significant challenges, including addressing infrastructure deficits, overcoming energy limitations, and investing in workforce development. Overcoming these obstacles and fostering a conducive business environment will be crucial for unlocking the potential of innovative manufacturing across the African continent. International partnerships and knowledge transfer initiatives will play a vital role in supporting these efforts and fostering sustainable growth.

National initiatives do not solely drive the development of innovative manufacturing hubs; regional clusters are also playing a significant role. For example, the Rhine-Ruhr region in Germany, long recognized for its industrial prowess, is undergoing a significant transformation into an innovative manufacturing powerhouse.

The region benefits from a highly skilled workforce, a strong research base, and a collaborative ecosystem of industry and academia. Similarly, the Silicon Valley region in the United States continues to be a hotbed of innovation, with many technology companies developing and deploying innovative manufacturing solutions. These regional clusters benefit from network effects, knowledge spillover, and the ease of collaboration among businesses, research institutions, and government agencies.

Understanding the dynamics of these regional clusters can provide valuable insights into how to create thriving ecosystems that support innovative manufacturing adoption.

The emergence of these diverse, innovative manufacturing hubs underscores the global nature of this technological revolution. Each hub possesses unique strengths and faces specific challenges, but collectively, they represent a powerful force driving innovation and efficiency across the manufacturing sector. Furthermore, the interaction and collaboration among these hubs are promoting the dissemination of knowledge and best practices, accelerating the pace of innovation worldwide. The future of manufacturing is undoubtedly global, interconnected, and increasingly intelligent.

The continuous evolution of these hubs, driven by technological advances, policy initiatives, and economic factors, will shape the future of global manufacturing for years to come. Continuous monitoring of these trends and proactive adaptation are vital for businesses and governments alike. A holistic approach, encompassing technological advancements, workforce development, supportive policies, and sustainable infrastructure investments, is key to ensuring successful innovative manufacturing adoption.

GLOBAL COLLABORATION AND KNOWLEDGE SHARING

The genuinely transformative potential of innovative manufacturing lies not just in the individual advancements made within isolated regions or nations but in the synergistic effects arising from global collaboration and knowledge sharing. The rapid pace of technological change demands a connected approach, allowing for the swift dissemination of best practices, the identification of emerging challenges, and the collaborative development of solutions that transcend geographical boundaries. This interconnectedness is not merely a desirable outcome; it's a necessity for realizing the full promise of Industry 4.0.

One crucial avenue for global collaboration is the establishment of international research consortia and collaborative projects. These initiatives bring together leading researchers, engineers, and industry experts from diverse backgrounds, fostering cross-pollination of ideas and accelerating the pace of technological innovation. For instance, projects focused on developing standardized communication protocols for innovative manufacturing systems are crucial for ensuring seamless interoperability between different equipment and software solutions from various manufacturers. Such standardization efforts necessitate the collaborative efforts of industry players worldwide, transcending competitive interests to achieve a common goal: a more efficient and interconnected global manufacturing landscape.

Furthermore, international conferences and workshops serve as invaluable platforms for knowledge exchange and the dissemination of best practices. These events provide opportunities for researchers and practitioners to present their findings, share their experiences, and engage in discussions that promote learning and collaborative problem-solving. The sharing of case studies from successful innovative manufacturing implementations, highlighting both successes and challenges, is particularly crucial. These real-world examples can provide valuable insights for others seeking to adopt similar technologies or address comparable challenges, potentially avoiding costly mistakes and accelerating the learning curve.

The role of international standards organizations, such as the International Organization for Standardization (ISO), is equally crucial. Developing universally accepted standards for data exchange, cybersecurity protocols, and other critical aspects of innovative manufacturing ensures interoperability and facilitates the seamless integration of technologies from different vendors. This standardization effort significantly reduces implementation costs and complexities, fostering wider adoption and accelerating the pace of global innovative manufacturing deployment. Furthermore, international standards help establish a common understanding of best practices, promoting safer and more reliable systems.

Beyond formal collaborations, informal networks and communities of practice are also vital for facilitating global knowledge sharing. Online forums, social media groups, and professional organizations provide avenues for engineers and practitioners to share information, exchange ideas, and learn from each other's experiences. These informal networks can be particularly effective in disseminating information about emerging technologies, addressing specific challenges, and connecting individuals with shared interests. The rapid evolution of innovative manufacturing demands ongoing learning and adaptation, and these informal networks help to facilitate this continuous learning process.

The exchange of skilled personnel through internships, training programs, and academic collaborations plays a significant role in disseminating knowledge and promoting global talent development.

Exchanges of engineers, researchers, and technicians allow for firsthand exposure to different approaches, technologies, and best practices, contributing to a richer understanding of the field and accelerating the pace of innovation. Moreover, fostering international collaboration in educational programs can cultivate a global workforce capable of navigating the complexities of a globally interconnected manufacturing landscape.

Governments have a pivotal role to play in promoting global collaboration and knowledge sharing. Through international agreements, funding for collaborative research projects, and support for participation in international initiatives, governments can foster an environment conducive to knowledge exchange and technology transfer. Strategic partnerships between nations can lead to the development of shared infrastructure, research facilities, and training programs, accelerating the adoption of innovative manufacturing technologies across borders. Governments can also facilitate the movement of skilled workers across borders, ensuring that talent is effectively utilized to drive innovation.

The private sector also has a crucial responsibility in fostering global collaboration. Multinational corporations, with their extensive global networks and resources, are uniquely positioned to facilitate knowledge exchange and technology transfer. By sharing best practices, collaborating on research and development, and investing in training programs, these companies can significantly contribute to the advancement of innovative manufacturing technologies worldwide. Such collaboration extends beyond direct competitors; sharing knowledge and experiences in areas like cybersecurity, supply chain optimization, and data analytics can help build a more robust and resilient global manufacturing ecosystem.

Furthermore, the effective utilization of digital platforms and technologies is crucial in facilitating global collaboration. Secure data-sharing platforms, virtual collaboration tools, and online training resources can significantly enhance the efficiency and reach of knowledge exchange initiatives. These digital tools are essential in connecting individuals and organizations across geographical boundaries, enabling real-time communication and collaborative problem-solving. Investing in such digital infrastructure and promoting its adoption is essential for ensuring that global collaboration efforts are practical and efficient.

Challenges, however, remain. Intellectual property rights protection can be a significant obstacle to open collaboration, especially in highly competitive sectors. Finding a balance between protecting intellectual property and promoting knowledge sharing is a crucial aspect of fostering successful collaborations. Likewise, differences in regulatory frameworks and standards across different nations can pose significant hurdles to seamless technology integration and interoperability.

Harmonizing regulations and promoting the adoption of global standards are essential for fostering effective global collaboration. Finally, language barriers and cultural differences can also impede communication and collaboration, requiring efforts to build trust and foster mutual understanding. Addressing these challenges requires a multi-faceted approach involving cooperation between industry, academia, governments, and international organizations.

In conclusion, the future of innovative manufacturing depends critically on a globalized approach that embraces collaboration and knowledge sharing. By leveraging international partnerships, fostering open communication channels, and addressing existing challenges, we can unlock the full potential of innovative manufacturing technologies and create a more efficient, sustainable, and globally connected manufacturing ecosystem. This requires a collective effort, with industry, academia, governments, and international organizations all playing their crucial roles in building a genuinely interconnected future for global manufacturing. The success of this endeavor will not only benefit individual nations but will drive global economic growth and prosperity for years to come.

ADDRESSING GLOBAL CHALLENGES IN INNOVATIVE MANUFACTURING

The global interconnectedness of modern manufacturing presents both immense opportunities and significant challenges for the implementation of innovative manufacturing strategies. While collaborative efforts are crucial for success, several key obstacles must be addressed to realize the full potential of Industry 4.0. One major hurdle is the vulnerability of global supply chains to disruptions. The COVID-19 pandemic starkly highlighted the fragility of these networks, revealing their susceptibility to geopolitical instability, natural disasters, and unforeseen events.

Innovative manufacturing, with its emphasis on data-driven decision-making and real-time visibility, offers potential solutions, but achieving resilience requires a coordinated global response.

This involves diversification of sourcing, the development of more robust logistics networks, and the implementation of advanced inventory management systems. Furthermore, fostering greater transparency and collaboration within supply chains, facilitated by technologies like blockchain, can enhance resilience by improving visibility and traceability. This shared visibility allows for quicker responses to disruptions and the proactive mitigation of potential risks. International collaboration on standardization and data-sharing protocols is essential for enabling seamless information flow across borders and different organizational systems. Governments play a crucial role in supporting the development of more resilient supply chains through strategic investments in infrastructure, technology, and workforce development programs. Incentivizing companies to adopt robust risk management strategies and promoting the adoption of international standards will bolster the resilience of the global manufacturing ecosystem.

Another critical challenge lies in the development of a globally skilled workforce capable of designing, implementing, and maintaining innovative manufacturing systems. The rapid pace of technological advancement requires continuous upskilling and reskilling of the existing workforce, as well as the education of a new generation of engineers and technicians proficient in areas like data analytics, artificial intelligence, and cybersecurity.

International collaboration is vital in addressing this skills gap. This involves developing shared educational programs, exchanging best practices in workforce development, and creating opportunities for cross-border knowledge transfer. Moreover, governments must invest in educational infrastructure and incentivize companies to invest in employee training programs. Promoting STEM education at all levels, from primary school to university, will build a strong pipeline of future talent in this field. Furthermore, creating international certification programs that recognize proficiency in innovative manufacturing technologies could facilitate the mobility of skilled workers and harmonize standards across countries.

Sustainability is increasingly recognized as a paramount concern in innovative manufacturing. The environmental impact of manufacturing processes, including energy consumption, waste generation, and carbon emissions, must be minimized to ensure the long-term viability of the industry. Innovative manufacturing technologies offer significant potential for enhancing sustainability, allowing for optimization of energy usage, reduction of waste through predictive maintenance, and improved resource efficiency. However, the implementation of sustainable, innovative manufacturing requires global collaboration to establish common standards, share best practices, and promote the adoption of environmentally friendly technologies. International cooperation in developing and implementing stricter environmental regulations will drive the adoption of sustainable practices across borders. The sharing of best practices in eco-friendly manufacturing through international conferences, collaborative projects, and online platforms is essential for accelerating the adoption of sustainability initiatives. Furthermore, funding collaborative research and development projects focused on green technologies can significantly contribute to developing more sustainable, innovative manufacturing solutions. Incentivizing companies to adopt sustainable manufacturing practices through tax breaks and other governmental support programs is also essential for making eco-friendly technologies a widespread practice.

Data security and cybersecurity are increasingly critical concerns within the context of innovative manufacturing. The extensive use of interconnected systems and the reliance on data-driven decision-making create vulnerabilities to cyberattacks, which can have severe consequences, including production disruptions, data breaches, and financial losses. Addressing this requires a multifaceted approach involving global collaboration on cybersecurity standards, best practices, and incident response protocols. The development of internationally recognized cybersecurity standards is essential for ensuring the interoperability and security of innovative manufacturing systems across borders.

Sharing information about cyber threats and vulnerabilities through international collaboration platforms can enhance collective preparedness and the speed of response to attacks.

Furthermore, governments must play a key role in promoting cybersecurity awareness, enacting regulations to protect critical infrastructure, and encouraging the development of robust cybersecurity measures by industry. International cooperation is necessary to prevent the spread of malware and to coordinate responses to global cybersecurity threats.

Ethical considerations are also increasingly important as innovative manufacturing systems become more sophisticated. The use of artificial intelligence and machine learning raises concerns about bias in algorithms, job displacement, and the potential for unintended consequences. Addressing these ethical challenges requires careful consideration and global dialogue. International collaboration can help establish ethical guidelines and standards for the development and deployment of innovative manufacturing technologies. This includes exploring the implications of algorithmic bias, developing mechanisms for ensuring fairness and transparency in decision-making processes, and addressing potential workforce impacts through retraining and reskilling programs.

Open discussions between policymakers, industry leaders, and researchers are crucial for ensuring that the benefits of innovative manufacturing are realized equitably and responsibly. The establishment of international ethics boards tasked with evaluating the societal and ethical implications of emerging technologies can help guide the responsible implementation of innovative manufacturing technologies globally.

In conclusion, the successful implementation of innovative manufacturing requires a global effort that addresses the multifaceted challenges inherent in a connected world. Overcoming issues related to supply chain resilience, workforce development, sustainability, cybersecurity, and ethics necessitates a collaborative approach involving industry, academia, governments, and international organizations. By fostering open communication, promoting knowledge sharing, and developing international standards and best practices, we can unlock the transformative potential of innovative manufacturing and build a more efficient, sustainable, and equitable global manufacturing ecosystem. The future of manufacturing depends on our collective ability to navigate these challenges and collaboratively shape a more sustainable and prosperous future for all. This continuous dialogue and engagement are not mere options; they are prerequisites for the successful and responsible deployment of innovative manufacturing technologies worldwide. The rewards of this collaboration far outweigh the challenges; a globally connected and sustainably driven manufacturing ecosystem will benefit all participants, accelerating innovation and improving global standards of living.

THE FUTURE OF GLOBAL MANUFACTURING IN AN INNOVATIVE WORLD

The transformative potential of innovative manufacturing extends far beyond individual factories and national borders. Its impact will be felt globally, reshaping the landscape of international competition and cooperation. To fully grasp the implications, we must look beyond the immediate challenges and envision the future of global manufacturing within this increasingly interconnected and intelligent environment. This necessitates a shift in perspective, moving away from a purely nationalistic view of manufacturing competitiveness towards a globally collaborative approach.

One of the most significant shifts will be the rise of global, collaborative production networks. Innovative manufacturing technologies facilitate the seamless integration of geographically dispersed operations, fostering a new era of distributed manufacturing. This paradigm shift will leverage the unique strengths of different regions, optimizing production processes for efficiency, cost-effectiveness, and resilience. For example, a company might design a product in one country, source raw materials from another, conduct assembly in a third, and distribute the finished goods globally, all coordinated through a sophisticated, interconnected, innovative manufacturing system. This necessitates the development of robust digital infrastructure capable of supporting the flow of data across borders, ensuring real-time visibility and collaboration across the entire supply chain. Standardization of communication protocols, data formats, and cybersecurity measures will be paramount in achieving seamless integration.

This collaborative model also implies a significant rethinking of traditional notions of intellectual property and trade secrets.

Increased reliance on shared platforms and open-source technologies will necessitate new mechanisms for protecting intellectual property while fostering collaboration and innovation.

This could involve the creation of secure data-sharing platforms that allow companies to collaborate while maintaining control over sensitive information. Similarly, new legal frameworks may be required to address the challenges of intellectual property protection in a globally distributed manufacturing environment.

The concept of "open innovation" will gain further traction, encouraging the sharing of knowledge and technologies to foster collective progress rather than pursuing competitive advantage in isolation.

The future of global manufacturing will also be profoundly shaped by advancements in artificial intelligence (AI) and machine learning (ML). These technologies will not only automate individual tasks within factories but will also play a crucial role in optimizing entire supply chains, predicting market demands, and mitigating risks. AI-powered predictive analytics can forecast disruptions in supply chains, allowing companies to proactively adjust their production plans and minimize the impact of unforeseen events. Furthermore, AI can enhance the efficiency of logistics and transportation networks, optimizing routes and schedules to reduce costs and delivery times. The integration of AI into quality control processes will lead to the production of higher-quality products with fewer defects, contributing to enhanced customer satisfaction and brand reputation. However, the ethical implications of using AI in manufacturing must be carefully considered, particularly concerning issues of bias, transparency, and accountability.

Sustainability will be a central theme in the future of global manufacturing. Increasing environmental concerns and tightening regulations will demand a shift towards more environmentally friendly manufacturing processes. Innovative manufacturing technologies provide powerful tools for achieving this goal. For example, predictive maintenance can optimize energy consumption by reducing equipment downtime and extending the lifespan of machinery. Real-time monitoring of resource usage can identify areas for improvement and reduce waste generation. The integration of renewable energy sources into manufacturing facilities, coupled with intelligent energy management systems, will minimize the industry's carbon footprint. These initiatives will not only reduce the environmental impact of manufacturing but will also offer economic advantages by lowering operating costs. However, the adoption of sustainable practices requires a concerted effort from governments, industry, and consumers alike. This includes the development of internationally recognized sustainability standards, the implementation of incentive programs to encourage green manufacturing practices, and consumer demand for environmentally friendly products.

The future of global manufacturing will also depend on the availability of a highly skilled workforce capable of designing, implementing, and maintaining innovative manufacturing systems. This necessitates a significant investment in education and training programs that focus on developing the skills needed in the Industry 4.0 era. These skills include proficiency in data analytics, AI, cybersecurity, robotics, and automation technologies. International collaboration in education and training will be essential in addressing the global skills gap. This can involve the creation of joint educational programs, the exchange of best practices in workforce development, and the creation of international certification programs that recognize proficiency in innovative manufacturing technologies. Governments and industries must collaborate to provide funding for education and training programs, ensuring that the workforce is equipped with the skills needed to succeed in the evolving manufacturing landscape.

The cybersecurity of innovative manufacturing systems will be a critical concern in the years to come. The increasing interconnectedness of manufacturing operations makes them vulnerable to cyberattacks, which can have devastating consequences, including production disruptions, data breaches, and financial losses. Addressing this requires a comprehensive approach that involves both technological and organizational measures. This necessitates the development of robust cybersecurity protocols and standards that are globally recognized and adopted. Furthermore, international collaboration on cybersecurity threat intelligence sharing and incident response protocols is essential. Governments and industries must work together to enhance cybersecurity awareness, implement stricter regulations to protect critical infrastructure, and invest in cybersecurity research and development.

In conclusion, the future of global manufacturing in an innovative world hinges on our collective ability to embrace collaboration, innovation, and adaptation. The development of global collaborative production networks, the integration of AI and machine learning, the adoption of sustainable practices, the development of a skilled workforce, and the prioritization of cybersecurity are all crucial elements in shaping a successful and sustainable future for the industry. This requires a concerted effort from governments, industries, educational institutions, and international organizations to foster a globally integrated and competitive manufacturing ecosystem that benefits all stakeholders. The challenges are substantial, but the potential rewards – a more efficient, sustainable, and equitable global economy – are immense. The journey toward this future requires a continuous commitment to dialogue, collaboration, and a shared vision for a globally prosperous and sustainable manufacturing landscape.

CHAPTER 15
CONCLUSION: EMBRACING THE
INNOVATIVE MANUFACTURING
REVOLUTION

SUMMARY OF KEY FINDINGS AND INSIGHTS

The preceding chapters have detailed the multifaceted revolution underway in global manufacturing, driven by the convergence of advanced technologies under the banner of "innovative manufacturing." This transformation isn't merely an incremental improvement; it's a fundamental reshaping of how goods are produced, distributed, and consumed worldwide. This final section synthesizes the key findings and insights, emphasizing the profound and far-reaching implications of this technological shift.

One overarching theme throughout this exploration has been the critical role of data. Innovative manufacturing's foundation rests upon the seamless collection, analysis, and utilization of data from every stage of the production process. From sensor data capturing real-time machine performance to supply chain data tracking materials and logistics, the effective management and interpretation of this data are paramount. This necessitates significant investments in robust data infrastructure, secure data storage, and sophisticated analytical tools capable of processing massive datasets.

Furthermore, the development of standardized data formats and protocols is crucial for facilitating interoperability between different systems and fostering collaboration across the entire value chain. The ability to extract meaningful insights from this data allows for proactive, rather than reactive, management of manufacturing operations. This predictive capability is revolutionizing aspects such as preventative maintenance, supply chain optimization, and quality control, leading to significant cost reductions and efficiency gains.

However, the data-driven nature of innovative manufacturing also introduces significant challenges. Data security and privacy are paramount. The interconnectedness of innovative factories and their reliance on cloud-based platforms create vulnerabilities to cyberattacks. Robust cybersecurity measures, including sophisticated intrusion detection systems, encryption protocols, and rigorous access control mechanisms, are not optional but rather essential components of any successful innovative manufacturing implementation. Furthermore, ethical considerations surrounding data usage must be carefully addressed. Transparency in data collection and usage, along with mechanisms for ensuring data integrity and preventing bias in algorithms, is crucial for building trust and ensuring responsible deployment of these technologies.

The development of robust regulatory frameworks and industry standards is vital to navigating these challenges and promoting responsible innovation.

Another recurring theme throughout this book has been the transformative power of artificial intelligence (AI) and machine learning (ML) in reshaping manufacturing processes. AI is not just automating individual tasks; it is enhancing the decision-making capabilities of entire organizations. Predictive maintenance algorithms can optimize equipment lifecycles, preventing costly downtime and extending the lifespan of machinery. AI-driven quality control systems can detect and correct defects in real-time, improving product quality and reducing waste. Moreover, AI is significantly impacting supply chain management, enabling more accurate demand forecasting, optimized logistics, and proactive risk management. These capabilities are not merely about cost reduction; they are about enhancing responsiveness, agility, and resilience in the face of ever-changing market conditions and global disruptions.

The integration of AI, however, requires careful consideration of its limitations and potential pitfalls. The "black box" nature of some AI algorithms can raise concerns about transparency and accountability. Ensuring that AI systems are free from bias and that their decisions are explainable is critical for maintaining trust and ensuring fairness. Furthermore, the implementation of AI requires a skilled workforce capable of developing, deploying, and maintaining these complex systems. This highlights the importance of investing in education and training to cultivate the necessary expertise in data science, AI, and related technologies. Bridging the skills gap is not just about training individuals; it's about fostering a culture of continuous learning and adaptation within manufacturing organizations.

Sustainability is another crucial aspect of the innovative manufacturing revolution. The increasing pressure to reduce carbon footprints and minimize environmental impact necessitates the adoption of more sustainable manufacturing practices. Innovative manufacturing technologies offer powerful tools for achieving this goal. Real-time monitoring of energy consumption, optimized resource utilization, and the integration of renewable energy sources can significantly reduce the environmental impact of manufacturing operations. Furthermore, the ability to predict and prevent equipment failures through predictive maintenance can minimize waste generation and optimize energy efficiency. This shift towards sustainability is not merely an ethical imperative; it is also a strategic advantage.

Consumers increasingly favor products from environmentally responsible companies, creating a robust market incentive for the adoption of sustainable practices. However, the transition to sustainable manufacturing requires concerted efforts from governments, industries, and consumers alike. Policy incentives, industry standards, and consumer demand are all crucial drivers of this transformative shift.

The global landscape of manufacturing is being fundamentally reshaped by innovative manufacturing. The rise of global collaborative production networks is breaking down traditional geographical barriers to manufacturing. Companies are increasingly leveraging the unique strengths of different regions, creating globally distributed production systems that optimize efficiency, cost-effectiveness, and resilience. This necessitates the development of robust digital infrastructure capable of supporting seamless communication and data exchange across borders. Standardization of communication protocols and cybersecurity measures is crucial for ensuring secure and efficient collaboration within these globally dispersed networks. This new model of global manufacturing also raises essential considerations regarding intellectual property rights and the sharing of knowledge and technologies. The exploration of models of open innovation and secure data sharing is vital for fostering collaboration while protecting sensitive information.

In conclusion, the innovative manufacturing revolution represents a profound and transformative shift in the global manufacturing landscape. The integration of advanced technologies, from AI and ML to advanced robotics and automation, is not merely improving efficiency; it is fundamentally reshaping how goods are produced, distributed, and consumed. The successful navigation of this revolution requires a multifaceted approach that addresses data security, ethical considerations, workforce development, sustainability, and global collaboration. The challenges are substantial, but the potential rewards – a more efficient, sustainable, and equitable global economy – are immense. The journey toward this future requires a continuous commitment to innovation, adaptation, and a shared vision for a globally prosperous and sustainable manufacturing landscape. The path forward necessitates a collaborative effort between governments, industry leaders, educational institutions, and international organizations, ensuring that the benefits of this technological revolution are broadly shared and the challenges are effectively addressed. The future of manufacturing is not predetermined; it is being shaped by the choices we make today.

THE IMPORTANCE OF CONTINUOUS INNOVATION

The preceding discussion has established the transformative potential of innovative manufacturing, emphasizing its impact on efficiency, sustainability, and global collaboration. However, the journey towards a genuinely innovative and resilient manufacturing ecosystem is not a destination but an ongoing process. Continuous innovation is not merely desirable; it's absolutely essential for sustained success in this rapidly evolving landscape. The technologies underpinning innovative manufacturing are not static; they are constantly advancing, presenting both opportunities and challenges. Companies that fail to embrace continuous innovation risk becoming obsolete, overtaken by more agile and adaptable competitors.

This imperative for continuous innovation extends beyond simply adopting the latest technologies. It encompasses a holistic approach that integrates research and development (R&D), talent acquisition and development, flexible manufacturing strategies, and a culture of experimentation and learning. A crucial aspect of this continuous improvement lies in fostering a robust R&D pipeline. This involves dedicated investment in research, exploring cutting-edge technologies like quantum computing, advanced materials science, and breakthroughs in artificial intelligence and machine learning. These investments are not simply about staying ahead of the curve; they are about shaping the future of manufacturing and defining the next generation of innovative factory capabilities.

Consider the potential of quantum computing, for instance. Its capacity to solve complex optimization problems far surpasses that of classical computers. In the context of innovative manufacturing, this translates to significantly more efficient scheduling, predictive maintenance, and supply chain optimization. Imagine a quantum algorithm capable of predicting equipment failures with near-perfect accuracy, minimizing downtime, and reducing waste to unprecedented levels. Or consider the application of advanced materials science in developing lighter, stronger, and more sustainable materials, reducing the environmental footprint of manufacturing processes and enhancing product performance.

These are not futuristic concepts; research and development in these areas are already underway, paving the way for future breakthroughs in innovative manufacturing.

Beyond technological advancements, continuous innovation necessitates a commitment to talent development. The successful implementation and management of innovative manufacturing systems require a highly skilled workforce capable of operating, maintaining, and further developing these sophisticated technologies. This necessitates investment in education and training programs that equip individuals with the necessary skills in data science, AI, robotics, cybersecurity, and related disciplines.

However, this is not a one-time investment; it's an ongoing process. The rapid pace of technological change demands continuous upskilling and reskilling initiatives to keep the workforce current with the latest advancements. Furthermore, fostering a culture of lifelong learning within manufacturing organizations is crucial. Encouraging employees to embrace new technologies and actively participate in training programs is essential for maintaining a competitive edge.

The ability to adapt manufacturing processes to meet evolving market demands and unforeseen disruptions is another critical aspect of continuous innovation. This requires the implementation of flexible manufacturing systems that can be quickly reconfigured to accommodate changes in product design, production volume, or material availability. Modular production lines, adaptable robotic systems, and agile software platforms are crucial components of this flexible approach. This ability to adapt swiftly is particularly critical in today's dynamic global marketplace, where consumer preferences, supply chain disruptions, and geopolitical events can significantly impact manufacturing operations. A company's responsiveness to these changes becomes a key differentiator, determining its survival and competitiveness.

The process of continuous innovation doesn't simply involve implementing new technologies; it requires a culture that actively promotes experimentation, learning from failures, and a willingness to embrace risk. This necessitates establishing robust feedback loops within manufacturing processes, enabling the continuous monitoring and evaluation of performance, identification of areas for improvement, and rapid iteration of solutions. A culture that embraces a "fail fast, learn fast" mentality is essential for driving rapid innovation. This mindset encourages employees to experiment with new ideas, learn from setbacks, and continually refine their approaches. Furthermore, data analytics plays a crucial role in this iterative process, providing valuable insights into the effectiveness of various strategies and informing future decision-making.

Another critical dimension of continuous innovation in innovative manufacturing is the focus on sustainability. The increasing emphasis on environmental responsibility necessitates the development of environmentally friendly manufacturing processes and the integration of renewable energy sources. This involves researching and implementing technologies that minimize waste generation, reduce energy consumption, and minimize the carbon footprint of manufacturing operations. Continuous innovation in this area involves exploring new materials, processes, and technologies that are both economically viable and environmentally sustainable. Circular economy principles, focusing on waste reduction, reuse, and recycling, become essential elements of a sustainable, innovative manufacturing strategy. Companies that integrate sustainability into their innovation strategies not only benefit the environment but also enhance their brand reputation and attract environmentally conscious consumers.

The successful adoption of innovative manufacturing necessitates robust collaboration between various stakeholders. This collaborative approach extends beyond internal teams; it encompasses partnerships with suppliers, customers, research institutions, and governmental agencies. Open innovation models, where companies share knowledge and resources, can accelerate the pace of technological advancement and foster the development of solutions. However, this requires careful consideration of intellectual property rights and the development of secure mechanisms for data sharing and collaboration. The establishment of industry consortia and collaborative research initiatives can facilitate knowledge exchange, accelerate technological breakthroughs, and address common challenges faced by the manufacturing sector.

Finally, continuous innovation in innovative manufacturing must be driven by a long-term vision. It is not a short-term cost-cutting exercise but a fundamental transformation that requires sustained investment, strategic planning, and a commitment to long-term growth. This requires leadership that understands the importance of innovation, invests in the necessary resources, and fosters a culture that values creativity and experimentation. Companies that adopt this long-term perspective are better positioned to weather market fluctuations, remain competitive, and capitalize on the transformative opportunities presented by the innovative manufacturing revolution. The path to a genuinely innovative and resilient manufacturing ecosystem is paved with continuous innovation, a journey that demands constant adaptation, learning, and a relentless pursuit of improvement. The future belongs to those who embrace this challenge and consistently strive for excellence.

NAVIGATING THE CHALLENGES AND CAPITALIZING ON OPPORTUNITIES

The transition to innovative manufacturing presents a complex tapestry of challenges and opportunities. Successfully navigating this transformation requires a strategic approach that goes beyond simply adopting new technologies. A holistic strategy, encompassing meticulous planning, robust risk mitigation, and a commitment to collaboration, is crucial for maximizing returns and minimizing disruption. Ignoring these crucial aspects can lead to significant setbacks, wasted investment, and, ultimately, failure to realize the full potential of innovative manufacturing.

One of the most significant challenges lies in the integration of legacy systems with new, innovative technologies. Many manufacturing facilities operate with aging infrastructure and processes, making the seamless integration of advanced technologies like AI, IoT, and robotics a complex undertaking. This often necessitates significant capital investment in new hardware and software, as well as extensive system re-engineering. Furthermore, data silos—a common problem in large organizations—can hinder the efficient flow of information needed for effective decision-making in an innovative manufacturing environment. Breaking down these silos requires a strategic approach to data management, potentially involving the implementation of enterprise resource planning (ERP) systems or cloud-based platforms capable of integrating data from various sources. The initial investment in upgrading infrastructure and integrating systems can be substantial, but the long-term benefits in terms of increased efficiency, reduced waste, and improved decision-making far outweigh the upfront costs.

Another key challenge is the lack of skilled labor. Innovative manufacturing relies heavily on advanced technologies, requiring a workforce with expertise in areas like data analytics, AI, robotics, and cybersecurity. The skills gap is a widespread issue, particularly in developed countries facing an aging workforce and a decline in technical education. Addressing this requires a multi-pronged approach, including investment in education and training programs, apprenticeship programs, and collaborations with universities and vocational schools to develop curricula aligned with the needs of the innovative manufacturing industry. Furthermore, organizations must invest in reskilling and upskilling their existing workforce to adapt to the changing technological landscape. This might involve providing employees with opportunities for continuous learning through online courses, workshops, and mentorship programs. Failing to address this skills gap will limit the potential of innovative manufacturing implementations, creating a bottleneck in the adoption and optimization of new technologies.

Cybersecurity is another critical concern in innovative manufacturing. The increasing connectivity and reliance on data exchange in innovative factories expose them to a broader range of cyber threats. Protecting sensitive data, intellectual property, and operational systems from cyberattacks is paramount. This requires the implementation of robust cybersecurity measures, including network

402

security protocols, data encryption, access controls, and intrusion detection systems. Regular security audits and penetration testing should be conducted to identify vulnerabilities and proactively address potential threats. Investing in cybersecurity training for employees is also essential to raise awareness of potential risks and best practices for safeguarding sensitive information. The cost of a successful cyberattack on an innovative manufacturing facility can be devastating, resulting in production downtime, data breaches, financial losses, and reputational damage. Therefore, a proactive and comprehensive cybersecurity strategy is an absolute necessity.

The implementation of innovative manufacturing technologies also raises ethical considerations. The increasing use of AI and automation raises questions about job displacement, algorithmic bias, and data privacy. Addressing these ethical concerns requires a thoughtful and responsible approach to the development and deployment of innovative manufacturing systems. Transparency in the use of data, fairness in algorithmic decision-making, and measures to mitigate potential job displacement through retraining and reskilling initiatives are crucial for building trust and ensuring the responsible use of technology. Ethical considerations should be integrated into the entire lifecycle of innovative manufacturing projects, from the initial planning stages to the ongoing operation and maintenance of the systems. Ignoring these ethical implications can lead to public backlash, regulatory scrutiny, and damage to an organization's reputation.

Capitalizing on the opportunities presented by innovative manufacturing requires strategic planning and collaboration. Developing a clear roadmap that outlines specific goals, timelines, and resource allocation is essential for successful implementation. This roadmap should be tailored to the specific needs and capabilities of the organization, taking into consideration its existing infrastructure, workforce skills, and business objectives. The roadmap should also incorporate a risk mitigation strategy to identify and address potential challenges proactively. This might involve conducting feasibility studies, piloting new technologies on a small scale, and establishing contingency plans to address unexpected issues.

Furthermore, successful innovative manufacturing initiatives rely heavily on collaboration. This involves partnerships not only within the organization but also with external stakeholders, such as suppliers, customers, research institutions, and government agencies.

Collaborating with suppliers can ensure the timely delivery of high-quality materials and components, while collaborating with customers can provide valuable feedback on product design and performance. Partnerships with research institutions can access cutting-edge technologies and expertise, and collaboration with government agencies can help secure funding and navigate regulatory requirements. Open innovation models, where companies share knowledge and resources, can accelerate the pace of technological advancement and foster the development of solutions. However, this requires careful consideration of intellectual property rights and the development of secure mechanisms for data sharing and collaboration.

The journey towards a genuinely innovative and resilient manufacturing ecosystem is not a destination but a continuous process of improvement and adaptation. Continuous innovation, coupled with a commitment to collaboration, risk management, and ethical considerations, will be key factors in determining success in this transformative era. Companies that embrace this holistic approach, investing in infrastructure, talent, and cybersecurity while proactively addressing ethical concerns and fostering robust partnerships, will be best positioned to capitalize on the opportunities and overcome the challenges of the innovative manufacturing revolution. The future of manufacturing belongs to those who embrace change, adapt swiftly, and continuously strive for excellence. The rewards are significant – increased efficiency, enhanced sustainability, improved product quality, and a strengthened competitive advantage in the global marketplace. The path is challenging, but the potential gains make the journey worthwhile.

THE FUTURE OF WORK IN AN INNOVATIVE MANUFACTURING ENVIRONMENT

The transformation to innovative manufacturing profoundly reshapes the nature of work, demanding a proactive and strategic response from organizations and individuals alike. The integration of advanced technologies like artificial intelligence (AI), the Internet of Things (IoT), and robotics significantly alters job roles and requires a workforce equipped with new skills and competencies. This necessitates a paradigm shift in workforce development strategies, moving beyond traditional training models towards a continuous learning ecosystem.

One of the most immediate impacts is the automation of repetitive and physically demanding tasks. Robots and automated systems are increasingly deployed across manufacturing processes, from assembly lines to material handling, leading to increased efficiency and productivity. While this automation may displace some workers performing these routine tasks, it simultaneously creates new opportunities in areas such as programming, maintenance, and system management. The workforce of the future will require a higher level of technical expertise coupled with strong problem-solving and critical-thinking abilities.

The rise of AI and machine learning (ML) introduces another layer of complexity to the future of work. AI-powered systems are capable of analyzing vast amounts of data to optimize production processes, predict equipment failures, and improve quality control. This leads to a greater demand for data scientists, AI specialists, and engineers capable of developing, implementing, and maintaining these complex systems. Furthermore, AI can enhance human capabilities by providing workers with real-time insights and decision-support tools, making them more efficient and effective.

However, the ethical implications of AI in the workplace need careful consideration. Algorithmic bias, data privacy concerns, and potential job displacement require a proactive and responsible approach to the integration of AI in the manufacturing sector.

The increasing connectivity in innovative factories via the IoT creates new opportunities for remote monitoring and control of production processes. This enables more flexible and agile manufacturing, allowing companies to respond quickly to changes in demand and optimize production schedules in real-time. However, this also necessitates a workforce proficient in cybersecurity and data management. The interconnected nature of innovative factories makes them vulnerable to cyberattacks, potentially causing significant disruptions and financial losses. Investing in cybersecurity training and implementing robust security protocols are crucial to mitigating these risks. This calls for a workforce skilled in managing and securing the vast amounts of data generated by the IoT.

The adoption of digital twin technology further transforms the nature of work. Digital twins are virtual representations of physical assets and processes, enabling companies to simulate and optimize operations before implementing them in the real world. This reduces the risk of errors and allows for faster prototyping and testing. The workforce in this environment will require expertise in simulation modeling, data analysis, and virtual reality technologies.

Furthermore, digital twins provide opportunities for remote collaboration and training, expanding the potential for global workforce participation.

Another significant aspect of the future of work in innovative manufacturing is the increased emphasis on collaboration and communication. The complex interplay of different technologies and systems requires a workforce that can work effectively across disciplines and share knowledge seamlessly. This necessitates a shift towards interdisciplinary teams, bringing together engineers, data scientists, technicians, and operations managers to solve complex problems collaboratively. Strong communication skills, both written and verbal, become essential for effective teamwork and efficient problem-solving.

The shift towards a more data-driven environment means that workers at all levels will need to be comfortable interpreting and using data to make informed decisions. Data literacy will become a critical skill, extending beyond specialized roles to encompass the entire workforce. This necessitates investing in data literacy training programs to equip workers with the necessary skills to understand, analyze, and utilize data effectively. Furthermore, the ability to adapt to rapidly evolving technologies will be crucial for sustained success. Continuous learning and professional development will be vital to remain competitive in this dynamic environment.

To prepare for this future, organizations must invest significantly in workforce development. This involves not only the recruitment of skilled professionals but also the reskilling and upskilling of existing employees. Implementing robust training programs that cover AI, robotics, data analytics, cybersecurity, and other relevant technologies is paramount. Partnerships with educational institutions and vocational schools are essential to develop curricula aligned with the evolving needs of the innovative manufacturing industry. Apprenticeship programs and mentorship initiatives can also play a significant role in bridging the skills gap.

The successful integration of innovative manufacturing technologies also requires a focus on fostering a culture of continuous improvement and innovation. This involves encouraging experimentation, celebrating failures as learning opportunities, and promoting a mindset of adaptability. Encouraging employees to embrace new technologies and actively participate in the development and implementation of innovative manufacturing initiatives is crucial for successful transformation.

The future of work in innovative manufacturing is not solely about technological advancements but also about the human element. Addressing potential job displacement through reskilling initiatives, promoting ethical considerations in AI and automation, and fostering a culture of collaboration and continuous learning are essential components of a successful transition. Companies that prioritize their workforce's development and create a supportive and engaging work environment will be best positioned to attract and retain talent in this increasingly competitive landscape. This also includes offering opportunities for career advancement and promoting a sense of ownership and purpose among employees, ensuring that the workforce feels valued and empowered as they navigate this evolving technological landscape. The future of innovative manufacturing depends not only on sophisticated technologies but also on a highly skilled, adaptable, and engaged workforce. This proactive and holistic approach to workforce development will be critical in unlocking the full potential of this transformative era.

Investing in human capital is just as essential as investing in technological infrastructure for the long-term success of innovative manufacturing.

A CALL TO ACTION: BUILDING A SUSTAINABLE AND MANUFACTURING FUTURE

The preceding chapters have detailed the transformative power of the innovative manufacturing revolution, highlighting its potential to reshape industries, enhance productivity, and foster innovation.

However, realizing this potential requires more than simply adopting new technologies; it necessitates a concerted, proactive effort from all stakeholders – manufacturers, policymakers, educators, and the workforce itself. The journey toward a truly sustainable manufacturing future demands a collective commitment to embrace change, invest wisely, and prioritize ethical considerations.

One of the most critical aspects of this call to action involves fostering a culture of continuous learning and adaptation. The rapid pace of technological advancement necessitates a workforce equipped not only with the skills required for today's tasks but also with the adaptability to learn and master emerging technologies.

This is not simply a matter of initial training; it requires a commitment to lifelong learning facilitated by accessible and comprehensive educational resources, reskilling initiatives, and robust apprenticeship programs. Manufacturers must play a leading role here, partnering with educational institutions to develop curricula aligned with industry needs and actively investing in the training and development of their employees. This investment should extend beyond technical skills, encompassing critical thinking, problem-solving, and collaborative skills – abilities equally crucial for navigating the complexities of the innovative factory.

Furthermore, embracing the innovative manufacturing revolution necessitates a significant shift in mindset. A culture of innovation must permeate the entire organization, from the shop floor to the executive suite. This entails creating an environment where experimentation is encouraged, failures are viewed as learning opportunities, and risk-taking is rewarded. Traditional hierarchical structures must give way to more collaborative and agile models, empowering employees at all levels to contribute ideas and participate in the decision-making process. This fosters a sense of ownership and shared responsibility, which is essential for the successful implementation of innovative manufacturing technologies.

The ethical implications of the technologies driving innovative manufacturing cannot be overlooked. The increasing use of AI and automation raises concerns about job displacement, algorithmic bias, and data privacy. Addressing these concerns requires a responsible and transparent approach to the development and deployment of these technologies. Manufacturers must prioritize ethical considerations throughout the entire lifecycle of their innovative manufacturing initiatives, ensuring fairness, accountability, and respect for human dignity. This includes implementing robust mechanisms to mitigate bias in AI algorithms, ensuring data privacy and security, and proactively addressing potential job displacement through reskilling and upskilling initiatives.

Policymakers also have a crucial role to play in shaping the future of innovative manufacturing. Supportive regulatory frameworks are needed to encourage innovation while addressing the ethical and societal implications of these technologies. Incentives for investment in innovative manufacturing technologies, along with policies that facilitate workforce development and upskilling, can accelerate the transition to a more sustainable manufacturing sector. This includes fostering collaboration between industry, academia, and government to create a coordinated approach to addressing the challenges and opportunities presented by the innovative manufacturing revolution.

The development of sustainable practices must also be at the forefront of this transformation. Innovative manufacturing offers the potential to significantly reduce waste, optimize energy consumption, and improve environmental performance. Adopting sustainable practices, such as circular economy principles and responsible sourcing, is not only ethically responsible but also economically advantageous, leading to cost savings and increased competitiveness. By integrating sustainability into the core of their innovative manufacturing strategies, companies can create value for both their businesses and the environment. This encompasses investing in energy-efficient equipment, implementing waste reduction strategies, and employing environmentally friendly materials. Transparency and accountability in supply chains are equally crucial for ensuring sustainable practices throughout the manufacturing lifecycle.

The adoption of standardized communication protocols and interoperability standards across different innovative manufacturing

413

systems is critical for realizing the full potential of this revolution. The lack of standardization can create significant challenges in data integration, system compatibility, and interoperability, hindering the efficiency and effectiveness of innovative manufacturing implementations. By promoting the development and adoption of universal standards, we can ensure seamless data exchange, improve system interoperability, and unlock the benefits of a fully integrated, innovative manufacturing ecosystem. This also reduces the costs associated with integrating disparate systems and promotes broader adoption of innovative manufacturing technologies across different industries and organizations.

Finally, the success of the innovative manufacturing revolution hinges on effective collaboration between all stakeholders. Open communication and knowledge sharing between manufacturers, suppliers, researchers, educators, and policymakers are crucial for accelerating innovation and addressing the challenges associated with this transformative technology. The formation of industry consortia, research collaborations, and public-private partnerships can facilitate this collaboration, enabling the rapid development and deployment of solutions. These collaborative efforts are instrumental in addressing the multifaceted challenges of integrating innovative manufacturing technologies and ensuring a smooth transition to a more sustainable and competitive manufacturing future. Through shared resources, expertise, and a collective vision, we can accelerate the adoption of best practices, foster innovation, and navigate the complexities of this technological transformation.

In conclusion, the innovative manufacturing revolution is not just about adopting new technologies; it's about creating a more sustainable and equitable future for the manufacturing industry. It requires a concerted effort from all stakeholders – businesses, governments, educators, and individuals – to embrace change, invest in workforce development, and prioritize ethical considerations. By fostering a culture of continuous learning, innovation, and collaboration, we can unlock the full potential of this transformative era, building a manufacturing sector that is both technologically advanced and socially responsible. The journey ahead demands commitment, adaptability, and a shared vision for a future where innovative manufacturing benefits all of society. The time for action is now. The future of manufacturing is not predetermined; it is being shaped by the decisions and actions we take today. Let us work together to create a future that is both prosperous and sustainable.

ACKNOWLEDGMENTS

This book would not have been possible without the contributions of many individuals who have supported, guided, and inspired me throughout my journey in **manufacturing, innovation, and technology**.

I want to express my deepest gratitude to **Mr. Ben Cutler**, who gave me the opportunity to join the **Faurecia IT Team**, setting the foundation for my career in the industry. A special thanks to **Eng. Tony Cantu** believed in me and provided me the opportunity to join the **engineering team as a Manufacturing Engineer** on one of the largest programs, the **F-150**, while continuously supporting and encouraging me. I am also profoundly grateful to **Eng. Mark Evans** for his patience in training me, guiding me through my **first steps in manufacturing**, and teaching me the essential fundamentals that have shaped my expertise.

Beyond my professional mentors, I extend my heartfelt appreciation to my **colleagues and peers** who have shared their insights and experiences, enriching my understanding of **innovative manufacturing, automation, and digital transformation**. Their discussions, challenges, and contributions have been instrumental in shaping the content of this book.

A special acknowledgment goes to my **dear friend Suzanne Chahine** for her **unwavering support, encouragement, and belief in me**. Her limitless motivation has been a pillar of strength throughout this journey.

Most importantly, my deepest gratitude goes to **my family**—my **wife, Tagrid**, whose patience, love, and support have been my most significant source of resilience; my **daughter, Alaa**, who has always inspired me with her strength and wisdom; and my **sons, Hamza and Adel**, who continue to make me proud every day. Their belief in me, especially during the long hours of writing and research, has been a source of strength and motivation.

To everyone who has played a role in my professional and personal growth—thank you. This book is a reflection of the collective knowledge, experiences, and guidance I have been fortunate to receive.

APPENDIX

Appendix A:

Case Studies in Innovative Manufacturing

This section presents real-world case studies of successful **implementations of Industry 4.0 technologies.**

1. **Automotive Sector**

   - Tesla's Innovative Factories: Tesla utilizes AI-driven automation, IoT sensors, and predictive analytics to optimize production efficiency and reduce downtime.

   - BMW's Digital Twins: BMW employs digital twin technology to simulate and optimize production lines before physical implementation.

2. **Aerospace Industry**

   - Boeing's Use of Augmented Reality (AR): Boeing integrates AR tools for aircraft assembly to improve precision and reduce human errors.

   - GE Aviation's Predictive Maintenance: General Electric employs IoT sensors and AI algorithms to predict engine component failures before they occur.

3. **Pharmaceutical Manufacturing**

- Pfizer's AI-Driven Drug Production: Pfizer uses AI algorithms to optimize drug formulation and ensure high-quality control during mass production.
- Moderna's Innovative Biomanufacturing: Moderna leverages cloud computing and automation to speed up vaccine production and supply chain efficiency.

Appendix B:

Overview of Innovative Manufacturing Technologies

A summary of the core technologies driving Industry 4.0, their **applications, benefits, and challenges**.

Technology	Description	Key Applications
AI & Machine Learning	Algorithms that analyze data and make predictions.	Predictive maintenance quality control.
Industrial IoT (IIoT)	Network of connected devices in a manufacturing setup.	Real-time monitoring process optimization.
Robotics & Automation	Use of robots to perform repetitive or complex tasks.	Assembly lines, logistics automation.
Digital Twin Technology	Virtual simulation of physical processes or products.	Product design, predictive analytics.
3D Printing (Additive Manufacturing)	Layer-by-layer manufacturing of components.	Prototyping, customized production.

Technology	Description	Key Applications
Augmented Reality (AR) & Virtual Reality (VR)	AR overlays digital information in the real world; VR creates a fully immersive digital experience.	Maintenance training, remote assistance.
Blockchain for Manufacturing	Decentralized, transparent transaction recording.	Supply chain tracking, cybersecurity.
Cloud Computing	On-demand access to computing resources via the internet.	Data storage, remote operations.

Appendix C:
Key Policies and Regulatory Frameworks

An overview of **global manufacturing policies, cybersecurity frameworks, and sustainability regulations** impacting Industry 4.0.

1. **Cybersecurity Frameworks**

   - **NIST Cybersecurity Framework**: Guidelines to protect manufacturing systems from cyber threats.
   - **ISO 27001**: International standard for information security in industrial environments.

2. **Government Initiatives for Innovative Manufacturing**

   - **Germany's Industrie 4.0 Program**: A national strategy supporting digital transformation in manufacturing.
   - **USA's Advanced Manufacturing Partnership (AMP)**: Collaboration between industry, academia, and government to foster innovation.
   - **China's Made in China 2025 Strategy**: Government policy aimed at transitioning China into a global leader in advanced manufacturing.

3. **Sustainability & Environmental Regulations**

   - **Paris Agreement & Carbon Neutrality Goals**: How manufacturing companies are aligning with carbon reduction targets.
   - **EU's Green Deal for Industry**: Policies promoting sustainable manufacturing and circular economy models.

GLOSSARY

This glossary defines key terms used throughout the book:

AI (Artificial Intelligence): The simulation of human intelligence processes by machines, particularly computer systems.

Automation: The use of technology to perform tasks without human intervention.

Big Data: Extremely large data sets that may be analyzed computationally to reveal patterns, trends, and associations, particularly useful in predictive maintenance.

Cyber-Physical Systems (CPS): Integrated systems that combine physical and computational components.

Digital Twin: A virtual representation of a physical object or process.

Industry 4.0: The current trend of automation and data exchange in manufacturing technologies and processes.

IoT (Internet of Things): A network of physical objects— "things"—that are embedded with sensors, software, and other technologies for the purpose of connecting and exchanging data with other devices and systems over the Internet.

Predictive Maintenance: Using data analytics to predict when equipment is likely to fail, allowing for proactive maintenance.

Innovative Factory: A manufacturing facility that uses data-driven insights and advanced technologies to optimize production processes.

Supply Chain Management (SCM): The management of the flow of goods and services, including all processes that transform raw materials into final products.

REFERENCES

Books & Journal Articles

Baur, C., & Wee, D. (2015). Manufacturing's next act. McKinsey & Company. Retrieved from https://www.mckinsey.com

Lee, J., Kao, H. A., & Yang, S. (2014). Service innovation and innovative analytics for industry 4.0 and big data environment. Procedia CIRP, 16, 3-8. https://doi.org/10.1016/j.procir.2014.02.001

Rüßmann, M., Lorenz, M., Gerbert, P., Waldner, M., Justus, J., Engel, P., & Harnisch, M. (2015). Industry 4.0: The future of productivity and growth in manufacturing industries. Boston Consulting Group.

Kagermann, H., Wahlster, W., & Helbig, J. (2013). Recommendations for implementing the strategic initiative INDUSTRIE 4.0: Final report of the Industrie 4.0 Working Group. German National Academy of Science and Engineering.

Xu, L. D., Xu, E. L., & Li, L. (2018). Industry 4.0: State of the art and future trends. International Journal of Production Research, 56(8), 2941-2962. https://doi.org/10.1080/00207543.2018.1444806

Zhou, K., Liu, T., & Zhou, L. (2015). Industry 4.0: Towards future industrial opportunities and challenges. Procedia Manufacturing, 6, 612-617. https://doi.org/10.1016/j.promfg.2015.07.312

Reports & White Papers

Deloitte. (2019). The innovative factory: Responsive, adaptive, connected manufacturing. Deloitte Insights. Retrieved from https://www2.deloitte.com

World Economic Forum. (2020). The future of manufacturing: A new era of opportunity and challenge for manufacturers. Retrieved from https://www.weforum.org

National Institute of Standards and Technology (NIST). (2020). Cybersecurity framework for the manufacturing industry. Retrieved from https://www.nist.gov

International Federation of Robotics (IFR). (2021). World Robotics Report 2021: Industrial Robots. Retrieved from https://ifr.org

Conference Papers

Monostori, L. (2014). Cyber-physical production systems: Roots, expectations, and R&D challenges. Procedia CIRP, 17, 9-13. https://doi.org/10.1016/j.procir.2014.03.115

Brettel, M., Friederichsen, N., Keller, M., & Rosenberg, M. (2014). How virtualization, decentralization and network building change the manufacturing landscape: An Industry 4.0 perspective. International Journal of Mechanical, Industrial Science and Engineering, 8(1), 37-44.

AUTHOR BIOGRAPHY

Dr. Ali Hamzeh Chalhoub is a technology and innovation expert with a deep background in **manufacturing engineering, IT governance, and industrial automation**. Holding a PhD in **Technology and Innovation Management – Engineering Management**, he has dedicated his career to bridging the gap between **cutting-edge technology and practical industrial applications**.

With extensive experience as an **IT Manager in the manufacturing sector**, Dr. Chalhoub has led numerous projects focused on **innovative manufacturing, AI-driven automation, and digital transformation**. His work in **sustainable innovation, process optimization, and data-driven decision-making** has positioned him as a thought leader in the field.

Beyond his professional expertise, Dr. Chalhoub is the founder of **Innovation Technology Engineering, LLC**, a company dedicated to developing **new and disruptive engineering solutions**. His passion for **technological advancement, automation, and strategic innovation** drives his continuous research in the evolving landscape of Industry 4.0 and beyond.

In **Innovative Manufacturing: The Future Now**, Dr. Chalhoub combines his **academic knowledge, hands-on industry experience, and visionary insights** to provide readers with a comprehensive understanding of the **future of manufacturing**. Through real-world case studies, strategic analyses, and in-depth discussions on **AI, IoT, and**

automation, he equips professionals, researchers, and industry leaders with tools to navigate the **next wave of industrial transformation**.

www.ingramcontent.com/pod-product-compliance
Lightning Source LLC
Chambersburg PA
CBHW071315210326
41597CB00015B/1238